Colección Támesis

SERIE A: MONOGRAFÍAS, 227

RHETORIC AND REALITY IN EARLY MODERN SPAIN

This collection of essays takes as its point of departure early modern Spain's insistent rhetorics of nation and kingship, of a monolithic body of shared values and beliefs, especially in respect of racial and gender stereotypes, and of a centralized and ostensibly absolutist legislative apparatus. These discourses, typically clothed in an authority borrowed from biblical and classical sources, furnished the 'official' ideological landscape of Habsburg Spain. But this does not mean that they mapped unproblematically onto the complex topography of everyday life, or the lived experience of Spaniards; nor did it preclude them from being subjected by other Spaniards to sceptical or even subversive commentary.

The volume explores the extent to which these rhetorics and the ideology they helped to construct or underpin, reflected or failed to reflect the realities of social, economic, and cultural life in the Spain of the period. It sets against their typically exorbitant claims the lived, messy, and sometimes contradictory experience of Spaniards across a broad social spectrum, both at the centre and at the margins, not just of peninsular society, but of the Hispanic world overseas. As these essays show, confronting ideology were questions of economic pragmatism, executive feasibility, jurisdictional competence, and, above all, the social and political complexity of the Spain of the period.

RICHARD PYM is Senior Lecturer in Hispanic Studies at Royal Holloway, University of London.

RHETORIC AND REALITY
IN EARLY MODERN SPAIN

Edited by

Richard J. Pym

TAMESIS

First published 2006
by Tamesis, London

ISBN 1 85566 127 6

Tamesis is an imprint of Boydell & Brewer Ltd
PO Box 9, Woodbridge, Suffolk IP12 3DF, UK
and of Boydell & Brewer Inc.
PO Box 41026, Rochester, NY 14604–4126, USA
website: www.boydell.co.uk

A CIP catalogue record for this book is available
from the British Library

This publication is printed on acid-free paper

Printed in Great Britain by
MPG Books Ltd, Bodmin, Cornwall

CONTENTS

CONTRIBUTORS

Trevor J. Dadson is Professor of Hispanic Studies at Queen Mary, University of London

Margaret Rich Greer is Professor of Spanish at Duke University, North Carolina

B. W. Ife is Principal of the Guildhall School of Music & Drama and Cervantes Professor Emeritus, King's College London

Alistair Malcolm is Lecturer in the Department of History at the University of Limerick

Melveena McKendrick is Pro-Vice-Chancellor for Education and Professor of Spanish Golden-Age Literature, Culture and Society at the University of Cambridge

Richard J. Pym is Senior Lecturer in Hispanic Studies at Royal Holloway, University of London

Helen Rawlings is Lecturer in Spanish at the University of Leicester

Alexander Samson is Lecturer in Golden-Age Literature at University College London

Jules Whicker is Lecturer in Hispanic Studies at the University of Birmingham

PREFACE

This collection of essays takes as its point of departure early modern Spain's insistent rhetorics of nation and kingship, of a monolithic body of shared values and beliefs, especially in respect of racial and gender stereotypes and hierarchies, and of a centralized and ostensibly absolutist state legislative apparatus.[1] These rhetorics, typically clothed (or disguised) in an authority borrowed from biblical and classical sources, furnished the 'official' ideological landscape of Habsburg Spain. As such, they inevitably found their way into the very fabric of most 'authoritative' texts of the period, whether legal, historical, economically, or morally focused, or, indeed, fictional. But this is not to suggest that they mapped unproblematically onto the complex topography of everyday life, or the immediate experience of Spaniards; nor did it preclude them from being subjected by contemporaries to sceptical or even subversive commentary, especially in fiction. The drama of the period, whose powerful ironies are only now coming fully to be recognized, provides an obvious case in point. This volume explores the extent to which these rhetorics and the ideology they helped to construct or underpin reflected or, just as commonly, failed to reflect, the realities of social, economic and cultural practice in early modern Spain. It sets against their typically exorbitant claims the lived, messy and sometimes contradictory experience of Spaniards across a broad social spectrum, both at the centre and at the margins, not just of peninsular society, but of the Hispanic world as a whole. Several chapters draw on contributors' recent archival work in Spain to examine how confronting the claims of ideology were thorny questions of economic pragmatism, executive feasibility, jurisdictional conflict, and, most important of all, social and political complexity, especially as glimpsed in specific regional or local inflections. Meanwhile, as one contributor argues, the experience of the New World challenged even the adaptive resources of what passed for 'authoritative' language itself. The volume explores how the familiar rhetorics of the day, whether related to Spain's much-vaunted martial prowess, the role of women,

---

1   The term 'rhetoric' should be understood not only in its formal sense of the use of devices such as amplification, repetition, hyperbole, and so on, but also in the more general sense of misrepresentation.

or the construction of ethnic, religious or cultural difference, could find themselves at odds, or simply incommensurate with lived experience, just as they might be subtly contested or subverted in the relatively protected space of the theatre. It is thus intended to make a contribution to the continuing process of revision by scholars of our understanding of the culture and society of early modern Spain, opening up and developing a range of perspectives which, it is hoped, may help to encourage and stimulate further research in the future.

Richard J. Pym

ABBREVIATIONS

ADR	Archivo de las Descalzas Reales
AGP	Archivo General del Palacio, Madrid
AGS	Archivo General de Simancas
AHN	Archivo Histórico Nacional, Madrid
AHNT	Archivo Histórico Nacional, Sección Nobleza, Toledo
AHPM	Archivo Histórico de Protocolos, Madrid
AHPZ	Archivo Histórico Provincial Zaragoza
ARCV	Archivo de la Real Chancillería de Valladolid
BL	British Library
BNM	Biblioteca Nacional, Madrid
CSIC	Consejo Superior de Investigaciones Científicas

Where early modern texts or documents are cited, spelling follows the source used in each case. Modern accentuation has however been added where absent, as has the occasional comma for purposes of clarification.

Official Rhetoric versus Local Reality: Propaganda and the Expulsion of the *Moriscos*

TREVOR J. DADSON

Propaganda has become such a part of twentieth- and twenty-first-century life that we sometimes forget that it is not a modern invention at all, but can be traced back many centuries, even to a time when public opinion barely existed as a notion, when governments did not have to face daily on the television or the radio probing journalists, their critics and their political opponents. The very modern concept of 'burying bad news' is not so modern as we might like to think, and even spin doctors spinning the news in artfully favourable ways have their counterparts in early modern Europe.

The expulsion of the *moriscos* from Spain from 1609 to 1614 is an excellent event from which to examine all of these issues, since official propaganda, burying bad news, and spin-doctoring were all to be found there to varying degrees and with varying degrees of success. The expulsion itself brought forth a multitude of propaganda works, favourable to the government position and in many cases instigated, aided and abetted by members of the government.[1] When things did not go as well as expected and the expulsion, which was meant to last for a few months, a year at most, dragged on year after year with no end in sight, attempts were made to gloss over the (many) failures and emphasize the (few) successes. The day that the expulsion was announced to the world as official government policy was itself a prime example of using the occasion to bury bad news, since the expulsion of the *moriscos* of Valencia was made public on the very same day, 9 April 1609, that the government of Philip III and the Duke of Lerma signed a humiliating twelve-year peace treaty with the Dutch rebels. The admission of failure in a war that had lasted for some forty years between the best and most experienced army in Europe and an assortment of rebels was intended to be a mere

---

[1] For a survey of anti-*morisco* literature, see Roger Boase, 'The Morisco Expulsion and Diaspora: An Example of Racial and Religious Intolerance', in *Cultures in Contact in Medieval Spain: Historical Survey and Literary Essays for L.P. Harvey* (London: King's College London Medieval Studies, 1990), pp. 9–28.

footnote to the grandiose announcement that the long-expected expulsion of the *moriscos* was about to begin. In the words of John Elliott:

> By the use of skilful timing, the humiliation of peace with the Dutch would be overshadowed by the glory of removing the last trace of Moorish dominance from Spain, and 1609 would be ever memorable as a year not of defeat but of victory.[2]

The total and definitive expulsion of the *moriscos* from Spain had been on the political agenda since the early 1580s and was energetically discussed during the time that the King, Philip II, and the Court spent in Lisbon after the occupation of Portugal. But however often the issue was raised, Philip II always in the end opposed it, usually, it is supposed, because his military commitments elsewhere (Northern Europe, the Atlantic, the Mediterranean) made it logistically impossible to contemplate the wholesale expulsion of part of the population, or because of his qualms of conscience over the idea of expelling people who had been baptised in the Christian faith. The expulsion of the Jews in 1492, which is often seen as a precedent, was not of course, since they were not baptised Christians and could therefore be expelled in good conscience. Expelling baptised Christians was another thing altogether, and the King and many of his councillors, and indeed leading churchmen, balked at the idea. No such qualms of conscience, however, appear to have affected his son and successor Philip III. Why this was so has been the subject of much investigation and speculation, but it is not the object of enquiry of this chapter.[3] What I want to explore is how the government sold its policy once a decision had been made to go ahead with the expulsion, how it manipulated public opinion to give a picture of the *moriscos* that was not based on fact or reality, and how it dealt with the opposition such a measure almost immediately drew, for opposition to the expulsion there certainly was and from a wide range of social classes and groups.

And it was precisely because there was this opposition that the government supporters and its propaganda machine swung into action. One of the most vehement supporters of government policy and one of its most polemical writers was the Valencian fray Jaime Bleda. He published one of the first

---

[2] J.H. Elliott, *Imperial Spain 1469–1716* (London: Edward Arnold, 1963), p. 300.

[3] Gregorio Marañón tries to make a case for seeing the expulsion as the inevitable result of the (failed) policies of Spanish kings since the Catholic Monarchs, none of whom had grasped or wanted to grasp the fact that national unity was impossible whilst there remained within the population a large and unassimilated group of followers of another religion, Islam, who were in constant and treacherous contact with either the Turk or the French. He thus writes: 'No son lícitas, después de tantas pruebas, las dudas respecto a que la expulsión de los moriscos fue un acto político justificado y no capricho de un Rey fanático y de sus consejeros' (G. Marañón, *Expulsión y diáspora de los moriscos españoles* (Madrid: Taurus, 2004), p. 65).

tracts in support of the expulsion, on 2 December 1609: *Defensio fidei in causa neophytorum, sive Morischorum Regni Valentiae, totiusque Hispaniae* [. . .] *Tractatus de iusta Morischorum ab Hispania expulsione*, published by Juan Cristóbal Garriz, in Valencia, although it had in fact been circulating in manuscript for a number of years, having been written initially in 1603 to convince Pope Clement VIII of the justification for the measure. Bleda was a constant thorn in the side of the supporters of the *moriscos*, always demanding more and harsher measures against them, and always on the alert for any potential backsliding among the royal councillors and nobles, from whom the *moriscos* got much of their support.

Since the expulsion was planned to take only a few months, with the expulsion of the *moriscos* from Valencia being followed immediately and in ordered stages by those from Aragon, Castile, Extremadura, Andalusia, and finally Murcia, no further pro-expulsion publications appeared nor, probably, were any felt necessary. But when it became clear that the expulsion was not going to be over in a matter of months and was certainly not going to be the ordered and uncontested event the government had hoped for and expected, a spate of pro-government publications began to appear: Pedro Aznar Cardona, *Expulsión justificada de los moriscos españoles y suma de las excelencias cristianas de Nuestro Rey Felipe Tercero* (Huesca: Pedro Cabarte, 1612); Damián Fonseca, *Justa expulsión de los moriscos de España, con la instrucción, apostasía y traición dellos: Y respuesta a las dudas que se ofrecieron acerca de esta materia* (Roma: Iacomo Mascardo, 1612); Antonio de Corral y Rojas, *Relación del [sic] rebelión y expulsión de los Moriscos del reino de Valencia* (Valladolid: Diego Fernández de Córdoba, 1613); Fray Marcos de Guadalajara, *Memorable expulsión y justísimo destierro de los Moriscos de España* (Pamplona: Nicolás de Assiayn, 1613), and *Prodición y destierro de los Moriscos de Castilla, hasta el Valle de Ricote* (Pamplona: Nicolás de Assiayn, 1614).

In case one is inclined to doubt the pro-government sympathies of these publications, it should be noted that Fonseca's book was dedicated to Don Francisco de Castro, Count of Castro and nephew of the Duke of Lerma, while Corral y Rojas's was dedicated to Don Rodrigo Calderón, Count of Oliva and principal (and notorious) henchman of the favourite.

The publications and pronouncements that surrounded the ongoing course of the expulsion are one of the best examples of how official propaganda and self-delusion took over from the reality on the ground; in fact, of how the propagandists came to believe their own propaganda even when everything and everyone was telling them that the opposite was true. A good example of this came at the end of 1610. By that stage only the *moriscos* of Valencia had been expelled; those from Aragon were being expelled and a small number of *granadinos* from across Castile had voluntarily made their way to France. Of the so-called *moriscos antiguos* (the former *mudéjares*) of Murcia, both Castiles, Extremadura and Andalusia, not one had left their town or village or showed any signs of doing so, and already a few hundred of the expelled *moriscos* were returning clandestinely from France and North Africa. Notwithstanding this, the Duke of Lerma proposed on 28 November that processions should take place all over Spain to celebrate the end of the expulsion and that they should set aside 'un día en que cada año se haga conmemoración de beneficio tan señalado con sermón en que se declare como se instituyó por la batalla naval y la de las Navas de Tolosa'.[4] Not surprisingly, no more was heard of this scheme.

This capacity for delusion ran all the way through those in charge of the expulsion, from the King to Lerma to the Count of Salazar to the army captains and commissars sent to expel the *moriscos*. But it particularly affected Don Bernardino de Velasco, Count of Salazar and the man put in charge of the expulsions from Castile, Andalusia, Extremadura and Murcia. Salazar was the typical middleman, the bureaucrat more than willing to carry out any orders received and not to question them. As a bureaucrat he believed in the power of figures, and was constantly sending in reports to his superiors with the number of *moriscos* expelled and boasting that the full and total expulsion was just around the corner. There is no better example of his self-delusion coming up against the wall of reality than in the case of the *moriscos* of the Campo de Calatrava. Salazar had been trumpeting his successes in the expulsion since the spring of 1611 and had in fact announced to the King in July that he had expelled some 50,000 *moriscos* from both Castiles, La Mancha and Extremadura, a vastly exaggerated figure since we know that the *moriscos* from many parts of New Castile and Extremadura had not been expelled by then. Their expulsion did not begin until the summer of 1611 and met with bitter resistance from not just the *moriscos* themselves but from the local authorities, local lords and indeed local *cristianos viejos*. Even Salazar was forced to recognize in early September that many of the *moriscos* expelled from the Campo de Calatrava were returning or had returned from their forced exile in France. But at the same time, so convinced were the authorities in Madrid that the expulsion was succeeding they ordered the return of many of their commissars: 'que ya es tiempo de que se vengan los caballeros que fueron a la de la expulsión de los moriscos, pues habrán echado todo lo que es notorio de aquella gente'.[5] In spite of what he knew to be true, Salazar went along with this rosy picture of events and on two occasions, 24 October and 3 December 1611, informed

---

4   AGS Estado, leg. 228–2ª, dated 28 November 1610. By 'batalla naval' he meant the victory at the Battle of Lepanto, in which for the first time Christian forces defeated the Turks in the Mediterranean. Las Navas de Tolosa was of course the famous battle and defeat of the Moors in 1212, which shifted the frontier from the Tagus to the Sierra Morena and opened the way to the conquest of Seville and Córdoba.

5   H. Lapeyre, *Geografía de la España morisca* (Valencia: Diputación Provincial, 1986), p. 217, n. 12, order dated 13 September 1611.

his superiors that he had accomplished his task: 'tengo acabado de echar todos los moriscos que lo son notoriamente'; the only *moriscos* remaining were, he said, 'los que pretenden ser cristianos viejos' and whose lawsuits 'se va[n] acabando muy a priesa' (Lapeyre, p. 217, n. 13; letter dated 3 December 1611). And yet on 23 December he was writing to the Secretary of the Council of State that more than 5,000 *moriscos* remained or had returned.

Throughout the expulsion Salazar sent in reports that were later found to be totally misleading or plain wrong. In many ways he found himself trapped by his own rhetoric and desires. On the one hand, he wanted to show that he was the man who had expelled the *moriscos* from Spain (hence the constant positive reports); on the other, he wanted to prolong as long as possible his role in the expulsion, a role that gave him enormous powers and prestige (hence his equally constant reports on the number of *moriscos* returning or still to be expelled). Even when the government called an end to the expulsions in 1614 Salazar continued to write in with dire reports of the numbers who had returned or who had been protected by their lords, and he never ceased to urge the need for more expulsions.

Salazar (and with him Philip III and Lerma) was defeated by a coalition of nobles, municipalities, ecclesiastics, normal *cristianos viejos* (not all of whom believed the negative propaganda put around about the *moriscos*), and the *moriscos* themselves. Aznar Cardona rather interestingly offered a glimpse of his reasons for writing in support of the expulsion, when he said that it was in order to:

> responder a ciertas proposiciones heréticas y escandalosas, que ohí en los días últimos de su execución, hallándome presente en la de Épila [. . .] Entendí por ciertos Christianos, senzillos y de pocas letras, las titubaciones y escrúpulos de dudas infieles, que avían causado en sus pechos, razones y acotaciones hereticales, afirmadas con ánimo desojado, por aquellos perros removidos ya para el viaje de su merecido destierro. Supe también como bolvieron a escriuir algunos dellos desde Francia a ciertos Cathólicos conocidos suyos, cosas semejantes a los que auían dicho de palabra [. . .] y de que tenían muchos amigos con quienes tratauan.
>
> (Aznar Cardona, I, fols 2v–3r)[6]

Much to Aznar Cardona's annoyance, the local population, upset by the expulsion of their *morisco* neighbours, was moved to help them, and these remained in contact with their Old Christian neighbours even from France. One of the central planks of the government's anti-*morisco* propaganda campaign – that they were universally disliked, hated even by the Old Chris-

---

6   In similar vein, Damián Fonseca's *Justa expulsión* observes in its title that it was in part intended as a 'respuesta a las dudas que se ofrecieron acerca de esta materia', so doubts there were.

tians among whom they lived, who saw them as nothing more than heretics – was thus already being questioned.

And these questions and doubts were raised right from the beginning of the expulsion – by councillors, nobles, prelates, town councils, and ordinary individuals. As early as 18 December 1609 a group of theologians meeting in Madrid to give their opinion on the matter (and presumably to calm the King's scruples of conscience) issued the following warning concerning the projected expulsion of the *moriscos* from Castile:

> Los antiguos de Castilla son los más entendidos de todos, todos reciben los sacramentos, tienen cofradías, traen armas, tienen oficios públicos como boticarios, médicos, graduados por universidades, letrados, escribanos públicos y reales; no saben cosa alguna de la lengua, y los hay del Rey Católico que les permite algunas de estas cosas como a los otros cristianos viejos. Hanse muchos de estos mezclado con cristianos viejos por los matrimonios [. . .] Y las razones que ha habido para la expulsión de los de Valencia no militan en los de Castilla, ni se pueden traer a consecuencia las pragmáticas del Rey Católico, ni la del año de 1492 ni la de 1515, porque se mandó salir los judíos primero y los moriscos después que no se convirtiesen, pero no los convertidos ni los bautizados [. . .] de manera que la expulsión de los moriscos de Castilla no puede regularse por las resoluciones que están tomadas.[7]

In spite of this setback and its explicit recognition of the full assimilation of the *moriscos antiguos* of Castile (those who had been there from the Middle Ages and had converted in 1502), the government pushed on with its plans and in early January 1610 all of those (nobles, prelates, municipalities) who had *moriscos* living on their lands received a letter from the King ordering them to publish the latest *bando* (proclamation), which encouraged the *moriscos* of Castile, Extremadura and La Mancha to leave voluntarily and to draw up a list of the *moriscos* on their estates. Unaware that this 'voluntary expulsion' was a trick, a mere delaying tactic until the *moriscos* of Valencia and Aragon (deemed the most dangerous and unassimilated) had been expelled, thus freeing men and ships for the rest, many nobles and *corregidores* (royal officials) sent in lists of *moriscos* with their responses. The one from the *corregidor* of Tordesillas is fairly representative: 'que, habiéndose publicado el bando, desean quedarse en sus casas'.[8] The *moriscos* of Martos (northern Andalusia) did not believe that they were included in the *bando*, while the *corregidor* said of those from Tobarra 'que de su voluntad ninguno se irá, según he entendido'.[9] When the *corregidor* of Écija asked the local *moriscos* (approximately 1,100) 'a qué partes quieren irse [. . .] no he

7   AGS Estado, leg. 250.
8   AGS Estado, leg. 227.
9   AGS Estado, leg. 227.

hallado quién diga que quiere salir a ninguna parte; antes publican todos que más quieren perder las vidas cumpliendo con el rigor del bando que salir de entre los cristianos, por serlo ellos'.[10] Although he tried to reassure them by saying that they would be sent to Christian lands and that it was not the intention of the King to send them to Africa (itself, an example of the inherent contradiction of the expulsion, for was not Spain a Christian land?), 'responden que, por lo menos adondequiera que vayan, corren gran riesgo y peligro sus mujeres e hijas en muchas ofensas de Dios [. . .] Conforme a esto y a lo que he colegido de sus ánimos, pienso que pocos o ninguno ha de querer salir de su voluntad.'[11] Much the same was true of the *moriscos* of Guadalajara: 'tampoco me parece se irá ninguno de ellos de su voluntad y están tan tenaces y firmes según muestran en no querer irse que no se irán [. . .] y me dicen que refieren que quieren ser esclavos y morir entre los cristianos como ellos y no irse a otras partes'.[12]

From all over Spain came similar responses to the King's letter, and at the same time, clear indications that the local authorities, whether seigniorial, Church or municipal, were not all going to see the expulsion of their *moriscos* go ahead without a struggle. An early defender was the Archbishop of Granada, Don Pedro de Castro, who, in an intelligently worded memorial, set out to destroy all the arguments in favour of their expulsion: (1) there were so few *moriscos* in Granada that they represented no danger whatsoever, least of all the women and elderly men, 'que éstos no son ya para alborotos ni para tomar armas'; (2) to separate husbands from wives, because one was an Old Christian and the other a Morisca was a civil and canonical abuse: 'casáronse con buena fe, con permisión de Vuestra Majestad y según sus leyes y las de la Santa Madre Iglesia. ¿Por qué les han de quitar sus mujeres, ni quién puede?'; (3) what was going to happen to the children, especially the orphans? They had committed no crimes, and there was no reason why they should suffer because their parents were Moors, and in any case, who was going to separate them from their parents?; and (4) quite a few *moriscos* were priests and soldiers, and these latter, he noted, 'sirvieron en la rebelión pasada; dejaron su parentela, sirvieron a Vuestra Majestad

10 BNM MS 9577, fol. 304.

11 The fear of being sent to North Africa came from the news that was beginning to filter back to the country about the reception afforded there to the Valencian *moriscos*: 'y están tan escandalizados del mal tratamiento y daño que han recibido los de Valencia en Berbería, habiéndose muerto más de las tres partes de los que fueron, que muy pocos se inclinaban a pasar allá' (L. Cabrera de Córdoba, *Relaciones de las cosas sucedidas en la Corte de España desde 1599 hasta 1614* (Madrid: Imprenta de J. Martín Alegría, 1857 [facsimile edition: Salamanca: Junta de Castilla y León, 1997]), p. 396: 'aviso' of 13 February 1610).

12 AGS Estado, leg. 227, cited in A. García López, *Moriscos en tierras de Uceda y Guadalajara (1502–1610)* (Guadalajara: Diputación Provincial de Guadalajara, 1992), p. 156.

señaladamente [. . .] fueron fieles cuando todo el reino se rebeló, estando ellos en medio del fuego con los suyos; no es de creer que ahora que están solos se rebelen hallándose entre nosotros'.[13]

Another ecclesiastical friend of the *moriscos* was the Bishop of Córdoba, who published his own interpretation of the latest *bando*, giving it the rather bold title of 'Memorial de las personas que el Rey nuestro señor manda reservar para que no tengan obligación de salir de estos reinos ni sean comprendidos en el bando'. Using the very words of the King's decree but in a positive and generous tone entirely absent from the original he managed to convey the sense that the majority would be allowed to stay and only a very few would have to leave.[14] Bishops, priests and cathedral chapters across Andalusia united to protest at the threatened expulsion of the *moriscos*.

And so did many towns and municipalities. Jaén, Úbeda, Baeza all wrote in defending their small *morisco* populations, and in the early months of the expulsion it was undoubtedly the local authorities who provided the *moriscos* with their greatest support, especially those of northern Andalusia, New Castile and Extremadura (who feared among other disasters a ruinous depopulation if the expulsion went ahead). The response of Cáceres is eloquent in this respect:

> es gente pacífica y humilde y tan pobres que no tienen tratos ni comercios ni más de lo que adquieren con su trabajo para su sustento. No solamente no se halla ninguno que quiera irse ni dejar la tierra, pero sentirían mucho que Vuestra Majestad los mandase salir de ella. Y porque sus oficios son a propósito para el bien de esta república y que si faltase esta gente, por no haber quien se ocupase en ellos, sería en daño de esta tierra, suplica a Vuestra Majestad humildemente esta villa se sirva de hacerles merced de no sacarlos de ella.[15]

The *corregidor* of Badajoz was even more explicit in his defence of the *moriscos* of the town:

> Siempre han vivido bien y cristianamente. Es gente muy pobre, humilde y corregida, y que no tienen otra hacienda de consideración sino lo que ganan cada día a jornal por su trabajo. De éste tiene esta ciudad mucha necesidad porque son los que más ayudan a la cultivación y labranza de la tierra y heredades de ella, y son ya naturales de esta ciudad porque todos han nacido y criádose en ella, y no hablan otra lengua sino la nuestra vulgar.[16]

---

[13] AGS Estado, leg. 220, memorial to the King dated 24 January 1610.
[14] AGS Estado, leg. 220.
[15] AGS Estado, leg. 220, letter dated 8 February 1610.
[16] AGS Estado, leg. 220, letter dated 30 January 1610.

In areas of such low population density as Extremadura, one can understand the fear of many towns and villages at the prospect of ending up depopulated and without a workforce. But there was also the very real problem of the assimilation of many of these *moriscos*, who had mixed in with the Old Christian population: these were not newly converted to the faith, and many could not even remember when they had converted it was so long ago. The reply of Doctor fray Juan Roco Campofrío, parish priest of Alcántara, is typical in this respect for many rural areas:

> Hago saber a Vuestra Majestad que las personas que en esta villa se dice tuvieron descendencia de los que antiguamente se convirtieron de moros son tan antiguos en su conversión que se dice por público inmemorial que por ninguna razón se alcanza el origen de ella, antes se tiene por cierto se hizo luego como esta villa se ganó de los moros, que ha sobre cuatrocientos años [. . .] y se han siempre tratado en hábito, nombres, lengua, comidas, casamientos, testamentos y otros actos sin hacer alguno de moriscos como los demás cristianos viejos sin distinción alguna.[17]

This priest (also Inquisitor of Valladolid and future Bishop of Coria), who knew the *moriscos* of Alcántara very well, ends his letter to the King reminding him that many *moriscos* had fought against the rebel Moors of Granada in 1568 on the side of the King, that others were soldiers and volunteers in the militia, that some were priests and others had married into Old Christian families. He begged the King to leave them in peace, a view seconded by the Prior of Alcántara (and chaplain to the King), Don Francisco de Ovando.

None of these views were listened to and the expulsions went ahead as planned. However, this did not stop individuals and institutions continuing to aid the *moriscos* in their efforts to avoid expulsion. This help could be subtle and difficult to detect (on the part of the authorities) or quite open. One method frequently used was delaying tactics: commissars and troops sent to deport the *moriscos* or to supervise the sale of their goods were often stopped at the gates of a town or village and told they could not enter until their papers had been thoroughly checked and validated. Sometimes they were simply turned away, refused entry because their papers had expired, as in the case of Juan de Castroviejo sent to Villarrubia de los Ojos in February 1612 to investigate the permits certain *moriscos* had obtained to escape expulsion because of old age or ill-health. The description of the event given by the notary Diego de Vergara shows how a village governor could thwart the government's intentions if he wished to (provided, of course, he had the support of his lord):

[17] AGS Estado, leg. 220, letter dated 27 February 1610.

> Yo, Diego de Vergara, escribano del Rey nuestro señor público de la villa de Torrejón de Velasco, doy fe y testimonio de verdad como, estando en la villa de Villarrubia de los Ajos de Guadiana que es del señor conde de Salinas, tomando residencia en ella con el señor Gabriel de Zurita, gobernador y juez de residencia en ella, llegó a ella Juan de Castroviejo, a quien doy fe conozco, con una comisión del señor conde de Salazar y señores de la Junta para averiguar las licencias falsas que tenían algunos moriscos expelidos, y la hizo notoria al señor gobernador y juez de residencia en mi presencia, y, vista por el dicho señor gobernador, constó por ella ser el término de la comisión cumplido y que el dicho Juan de Castroviejo no podía usar de ella como por ella parecerá, a que me refiero.[18]

Eventually the commissars were able to enter Villarrubia, but the delay of some months gave the *moriscos* sufficient time to prepare themselves, to hide their goods or to hand them over to neighbours in the expectation or hope of getting them back at a later date.

However, a far more daring and outright opposition to the authorities came during the summer of 1612 from the town of Plasencia in the province of Cáceres. Because the expulsion of the *moriscos* from Plasencia was not going as planned, Salazar had asked the *corregidor* to give him a list of all those who defended the *moriscos*; unhappy with the response, he had sent in one of his *receptores* Francisco Rodríguez Losa to draw up secretly a full list of the *moriscos* in Plasencia. Although trying to do the job discreetly, Rodríguez Losa managed to offend almost everyone, since he included many true Old Christians in his list as well as *moriscos* who considered themselves true Christians. All might have been well had not a copy of the list been made public by two *regidores* sympathetic, according to the *receptor*, to the *moriscos*. The *corregidor* immediately imprisoned Rodríguez Losa, as much to protect him as to punish him, and took away all his papers. Salazar was outraged at what he saw as an affront to royal authority and demanded that his official be set free. On 17 July he wrote to the King:

> En la ciudad de Plasencia se ha tomado muy mal la expulsión de los moriscos antiguos y los han ayudado y defendido dos regidores que aquí han estado en negocios de aquella ciudad [. . .] y no se cumplió con esto con la puntualidad que deseaba, y el corregidor prendió un receptor que estaba allí haciendo una información y el que servía de fiscal, por decir que ellos eran los que habían dado la memoria que he referido, y los quitó los papeles y tiene en un calabozo. Yo no los tengo por libres de culpa, pero paréceme que sería mucha desautoridad de la Junta que se castigasen por otra mano y mucho más si fuera por la del Consejo Real, como pretenden los contenidos en la memoria.[19]

---

[18] AHPZ Híjar, 3ª–16–12.
[19] AGS Estado, leg. 244, doc. 58.

In the meantime, the *corregidor* of Plasencia Don Antonio Pacheco had also written to the King, justifying the imprisonment of Salazar's *receptor* and explaining the difficult and tense situation in the town, where the Old Christians had made common cause with the *moriscos* against the conduct of Rodríguez Losa. Back in Madrid, the Council of State took up the case of Plasencia and used it as yet another example of how Salazar had abused his powers and jurisdiction:

> que es muy justo y conveniente que la Junta tenga fin, desde luego, pues ha ocho meses que expiró el último plazo que se le dio, y lo que después acá ha hecho es sin jurisdicción, y el caso presente de Plasencia es muy grave, y lo fue haber enviado aquella memoria al corregidor siendo la real intención de Vuestra Majestad que no se trate sino de lo muy notorio, sin escarbar lo que no lo es . . .[20]

This continued for many months, though not without incident: 'el susodicho [Rodríguez Losa] pretendió romper la cárcel real de esta ciudad e irse de ella, y para ello se le hallaron unas escalas y quitadas las prisiones y hechas otras prevenciones para ello'.[21] Salazar justified this desperate action because his men were 'presos dos meses ha, y en un calabozo y muriendo de hambre'.[22] It seems that they were still in prison more than a year later, for in November 1613 Salazar asked for the intervention of the Council of Justice to get them freed.[23] There can be no doubt that the local authorities and the general populace of Plasencia did all in their power to protect and help their *moriscos* and thus subvert the intentions of the central government.

Finally, the *moriscos* found many supporters among the nobility. This support is usually ascribed to motives of greed and self-interest on the part of the nobles who did not wish to lose a very productive workforce from their lands. This may well be true of some of the nobles, but it was not true of all, and in any case had a *morisco* of the time been asked whether he was worried that his lord's support for him was based on narrow self-interest, it is doubtful that he would have worried too much, provided that it allowed him to remain in Spain. As for the nobles, deciding to come out in support of their *moriscos* was risky, for it meant going expressly against the wishes of the King and Council and threatened that intangible but strong link that bound the nobility to the monarchy. The link proved too strong for the Valencian nobles, who in spite of their much-vaunted support of the *moriscos* working on their lands very quickly abandoned them to their fate, especially when

---

[20] AGS Estado, leg. 2642. By *Junta* they mean the 'Junta de Moriscos' set up by Salazar to judge all Morisco cases, something the Council of State was never happy about.

[21] AGS Estado, leg. 245, doc. 56.

[22] AGS Estado, leg. 245, doc. 53.

[23] Letter by Salazar in AGS Estado, leg. 253, 30 November 1613.

Lerma stepped in promising to make good their economic losses (though he never did).

But there were nobles prepared to stand up to the government, such as the Duchess of Cardona, who, in the absence of her husband away on his estates in Catalonia, wrote to the King urging him to imitate the example of Christ and show justice and mercy to these people who, far from doing anything wrong, had done their best to assimilate to the local Christian population:

> de todos éstos han procedido hijos e hijas que, como se han criado con la buena doctrina y ejemplo de los cristianos viejos, han vivido y viven como buenos cristianos; unos han casado con cristianas viejas, los varones, y las mujeres con cristianos viejos, de cuyos matrimonios hay hijos e hijas de pequeña edad. Algunos hay tan viejos y pobres que son inútiles y están imposibilitados e impedidos de poder caminar; otros huérfanos sin tener quién les acuda ni haga elección por ellos, sirven a cristianos viejos que los tienen bien doctrinados e instruídos en las cosas de la fe, y muchos con privilegios y probanzas de cristianos viejos y descendientes de tales, y es cosa lastimosa los clamores que todos hacen y protestaciones que son cristianos y quieren vivir y morir como tales y cumplir como fieles vasallos de Vuestra Majestad lo que se les manda.[24]

Others inevitably tried to benefit from the situation, expressing outward signs of distress at the expulsion of their *moriscos* while inwardly rejoicing at their departure provided the state would indemnify them against the economic disaster that the loss of so many vassals would bring. Among such was the Count of Aranda, as his weasel words written on 28 August 1610 reveal:

> Y aunque esta expulsión me deja sin hacienda por consistir toda la que tenía en lugares de moriscos y la miseria que me queda no basta para la cuarta parte de los censos con que hallé cargada mi casa, y aún esto me quiere quitar el arzobispo con la pretensión que en tan apretada ocasión ha movido a pedir diezmos de las tierras que jamás las han pagado [. . .] con todo quedo contento con haber cumplido el mandato de Vuestra Majestad y con esperanza cierta de que en consideración de la voluntad y fidelidad con que he obedecido y de lo mucho que mis antecesores han servido a la real corona y de las obligaciones grandes en que por mi calidad estoy puesto y de la poca hacienda que me queda, Vuestra Majestad se ha de servir hacerme merced según su grandeza, de manera que con ella se repare el daño que de quedar sin vasallos y hacienda tengo.[25]

One group of nobles who consistently and persistently resisted the government before, during and after the expulsions was the extended

---

[24] AGS Estado, leg. 220, letter dated 18 January 1610.
[25] AGS Estado, leg. 224.

Mendoza family, and their efforts to protect their *moriscos* remind us, in a very timely fashion, of the power of lineage, of clan, of family. Indeed, so strong were these blood ties that neither the King nor Lerma nor his faithful lieutenant the Count of Salazar could do anything against them and by and large they were successful in their efforts to minimize the danger. The Mendozas were a family in which tradition played a strong role: for more than a century they had shown an attitude of tolerance towards the *moriscos*. The second Count of Tendilla, Íñigo López de Mendoza (nephew of the Great Cardinal and grandson of the Marquis of Santillana), had distinguished himself in Granada as Captain General at the time of the conquest and had worked hard with Archbishop Talavera to pacify the conquered Moors and to resist the fanaticism of Cisneros. His descendants had convinced Charles V of the merits of a restrained approach towards the inhabitants of the Kingdom of Granada and for half a century Granada enjoyed a relative peace. When Philip II embarked on a policy of intransigence towards the *moriscos*, determined to enforce pragmatics on dress, speech and customs that his more sensible father had allowed to lapse, it was the Mendozas, through the Marquis of Mondéjar, who forecast the probable results of such a policy. The uprising of the Alpujarras in 1568 was the direct result of the King ignoring such sensible advice. Under a new king, Philip III, it was once again a Mendoza, Juan Hurtado de Mendoza, fifth Duke of the Infantado, who as a Councillor of State consistently urged a policy of toleration. His voice in support of the *moriscos* never wavered.

He was joined and supported by other members of the family: his cousin, Diego de Silva y Mendoza, Count of Salinas, was President of the Council of Portugal and lord of a village, Villarrubia de los Ojos de Guadiana, with a substantial *morisco* population; Salinas's nephew was Ruy Gómez de Silva, third Duke of Pastrana, a town also noted for its large *morisco* community, encouraged to settle there in 1570 by Ruy Gómez, Prince of Éboli, as part of his efforts to establish a thriving silk industry in the Alcarria. Salinas's brother-in-law was Alonso Pérez de Guzmán el Bueno, seventh Duke of Medina Sidonia and Captain General of the coasts of Andalusia. He was charged with watching over the coasts and preventing the *moriscos* returning from North Africa; at the same time, he also had substantial numbers of *moriscos* on his estates in Andalusia. Linked to Medina Sidonia through the marriage of his daughter to Medina Sidonia's heir was Don Pedro de Toledo, Marquis of Villafranca and *Comendador* of the Val de Ricote in Murcia, perhaps, thanks to Cervantes, the most famous concentration of *moriscos* in the Peninsula. He was also Captain General of the Galleys and in permanent contact with the Duke over events in the Mediterranean, and as a Councillor of State almost always voted with Infantado on the side of the *moriscos*.

Infantado in Guadalajara, Ruy Gómez de Silva in Pastrana, Salinas in Villarrubia and his encomienda of Herrera (near Alcántara), Medina Sidonia in Andalusia, Villafranca in Murcia: these men formed a powerful alliance of family and common interests that Salazar could never break down. It is no surprise to discover therefore that large numbers of *moriscos* managed to remain in Spain, on their estates, after the expulsions. And paradoxically, their support of the *moriscos* did not bring them the loss of royal favour that we might expect. Not one lost his court or government positions; indeed, Salinas went on to become Viceroy and Captain General of Portugal, Pastrana led an embassy to France in 1612 to arrange the double marriage of Philip's son and daughter (Philip and Ana) to the daughter and son of Henri IV (Isabel and Louis), Infantado remained a Councillor of State and Medina Sidonia kept control of the coasts of Andalusia. Salazar had constantly railed against those whom he called the 'favorecedores' of the *moriscos*, nobles who got away with opposing the royal decrees, and he always had in his sights the Mendozas, in particular the Count of Salinas, but in fact the only individual to suffer real diminution in his power was Don Bernardino de Velasco, Count of Salazar, architect of the expulsions, who after 1615 found himself out of a job and removed from Court to his estates in the country.

It was thanks to the efforts of such nobles, and the municipal and ecclesiastical authorities mentioned earlier, that so many *moriscos* were able to beat the expulsion decrees and remain in Spain. And to these must be added the *moriscos*' Old Christian neighbours, not all of whom hated the *moriscos* or wanted to see them leave. In the celebrated meeting between Ricote and Sancho Panza, Cervantes depicted the sort of neighbourly relations that could exist even between an educated *morisco* and an illiterate Old Christian peasant, relations that extended to the whole of the village according to Sancho, who recounts to Ricote how they all came out of their houses to see the departure of the *moriscos* and show their solidarity with them:

> séte decir que salió tu hija tan hermosa, que salieron a verla cuantos había en el pueblo, y todos decían que era la más bella criatura del mundo. Iba llorando y abrazaba a todas sus amigas y conocidas, y a cuantos llegaban a verla, y a todos pedía le encomendasen a Dios y a Nuestra Señora su madre; y esto, con tanto sentimiento, que a mí me hizo llorar, que no suelo ser muy llorón. Y a fee que muchos tuvieron deseo de esconderla y salir a quitársela en el camino; pero el miedo de ir contra el mandado del rey los detuvo.[26]

Such scenes were repeated all over Spain and, as we have seen, Aznar Cardona hinted at one such in the village of Épila. Once deported, many *moriscos* did keep in touch (or try to) with their former neighbours and very quickly a clandestine postal service was in operation (one of its centres of operations was in fact the palace of the Duke of Pastrana in Madrid). After having been robbed and shipwrecked off Africa with his young family, the

---

[26] *Don Quijote*, II, 54 (Madrid: Castalia, 1978), pp. 453–4.

Granadine *morisco* Pedro Hernández wrote on 2 November 1610 from Tetuan to his former Old Christian mistress Doña Catalina de Valdés in Málaga asking for her help and 200 ducats to enable him to get to Marseille, 'para que yo pueda salir de entre tan mal[a] gente'; he finished his letter with these heartfelt words: 'nosotros estamos padeciendo entre la más bella nación que hay en el mundo'.[27] Antonio de Ávila wrote on 30 March 1611 to his Old Christian neighbour and friend Sebastián Redondo recounting his exile in the south of France and noting 'el sentimiento que yo tengo de mi patria y amigos como el señor Sebastián Rredondo, ssiento mucho su avsencia'.[28] In similar terms the *morisco Licenciado* Don Ángel Molina wrote to his Old Christian neighbour Don Jerónimo de Loaisa of Trujillo on 25 July 1611 from Algiers: 'El no haber hecho esto por extenso antes de agora, no ha sido haberme olvidado de la mucha merced que siempre de su casa he recibido porque esto he tenido y tengo en la memoria mientras viviere.'[29] Diego Luis Morlem from the *Cinco Villas* of the Campo de Calatrava also sent a letter back from France, on 10 November 1611, full of news about his contingent of expelled *moriscos* for the folks back home and with a final patriotic flourish worthy of Ricote: 'viéndonos en tierra extraña, fuera de nuestro natural, que estamos llorando por él lágrimas de sangre'.[30] Thus the official propaganda that made out that the *moriscos* were not really Spaniards at all, that they had no support in Spain, that everyone was glad to see the back of them, was in many cases just that: propaganda, not reality.

Another area where official propaganda was rife was in the depiction of the *moriscos*: negative, stereotyped and dehumanizing. In order to separate the *moriscos* from the rest of the population the government needed to make them different, distinct, less than the rest, a people not worth defending. A good example of such propaganda is provided by Aznar Cardona's *Expulsión justificada de los moriscos españoles*, where we find the following description of the *moriscos*:

> [E]ran una gente vilísima, descuidada, enemiga de las letras y ciencias ilustres, compañeras de la virtud, y por el consiguiente ajena de todo trato urbano, cortés y político. Criaban sus hijos cerriles como bestias, sin enseñanza racional y doctrina de salud, excepto la forzosa [. . .] Eran torpes en sus razones, bestiales en su discurso, bárbaros en su lenguaje, ridículos

---

[27] AGS Estado, leg. 247.

[28] AHN Inquisición, leg. 3205, exp. 1, cited in Serafín de Tapia, 'Los moriscos de Castilla la Vieja, ¿una identidad en proceso de disolución?', *Sharq al-Andalus. Estudios Mudéjares y Moriscos*, 12 (1995), 179–95 (pp. 194–5).

[29] Letter published by Florencio Janer, *Condición social de los moriscos de España: Causas de su expulsión, y consecuencias que ésta produjo en el orden económico y político* (Madrid: Imprenta de la Real Academia de la Historia, 1857 [facsimile edition: Barcelona: Editorial Alta Fulla, 1987]), p. 350.

[30] AGS Estado, leg. 233.

> en su traje [. . .] Eran brutos en sus comidas; comiendo siempre en tierra (como quienes eran), sin mesa, sin otro aparejo que oliese a personas, durmiendo de la misma manera, en el suelo . . .[31]

Accustomed as we are to modern-day propaganda we can recognize immediately the strategies that the Aragonese theologian employs: he reduces the *moriscos* to the level of animals (who eat and sleep on the floor), of irrational beasts, a people without education. We note the language that he uses: *gente vilísima, enemiga, [gente] ajena, hijos cerriles, bestias, torpes, bestiales, bárbaros, ridículos, brutos,* etc. As the Nazis taught us, once you have converted your enemy into an irrational animal, a dehumanized being, his extermination becomes so much easier.

Such was the power of this propaganda that we find echoes of it not just in the apologists for the expulsion, but also in other writers of the time, as we see in this extract: 'No gastan con sus hijos en los estudios, porque su ciencia no es otra que la del robarnos . . .'. These words are spoken by Berganza about his *morisco* master in Cervantes's *El coloquio de los perros*.[32] And yet elsewhere, we find that the *moriscos* were criticized for precisely the opposite, for social climbing and trying to merge into the general population:

> armados y vestidos como cristianos, y hablando la misma lengua [. . .] Que se hacían dueños del dinero porque estaban apoderados de todos los tratos y contrataciones, mayormente en los mantenimientos, que es el crisol donde se funde la moneda. Y, para mejor usar de ello, se habían hecho tenderos, despenseros, panaderos, carniceros, taberneros, y aguadores, pasteleros, buñoleros y hortelanos, y que era inconveniente que nuestros enemigos declarados se hiciesen dueños de lo que es dinero, consistiendo en él la mayor parte de la conservación y prosperidad de la cosa pública.[33]

Naturally, the *moriscos* could not win in this dialectical struggle: if they did not speak Castilian and persisted in dressing in an Arab style, they were deemed to be inassimilable; if they did speak the language and dressed like any other Christian, then they were potential spies, a fifth column bent on helping the enemies of the Crown. If, on top of that, they dared to climb socially and hold important posts in their communities or villages, then they were doing it solely in order to control the local economy. Such was the fear

---

[31] Pedro Aznar Cardona, *Expulsión justificada de los moriscos españoles y suma de las excelencias cristianas de Nuestro Rey Felipe Tercero* (Huesca: Pedro Cabarte, 1612), II, fols 32v–33r.

[32] *Novelas ejemplares*, ed. Harry Sieber, 2 vols (Madrid: Cátedra, 1980), II, p. 350.

[33] The words of the Patriarch Juan de Ribera, cited in Jaime Bleda, *Corónica de los moros de España* (Valencia: Felipe Mey, 1618), p. 893 [facsimile edition with introduction by Bernard Vincent and Rafael Benítez Sánchez-Blanco: Valencia: Biblioteca Valenciana-Ajuntament de València-Universitat de València, 2001].

that educated *moriscos* inspired among some of the local population that the *diputado* Pedro de Vega petitioned the King in the *Cortes* of Castile of 1607 to prevent *moriscos* gaining access to the Faculties of Medicine, since 'estudian y practican muchos en las Universidades de Alcalá y Toledo y de otras [. . .] de suerte que en poco tiempo todos o los más médicos serán moriscos'.[34]

This fear of the educated *morisco* flies in the face of views expressed by Aznar Cardona and other apologists of the expulsion that the *moriscos* were no more than uneducated animals, 'bestias torpes, cerriles' as he calls them. Even today, historians continue to peddle the same stereotypical image: '[Con la expulsion de los moriscos] no hubo efectos culturales, a diferencia de lo que sucediera con la expulsión de los judíos. El nivel educativo de los moriscos era bajo.'[35] The fact is that there were many educated *moriscos* in Spain, who sent their children to the local schools and from there to university.[36] If you know their names and surnames it is not difficult to find them in the matriculation records of the University of Alcalá, for example. Because they all had normal Castilian names at this period, they do not stand out in the records; they merge happily with the rest of the population, exactly what they wanted. As a result, many *morisco* communities in New Castile and Extremadura were led by an educated élite of university graduates, lawyers, doctors, teachers, priests, who held many of the key posts in their towns and villages, such as *alcalde, regidor, escribano, notario* and so on, as this extract from a memorial sent to Philip III in May 1611 shows:

> Y es ansí que los [moriscos] que hay en la dicha villa de Villarrubia de los Ajos son del tiempo del Católico Rey don Fernando de gloriosa memoria, todos ellos habidos y tenidos por cristianos viejos y como tales admitidos a todos los oficios honrosos de la república, porque han sido y ejercido los oficios de alcaldes y regidores y los demás honrosos de la república de tiempo inmemorial a esta parte, y son clérigos presbíteros y letrados graduados en las universidades de estos reinos, y muchos de ellos son escribanos públicos y notarios apostólicos, y han servido y de presente sirven a Vuestra Majestad en la guerra con oficios de capitanes, alférez y

---

34 Cited in A. Galmés de Fuentes, 'La conversión de los moriscos y su pretendida aculturación', in *La política y los moriscos en la época de los Austria*, dir. Rodolfo Gil Grimau (Madrid: Comunidad de Madrid, 1999), pp. 157–74 (p. 164).

35 Luis Suárez Fernández, 'Repercusiones políticas de la cuestión morisca', in Marañón, pp. 143–57 (p. 156).

36 Serafín de Tapia showed well over a decade ago that literacy was higher among the *moriscos* of Ávila than among the Old Christian population: 'Es sorprendente que los varones convertidos tuvieran más facilidad para firmar que sus coetáneos cristianos viejos, incluso desde el momento de su conversión en 1502. Tal fenómeno no deja de ser chocante, pues ha sido lugar común hablar del ínfimo nivel cultural de los moriscos' (*La comunidad morisca de Ávila* (Salamanca: Ediciones Universidad de Salamanca, 1991), p. 338).

sargentos y soldados, puestos en presidio de la costa de la mar con muchas ventajas y premios de Vuestra Majestad. Y los demás son casados con cristianos viejos y vividos y conformes con ellos en todo el trato y comunicación . . .[37]

Another memorial sent to the King in November 1611 lists the most important *moriscos* of the village, 'entre los cuales hay dos clérigos presbíteros, dos letrados, un notario apostólico y un maestro de niños'.[38] Fortunately, we can identify this *morisco* élite in Villarrubia: the two presbyters were Pedro Naranjo and Alonso Rodríguez; the two lawyers were Lope el Niño and Alonso Herrador; the apostolic notary was Juan Mellado (brother of Lope el Niño), and the primary school teacher was Gabriel Peras. These families and others related to them, like the descendants of Alí de Mariota, who changed his name to Pedro López de Mariota when he converted in 1502, exercised considerable power in a village that never had a population of more than 4,000 souls during this period. And obviously, they do not correspond to the typical portrait of the rural *morisco*, this 'grey de labradores y artesanos analfabetos, ignorantes' (Galmés de Fuentes, p. 162), a description that is so often bandied about and which Aznar Cardona and others reproduce in their anti-*morisco* diatribes.[39] The *moriscos* of Villarrubia (and other towns and villages in the Campo de Calatrava, such as Almagro and Daimiel) had seen and grasped the benefits of education, and it was of course the presence of an educated élite in their ranks that helped many of these communities to fight the edicts of expulsion and thus remain in the country after 1614.[40]

Another topical complaint levelled against the *moriscos* is their supposed fertility: they married younger and had more children than their Old Christian neighbours, their sons did not enlist in the army and thus die in battle as

---

[37] AHPZ Híjar, 1ª–36–74.

[38] AGS Estado, leg. 235.

[39] Galmés de Fuentes cites this topic in order to demonstrate the contrary, as he says in another study: 'Porque, si es cierto que muchos moriscos fueron "rudos e ignaros", entre ellos, lo mismo que entre sus contemporáneos de las otras dos castas, existió una elite burguesa y culta' (*Los moriscos [desde su misma orilla]* (Madrid: Instituto Egipcio de Estudios Islámicos en Madrid, 1993), p. 38).

[40] On the education of the *moriscos* of Villarrubia, see my studies 'Un Ricote verdadero: el licenciado Alonso Herrador de Villarrubia de los Ojos de Guadiana – morisco que vuelve', in *Memoria de la palabra. Actas del VI Congreso de la AISO, Burgos-La Rioja, 15–19 de julio 2002*, eds María Luisa Lobato and Francisco Domínguez Matito, 2 vols (Madrid: Iberoamericana-Vervuert, 2004), I, pp. 601–12; 'Literacy and Education in Early Modern Rural Spain: the Case of Villarrubia de los Ojos', in *The Iberian Book and its Readers. Essays for Ian Michael*, eds Nigel Griffin, Clive Griffin and Eric Southworth, *Bulletin of Spanish Studies*, 81 (2004), 1011–37; and 'Educación y movilidad social entre los moriscos del Campo de Calatrava', in *Actas del XV Congreso de la AIH, Monterrey, julio de 2004* [in press].

did so many Spaniards of this period, and few if any of their children entered the Church or religious orders. In short, they would soon outnumber the rest of the population, a view expressed with admirable simplicity and clarity by Damián Fonseca in 1612:

> Iban creciendo en ella [*España*] mucho más que el número de los amigos [*españoles*] y así, aunque por aquel tiempo fuesen muchos menos, la buena cuenta dice que dentro de pocos siglos habían de ser ellos los más, porque se casaban antes de los 20 años y no los consumían las guerras, ni las Indias, ni los presidios de Flandes o de Italia; ni de su casta había frailes ni monjas ni beatos y los clérigos eran muy raros; y todos multiplicaban como conejos; y por esta cuenta no es mucho que se doblase el número cada diez años, y siendo así, de cada mil se harían más de un millón dentro de 100 años.[41]

While Fonseca saw the *moriscos* breeding like rabbits, Aznar Cardona viewed them as weeds sprouting up all over the place, for their intention, he said, 'era crecer y multiplicarse en número como las malas hierbas [. . .]. Todos se casaban, pobres y ricos, sanos y cojos' (*Expulsión*, II, fol. 37). Once again, Cervantes echoed this chorus of complaints via his anti-*morisco* mouthpiece Berganza: 'Entre ellos no hay castidad, ni entran en religión ellos ni ellas; todos se casan, todos se multiplican, porque el vivir sobriamente aumenta las causas de la generación. No los consume la guerra, ni ejercicio que demasiadamente los trabaje.'[42] The notable degree of similarity in the language used by these different authors would suggest that they were simply repeating well-rehearsed commonplaces. The reality of course is that the *moriscos* were no more fertile than their Old Christian counterparts. Where detailed studies have been carried out on local populations, size of family and birth rates, the figures if anything suggest that the *moriscos* had smaller families than their Old Christian neighbours. As Juan Aranda Doncel has concluded from the evidence found for Córdoba: 'se puede colegir que la fecundidad morisca, al igual que ocurre en Cáceres, es inferior a la cristiana'.[43] To this can be added the more detailed information available for the Albaicín of Granada: 'Les Morisques sont en moyenne 4 par foyer, chiffre inférieur à celui des foyers chrétiens [. . .] Il semble bien que l'on doit appliquer le coefficient 4 para *vecino* morisque et 4,5 par *vecino* chrétien.'[44]

---

41 *Justa expulsión de los moriscos de España, con la instrucción, apostasía y traición dellos* (Roma: Iacomo Mascardo, 1612), p. 174.

42 *Novelas ejemplares*, II (Madrid: Cátedra, 1982), p. 350.

43 *Los moriscos en tierras de Córdoba* (Córdoba: Publicaciones del Monte de Piedad y Caja de Ahorros de Córdoba, 1984), p. 93.

44 Bernard Vincent, 'L'Albaicín de Grenade au XVIe siècle (1527–1587)', *Mélanges de la Casa de Velázquez*, 7 (1971), 187–222 (pp. 195–8). In 'Amor y matrimonio entre los moriscos', in *Minorías y marginados en la España del siglo XVI* (Granada: Diputación Provincial, 1987), pp. 47–71, Vincent gives a very useful picture of the size of Morisco

When a similar picture emerged in respect of the *moriscos* of Cuenca, Mercedes García-Arenal was led to observe: 'desde luego parece absolutamente desmesurada y exagerada, probablemente a causa de la desconfianza y el temor, la insistencia en la fecundidad morisca'.[45]

The danger with official propaganda is not so much that those who purvey it end up believing it, which is bad enough, but that those who come later do so. Too much *morisco* historiography in fact has been based on what the government of Philip III and Lerma wanted us all to believe. By relying so much on the 'official' version of events to be found in the State papers of Simancas or those of the Inquisition (or, indeed, in the diatribes of writers such as Bleda, Fonseca, Aznar Cardona *et al.*), many historians have willingly gone along with that 'official' view, rarely questioning the validity or reliability of what they were reading. As Gregorio Colás Latorre has stated:

> Finalmente una parte de la historiografía ha sido víctima de un craso error. Ha otorgado a los papeles 'estatales' e inquisitoriales una credibilidad que nunca debió conceder. Como toda documentación política, la del Consejo de Estado responde, ante todo, a unos determinados intereses, en este caso a los de la monarquía hispana del Quinientos. En ningún momento pretende ser testigo o dar testimonio de la realidad de su tiempo. La Inquisición, por su parte, necesita herejes para sobrevivir además de conseguir las confesiones de sus víctimas, si es preciso, mediante tortura. Y siempre queda la duda, que nunca parece haberse planteado en el caso concreto de los moriscos, de la validez de un testimonio conseguido por la violencia . . .[46]

And yet, even here, while agreeing with the main thrust of Colás Latorre's arguments, we have to be careful. The Council of State was made up of men of quite varying and often opposed opinions: at the one extreme was the Cardinal Archbishop of Toledo, Lerma's uncle Don Bernardo de Sandoval y Rojas, who, unsurprisingly, never wavered in his support of the expulsion; at the other were the Duke of the Infantado and the Duke of Albuquerque who almost always spoke up for the *moriscos*, especially the *antiguos*. Between the hawkish Cardinal and the dove-like Dukes we can place the rest of the councillors, with some, like the *Comendador Mayor* of León, changing his

---

families in different areas (pp. 50–1). The average is approximately 3.6 persons per family: Cáceres, 3.5; Córdoba, 3.6; Cuenca, 3.6; Extremadura, 3.7; Salamanca, 3.6. Clearly there is nothing here to suggest an excessive fertility or overbreeding; the opposite in fact is the case, since an average family size of 3.6 members is insufficient to maintain the population, let alone overtake the Old Christian one.

[45] 'Los moriscos de la región de Cuenca según los censos establecidos por la Inquisición en 1589 y 1594', *Hispania*, 38 (1978), 151–99 (p. 170).

[46] 'Los moriscos aragoneses: una definición más allá de la religión y la política', *Sharq al-Andalus. Estudios Mudéjares y Moriscos*, 12 (1995), 147–61 (p. 148).

opinion on the matter over time. The Council of State was not then a mono-lithic body one hundred percent in support of the expulsion. The Council minutes show that every single meeting threw up intense debate and disagreement, which increased the longer the expulsion went on. The Council of State was also engaged in a running battle with the Count of Salazar over the extent of his powers, especially those he had arrogated to himself and his Junta to judge the legitimacy of the *moriscos'* claims to be good Christians. The Council saw this as an assault on its own powers and those of the Royal Council, which had always judged these legal matters, and constantly petitioned the King to have Salazar put in his place.

For the *moriscos*, the internal disagreements of the Council of State and its relentless battle with Salazar proved to be a godsend, since they meant that every edict, every new move in the expulsion was heavily contested and its implementation delayed. Effectively, the longer the expulsions dragged on, the more chance the *moriscos* had of remaining in Spain, as indeed proved to be the case. However united and determined the King, Lerma and Salazar were in their efforts to expel all the *moriscos* without exception, they were opposed by people equally determined if not to thwart their efforts, then at least to delay them and ameliorate their worst effects. By the end, even the hawkish members of the Council of State were coming round to the view that the expulsion had gone on too long and an end to it had to be called. A memorandum the Council sent to the King on 20 February 1614 left no doubt as to its feelings on the matter:

> se ha platicado en el Consejo sobre lo mucho que conviene al servicio de Dios y de Vuestra Majestad que cesen ya las delaciones y jurisdicciones que hay en esta matera de expulsión, y que, teniéndola por concluida, se trate solamente de que no vuelvan los que han salido, y castigar a los que lo hicieren por medio de las justicias ordinarias [. . .] y que se ordene al conde de Salazar que alce la mano de esta negociación . . .[47]

In short, they were content for those who had not been expelled to remain and to be left alone in peace and quiet. Many *moriscos* who found them-selves in this category must have heaved a sigh of relief, as must their many supporters, and the large numbers of *moriscos* waiting in North Africa and southern France for the right moment to return to their homeland, for they knew as did the Council of State (and Salazar who was apoplectic at the deci-sion) that almost no *moriscos* had been punished for returning to Spain nor any who had aided them, in spite of the threats contained in every *bando*. And this is another side of the expulsion that has not received the attention it deserves, because, again, it goes against the 'official' view.

Finally, too much reliance has been placed on the supposed ingrained

[47] AGS Estado, leg. 2644.

Islamic faith and culture of the *moriscos* (whereby all *moriscos* without exception were crypto-Muslims), thereby ignoring the fact that they were also economic and social entities and thus a part of the political and socio-economic fabric of Christian society that surrounded them and into which they were inserted. Many *morisco* groups had lived for centuries side by side with their Christian neighbours in peace and harmony, to such an extent that by the sixteenth century racial, ethnic and religious divisions rarely came into play or were barely visible. The evidence for this will not come from the papers held in Simancas or the Archivo Histórico Nacional in Madrid, but from local and seigniorial archives where the voice of the *morisco* can still be heard, if one knows where to look for it.

The same is true if we are looking for evidence of their survival post-1614. Many historians have denied that the *moriscos* could have stayed behind or returned from exile, even when their own investigations seemed to show the opposite. They have swallowed the government propaganda that wanted us to believe that they had all been expelled, and expelled because they were inassimilable and/or a danger. As Rafael Benítez Sánchez-Blanco has pondered (my italics):

> Pero me pregunto si, en el fondo, no se habrá invertido el orden lógico y aceptado que *ya que se les expulsó debían ser inasimilables y un peligro*. Si no habremos admitido buenamente como explicación histórica la excusa oficial para expulsarles. Si no nos hemos dejado intoxicar con la verdad oficial.[48]

The demographic and economic evidence for their survival in Spain has been largely overlooked, although it is there. When Earl J. Hamilton studied the economy of Andalusia to see the effects of the expulsions, he came to the conclusion that the only explanation for the lack of a significant downturn in the economy was that many of the *moriscos* had managed to stay or return soon after their expulsion.[49] My own studies of the economy of Villarrubia de los Ojos have come to the same conclusion. Had the *moriscos* of Villarrubia (some 40–50% of the population in 1611) been expelled, the effects on the local economy would have been disastrous and long-lasting, but neither is the case. Demographic evidence – the continuance of the same families and names well after the expulsions of 1609–14 as well as little or

---

[48] 'Las relaciones moriscos–cristianos viejos: entre la asimilación y el rechazo', in *Disidencias y exilios en la España moderna. Actas de la IV Reunión Científica de la Asociación Española de Historia Moderna*, eds Antonio Mestre Sanchis and Enrique Giménez López (Alicante: CAM/Universidad de Alicante, 1997), pp. 335–46 (p. 336).

[49] Earl J. Hamilton, 'Las consecuencias económicas de la expulsión de los moriscos', in *Actas del I Congreso de Historia de Andalucía. Andalucía Moderna (Siglos XVI–XVII)*, vol. II (Córdoba: Publicaciones del Monte de Piedad y Caja de Ahorros de Córdoba, 1978), pp. 69–84.

no downturn in the number of baptisms – also supports the view of a continuing *morisco* presence in Spain. Apart from the Campo de Calatrava and the Val de Ricote, where even contemporaries agreed that the *moriscos* had returned en masse, documentary evidence suggests that some of them stayed on in Ciudad Rodrigo, in Valladolid, in Ávila, and in many parts of Andalusia, Extremadura and Aragon. It may well be the case that the only part of the country where the expulsion was at all successful was Valencia.

It is also true that the evidence available can present two quite opposite pictures, depending on the prejudices of the researcher. Let us take the example of baptismal records. Since I knew that Villarrubia had a large *morisco* population, which by the time of the expulsions constituted almost one-half of the village total (some 300 families out of c. 650), I expected to find a significant drop in the number of baptisms and marriages recorded for the period during and after the expulsion, i.e. 1611–15, assuming that the *moriscos* had in fact been expelled. When I found that the number of baptisms and marriages did not diminish but actually increased (for baptisms) and remained steady (for marriages), I had no alternative but to assume that the *moriscos* had not been expelled from Villarrubia, a point of view confirmed by studying the names of those baptised and married. María del Carmen Ansón Calvo similarly studied the baptismal records of various villages in the Campo de Cariñena of Aragon to test the existence of *moriscos* there.[50] When she discovered in some of her sample almost no diminution in the number of baptisms between 1610 (when the expulsions began in Aragon) and later years, she came to the conclusion that in these villages there were no *moriscos* to be expelled, hence no drop in the birth rate. She might be right, but her findings would have been exactly the same if these villages had had *moriscos* who either managed to escape the expulsion or returned after being expelled. Unfortunately, she did not consider this possibility, one has to presume because she had accepted without question the official version that all the *moriscos* of Aragon were expelled.

It is high time therefore to begin to mistrust the official version of events, to put the stereotypes to one side, to look for signs of coexistence and co-operation between *morisco* and Old Christian rather than hatred and separation, to judge the *moriscos* not just as imagined crypto-Muslims and therefore an inassimilable fifth column but also as political and socio-economic entities fully involved in the communities that surrounded them and in which they played their part, religious as well as social.[51] How else can we explain the otherwise bizarre episode where the *moriscos* of Gea de Albarracín, near

[50] 'La expulsión de los moriscos en el Campo de Cariñena', in *Destierros aragoneses. I. Judíos y Moriscos* (Zaragoza: Institución Fernando el Católico, 1988), pp. 261–72.

[51] See my 'Convivencia y cooperación entre moriscos y cristianos del Campo de Calatrava: De nuevo con Cervantes y Ricote', in *Siglos Dorados. Homenaje a Augustin Redondo*, ed. Pierre Civil, 2 vols (Madrid: Editorial Castalia, 2004), I, pp. 301–14.

Teruel, complained to the Church authorities about the village priest allotted
to them who was so ignorant that the *moriscos* themselves had to teach him
the catechism (they asked for one to be sent who could instruct them, rather
than the other way around);[52] or the situation in many villages of Valencia
where it was the majority *morisco* parishioners who had to certify the efficacy and dedication of the local priest – the quality of his sermons, teaching
of the catechism, administration of the sacraments – before he could be
paid.[53]

The picture that evolves as we move away from the 'official' version of
events is one of a more pluralist Spain than we have ever been led to believe
existed at this time, a Spain where central authority was heavily circum-
scribed and wholly dependent on local goodwill for implementation of its
edicts and decrees. Early modern Spain was not a monolithic state following
a single ideology; it was made up of myriad little states where the writ of the
government often did not run at all. Like many other nobles and local municipal authorities, the Count of Salinas as Lord of Villarrubia was able to
ignore, when not subvert, the orders he received from Madrid regarding the
expulsion of his *moriscos*, yet he suffered no unwelcome consequences.
Salazar might have railed against his unwillingness to follow orders and
demanded an example be made of him, Lerma might have been annoyed by
his behaviour, the King might have wished for more compliance, but in the
end Salinas held on to his post as President of the Council of Portugal, and
just two years after the end of the expulsions was promoted to Viceroy and
Captain General of Portugal. It is well not to lose sight of this fact: the
government of early modern Spain did not have the resources or the political
structures to impose its will on all its subjects; government operated through
a client system and largely by consent, and with regard to the expulsion of
the *moriscos* consent from many individuals and groups was simply not
forthcoming. Local reality proved in the end to be stronger than official
rhetoric and the propaganda that it spawned.

[52] Quoted in Jesús Maiso González, 'La cuestión morisca en Bulbuente, 1576–1700',
in *Estudios del Departamento de Historia Moderna. Facultad de Filosofía y Letras,
Zaragoza* (Zaragoza: Universidad, 1976), pp. 247–77 (p. 258). It is also worth pointing out
that the *moriscos* of this area of Aragon voluntarily accepted baptism in 1502, even
though they were not required to (forcible conversion in Aragon did not take place until
1526).

[53] See Santiago La Parra-López, 'Los moriscos y moriscas de los Borja', in
*Disidencias y exilios en la España moderna. Actas de la IV Reunión Científica de la
Asociación Española de Historia Moderna, Alicante, 27–30 de mayo de 1996*, ed. Antonio
Mestre Sanchis (Alicante: Universidad de Alicante, 1998), pp. 435–46 (pp. 440–1).

Arbitrismo and the Early Seventeenth-Century Spanish Church: The Theory and Practice of Anti-Clericalist Philosophy

HELEN RAWLINGS

The opening decades of the seventeenth century, in particular the period 1615–25, witnessed the publication of an unprecedented volume of polemical literature in Spain that focused on the acute crisis – demographic and economic in its broad dimensions – engulfing its kingdoms. The authors were a heterogeneous group of commentators, collectively known as the *arbitristas*, who, via their treatises, put forward a range of expedients (*arbitrios*) for curing the ills afflicting the body politic. Foreign observers, political theorists and members of the *Cortes*, among others, also presented their advice to the monarch and his ministers within what was a remarkably open forum of public debate. Although the *arbitristas* were criticized by their contemporaries for being irrational in their judgements, and indeed were satirized in the writings of Cervantes and Quevedo, their role has been favourably reassessed by modern scholars. The *arbitristas* included academics, clergymen and merchants, as well as members of central and local government. Accordingly their approaches varied, encompassing a broad social, political and intellectual spectrum. When viewed collectively, their treatises provide historians with a unique insight into how Spaniards perceived their nation's decline.[1]

One of the common concerns to which the *arbitristas* drew attention in their writing, little studied to date, is the contribution that the Spanish Church made to the crisis in which the country found itself. The excessive growth of the clerical estate, so they argued, had created a demographic

---

[1]   J.H. Elliott, 'Self-perception and decline in early seventeenth century Spain', in *Spain and its World, 1500–1700* (New Haven: Yale UP, 1989), pp. 241–61; Henry Kamen, *Spain, 1469–1714* (London: Longman, 1999), pp. 231–36; Jean Vilar, *Literatura y Economía. La figura satírica del arbitrista en el Siglo de Oro* (Madrid: Revista de Occidente, 1973), pp. 59–102. This chapter incorporates some material originally published in chapter 6 of my *Church, Religion and Society in Early Modern Spain* (Basingstoke: Palgrave, 2002) and reproduced here with kind permission of Palgrave Macmillan.

imbalance, seriously reducing the size of the potential labour force. As a profession, the Church encouraged idleness and a lack of interest in economically productive activities. The exemptions and privileges enjoyed by the clerical estate were regarded as having a polarizing effect on society, protecting its own members while accentuating the plight of those who carried the burden of service and tribute. Contemporaries observed that a disproportionate amount of wealth had been absorbed by the Church, instead of being channelled into more productive areas of investment. At certain levels, they claimed, it had also allowed itself to succumb to corrupt practices of preferment. Beyond the small *arbitrista* circle, many Spaniards' fundamental perception of the Spanish Church was that of an institution responsible for taking away the potential force and vitality of an ailing nation, for widening the contrast between privilege and poverty in society, and for readily accepting those without training or calling into its ranks. Although it might appear paradoxical that controversial opinions in respect of the Church were allowed to enter into the public debate at a time in Spain's history when Catholicism held such political as well as ideological sway, the publication of anti-clerical views of this sort (along with other *arbitrista* remedies) was essentially designed to alert and advise the King and his government on ways to turn around the nation's declining fortunes. This kind of writing was by nature exaggerated and rhetorical in order to achieve its desired effect and acquired a special intensity in early seventeenth-century Spain, where criticism of the Church was not necessarily incompatible with a fervent devotion to its teachings.

Many *arbitristas*, significantly, were members of the clerical profession itself. Sancho de Moncada was a priest and professor of theology at the University of Toledo. In his *Restauración política de España* of 1619, he presented a series of proposals designed to increase Spain's prosperity. He drew a direct parallel between the harshness of economic circumstance and the increase in clerical recruitment. 'Muchos son eclesiásticos o religiosos', he wrote, 'por no poder pasar en el siglo, y así lo que causa [*la*] pobreza del reino es lo que los obliga a ser religiosos y eclesiásticos, por no poder tomar otro estado, y eso es lo que tiene la culpa.'[2] In his view, the plethora of ill-prepared religious, as well as diminishing respect for the Church, was seriously reducing the size of the nation's workforce. Reiterating the recommendations of the Council of Trent (1545–63) on Catholic reform, Moncada urged that a stricter control be exercised on the educational qualities of those seeking entry to the priesthood; likewise, only those with a true sense of vocation and the means to fund their own living should join the religious orders. These measures, he argued, would serve to restore the social and

---

[2] *Restauración política de España*, ed. Jean Vilar (Madrid: Instituto de Estudios Fiscales, 1974), p. 136.

fiscal imbalance, by providing more people to engage in labour, commerce and agriculture and contribute to the economy.

Licenciado Jerónimo de Ceballos, a Toledan lawyer and local councillor (*regidor*), published in 1620 his *Discurso sobre el remedio de la Monarquía Española* – a treatise addressed to the monarch on how he might arrest Spain's decline, including a recommendation to reduce the size of the clerical estate. In it he drew attention to 'el gran número de personas que entra cada día en las Religiones, en las quales con sólo un saco de sayal se halla honra y provecho con la mayor dignidad del mundo, teniendo licencia para recibir de todos, pero no para dar a nadie'.[3] Ceballos argued that there were too many clergy for Spain's needs, many of them unworthy of the profession, and that the Church provided the opportunity to escape social denigration in menial occupations, as well as conferring protection under ecclesiastical as opposed to secular law. Ironically, though, he eventually became a beneficiary of ecclesiastical office himself. In 1625, following two unsuccessful applications, he was preferred to a prestigious New Kings chaplaincy within Toledo cathedral – an honorary appointment reserved for loyal Toledan citizens.[4]

The Cistercian friar and university professor, Ángel Manrique, published a discourse in 1624, called *Socorro del clero al estado*, in which he criticized the Crown for encouraging the growth of the clerical estate in disproportion to the needs of secular society: 'No hay año en que no se instituyan de nuevo gran cantidad de capellanías y otros beneficios, ni ciudad donde de cinquenta años a esta parte no se hayan fundado tres doblados conventos que tenía antes. Viene a ser que en algunas haya menos vecinos que eclesiásticos.'[5] How could God be calling so many more men to his ministry? Ambition, greed and a desire to move up the social ladder were all identified by Manrique as being motivating forces: 'Que algunos hacen vanidad del estado eclesiástico; y les parece que el hijo cura hace hidalgo al padre labrador; el canónigo caballero al mercader, y que si alguno llega a ser obispo será el lustre de todo su linage' (Manrique, fol. 31). But, significantly, these controversial views on the distorted honorific value attached to ecclesiastical office did not deter his own rise up the career ladder, culminating in his appointment to the bishopric of Badajoz in 1645.

The canon of Santiago, royal chaplain and secretary, Pedro Fernández de Navarrete, published a treatise on the condition of the monarchy in 1626, entitled *Conservación de Monarquías*, in which he criticized the Church for accepting men of little talent into the profession. Over sixty years after the

---

3   Jerónimo de Ceballos, *Discurso sobre el remedio de la Monarquía Española* (Toledo: n. pub., 1620), BNM MS 5791, fols 263–70.

4   AHN Consejos Suprimidos, leg. 15224, doc. 24 (appointment to New Kings chaplaincy, 10 October 1625).

5   Ángel Manrique, *Socorro del clero al estado* (Salamanca, 1624, repr. Madrid: n. pub., 1814), BNM R/61605, fol. 17.

Council of Trent's recommendations on ecclesiastical reform, Church offices were still being dispensed too freely, without proper regard for the calibre or background of candidates, resulting in a lowering of moral and educational standards within its ranks:

> Vaya creciendo tanto el número de clérigos seculares, siendo muchos los que con menos letras y suficiencia entran a estado en que tan necesaria es la sabiduría. Son asimismo muchos los que entran al sacerdocio, sin tener competentes beneficios, o suficientes patrimonios con que sustentarse; de que resulta verse ya en España tanto número de clérigos mendicantes en oprobio del sacerdocio, para cuya estimación es necesaria si no riqueza, al menos congrua pasada.[6]

Like other commentators, Navarrete called for a reduction in the foundation of religious houses and a more thorough examination of all those seeking admittance into holy orders. He also observed that while the Church amassed increasing amounts of material wealth from the bequests of the deceased, it gave very little back in the form of charity. It thus represented a negative form of investment and contributed to the stagnation of the economy. These were harsh judgements that reveal something of the internal dilemmas that existed within the ecclesiastical estate over its own condition, reinforcing those concerns raised in the public debate.

Criticism of the Church also surfaced from within the heart of government. The *Junta de Reformación*, a sub-committee of the Council of Castile, was commissioned by the Crown in 1618 to make recommendations on how to resolve the crisis affecting the kingdom. It was to place the reduction in size of the clerical estate high on the political agenda. In its famous *consulta* of 1 February 1619, the *Junta* remarked upon the dangers of excessive recruitment to the religious orders and how this inevitably led to a relaxation of their rule, thereby overturning the objectives of reform. In its judgement, 'muchas personas [. . .] entran huyendo de la necesidad y con el gusto y dulzura de la ociosidad que por la devoción que a ella les mueve'.[7] The *Junta* advised that, in accordance with Trent's decrees, novices should not be allowed to enter a religious order before the age of sixteen or take their vows before they were twenty. The *Junta* presented even more forceful observations to Philip IV on the low moral and intellectual calibre of the clergy on his accession in 1621:

---

6 *Conservación de Monarquías y discursos políticos*, ed. Michael D. Gordon (Madrid: Instituto de Estudios Fiscales, 1982), discurso XLIV, p. 351.

7 Ángel González Palencia (ed.), *Archivo Histórico Español*, vol. V (Valladolid: n. pub., 1932), *La Junta de Reformación, 1618–1625,* doc. IV, *El Consejo Real a Felipe III*, 1 febrero 1619, pp. 12–30 (pp. 27–8).

La mayor parte de clérigos que hoy hay en estos Reynos han procurado este estado más como oficio y arte para ganarse de comer que por vivir en el con [*la*] mayor perfección cristiana, y así hay entre ellos gran multitud de idiotas sumamente viciosos y escandalosos, y algunos tan pobres y miserables que la necesidad les obliga a hacer muchas cosas en oprobio y afrenta del estado eclesiástico.[8]

But how do the criticisms made by contemporary commentators in respect of the condition of the early seventeenth-century Spanish Church, including its excessive size, wealth and declining standards of clerical recruitment, measure up against modern historical evidence? How far did commonly accepted theories on the causes of decline meet with practice? When we examine the qualitative judgements of the *arbitristas* and other observers alongside the quantitative evidence now at our disposal, certain factors emerge to reshape the debate.

As suggested, the *arbitristas* were commonly concerned about the clericalization of Spanish society. A close examination of the 1591 fiscal census drawn up for the kingdom of Castile (and whose general trends can be applied to the Aragonese territories), suggests that these concerns may well have been exaggerated.[9] At the end of the sixteenth century there were 91,000 secular and regular clergy in Spain, 74,000 or 81 per cent of whom were concentrated in the kingdom of Castile and 17,000 or 18.6 per cent in the crown of Aragón. The ecclesiastical estate made up just over 1.1 per cent of the total population - hardly an exceptional figure (see Table 1). In broad geographical terms there was one member of the clerical estate for every eighty-eight inhabitants. However, their regional distribution was distinctly uneven. The northern coastal areas of Galicia, Asturias and the Basque Country, together with parts of the kingdom of Aragón, had the lowest proportion of clergy relative to inhabitants: a figure of up to 1 per cent. In the central Castilian provinces of León, Ávila, Cuenca. and Segovia, as well as in Valencia and Cartagena in the south-east, the concentration of clergy was slightly higher. Here they represented between 1 and 1.5 per cent of the population. In Catalonia, Extremadura, Salamanca, Toledo, and Seville, the size of the clerical component of society exceeded 1.5 per cent. In the majority of diocesan capitals this figure was further surpassed. Around 75 per cent of clergy were based in towns, whereas well over 80 per cent of the population lived in the countryside. Overall there was a slightly higher presence of clergy, both secular and regular, in the southern half of the kingdom

8   González Palencia, *La Junta*, doc. XLII (*Anónimo a Felipe IV*, 1621?), pp. 227–63 (p. 256).
9   *Censo de la Corona de Castilla, 1591*, facsimile edition (Madrid: Instituto Nacional de Estadística, 1984); Eduardo García España and Annié Molinié-Bertrand, eds, *Censo de Castilla de 1591: Estudio Analítico* (Madrid: Instituto Nacional de Estadística, 1986).

of Castile than in the northern half. The following century witnessed a considerable alteration in the balance between the clerical and non-clerical components of Spanish society.[10]

Table 1. The clerical population of Castile and Aragón in 1591

Clergy	Castile		Aragón		Spain	
	No.	%	No.	%	No.	%
Secular	33,087	0.50	7,512	0.49	40,599	0.50
Regular (m)	20,697	0.31	4,748	0.31	25,445	0.31
Regular (f)	20,369	0.31	4,672	0.31	25,041	0.31
Total number of clergy	74,153	1.12	16,932	1.11	91,085	1.12
Total number of inhabitants	6,534,098	100	1,503,086	100	8,046,184	100

Sources: Felipe Ruiz Martín, 'La población española al comienzo de los tiempos modernos', *Cuadernos de Historia*, I (1967), pp. 189–202 and 'Demografía Eclesiástica', in *Diccionario de Historia Eclesiástica de España*, II (Madrid: CSIC, 1972), pp. 682–733.
Note: A coefficient of 5 inhabitants per household has been used in calculating the size of the lay population.

A recurrent series of demographic catastrophes devastated the Spanish kingdoms during the first quarter of the seventeenth century, beginning with the great plague of 1596–1602. Close on three-quarters of a million Spaniards (some ten per cent of the total population) fell victim to pestilence in the period up to 1614. The kingdom of Castile was worst affected by this crisis, set to intensify in the second quarter of the century in the wake of crop failures and famine. A further wave of plague hit Andalusia in the south and the Levant regions in the east between 1647 and 1652 and carried with it half a million lives. Taking into account all demographic losses, including those attributed to emigration, expulsion and warfare, the Castilian lay population is estimated to have fallen by one and a half million from around six and a half million inhabitants in 1591 to one of five million in 1665, while Spain as a whole may have lost two million inhabitants over this same period. Against this background, the clerical estate underwent a rapid expansion in size. By the mid-1660s there were an estimated 160,000 clergy in Spain, making up

[10] Felipe Ruiz Martín, 'La población española al comienzo de los tiempos modernos', *Cuadernos de Historia*, I (1967), pp. 189–202 and 'Demografía Eclesiástica', in *Diccionario de Historia Eclesiástica de España* [henceforth DHEE], eds Q. Aldea, T. Marín and J. Vives, 4 vols (Madrid: CSIC, 1972–5), II, pp. 682–733; Annié Molinié-Bertrand, 'Le Clergé dans le Royaume de Castille à la fin du XVIe siècle', *Revue d'histoire économique et sociale*, 51 (1978), 5–53.

2.5 per cent of the population. Each member of the clerical estate now served on average forty members of secular society, more than double the figure for the end of the sixteenth century.

No detailed census of the clerical estate, equivalent to that drawn up for Castile in 1591 was available to early seventeenth-century commentators. They sensed growth rather than having actual numerical proof of it. Their calculations thus provide us with a somewhat speculative interpretation of clerical demography. In his treatise of 1619, Sancho de Moncada suggested that a quarter to a third of Spain's population was made up of clergy whereas the late sixteenth-century figure stood at just over 1 per cent. Fray Ángel Manrique wrote in 1624 of a doubling in the size of the clerical estate. At most it grew by 75 per cent over the period 1591 to 1665. He also referred imprecisely to a tripling in the number of monasteries and convents. There were a total of 1,326 religious communities (841 male and 485 female) in Castile at the end of the sixteenth century. By 1623 there were reported to be 2,141 in Spain as a whole; this figure may have risen to 3,000 by 1700.[11] Observers clearly had little or no conception of the relationship between secular and clerical demographic trends, nor were they apparently aware of the diversity affecting the geographical distribution and structural composition of the Church's membership. Their generalizations, therefore, have to be treated with some caution in the absence of more accurate data. Furthermore, it should be noted that the size of the clerical estate peaked in the mid-1660s, after which lay society began to recover its losses. By 1700 Spain had a population – once again on the increase – of some seven million, while the number of clergy had stabilized at around 150,000. Taking into account all these variable factors, the statistical evidence currently available to historians, while confirming in broad terms the view of early seventeenth-century contemporaries that the growth in size of the clerical estate was excessive and unnecessary, nevertheless suggests that the real expansion took place over the longer period of 1600–50 rather than the shorter one of 1600–25. Furthermore, certain sectors of the Spanish Church grew, while others remained stable in size.

Gil González Dávila, a priest and prebendary of Salamanca and court historian to Philip III, acknowledged in 1619, 'Sacerdote soy; confieso que somos más de los que son menester.'[12] The expansion of the ecclesiastical estate, to which he and other contemporaries referred, was not a general phenomenon, but rather one specific to its lower reaches. As far as its secular branch was concerned, there was no major increase in the size of the

11 Ruiz Martín, 'Demografía', pp. 682–9; Antonio Domínguez Ortiz, *Las Clases Privilegiadas en el Antiguo Régimen* (Madrid: Istmo, 1979), p. 274.

12 Gil González Dávila, *Historia de la vida y hechos del inclito monarca, amado y santo Don Felipe Tercero*, in Pedro Salazar de Mendoza, *Monarquía de España* vol. III (Madrid: Ibarra, 1770–1) p. 215.

Church's body of senior stipended clergy (archbishops, bishops, cathedral, and collegiate clergy) during the first half of the seventeenth century. Nor does there appear to have been any significant new recruitment of parish clergy. Indeed, there were continued reports of a shortage of priests in some remote parts of Spain, as well as in those areas worst affected by depopulation. In the diocese of Barcelona, 4,502 men received the tonsure – the first grade of clerical status – over the period 1546–70, but only 284 entered the priesthood (an average of eleven priests per year). In the later period 1635–1717, the number of priests being ordained declined to an average of seven per year.[13]

The calibre of pastoral leadership to be found in early seventeenth-century Spain – about which the *arbitristas* expressed considerable disquiet - varied enormously and was determined by a number of factors including geography, powers of patronage and the provision of clerical training. In the Calahorra region in northern Spain noble patrons acquired the reputation for appointing their own sons to office and for appropriating the tithe for personal gain. In 1616, following a visitation of his diocese, the bishop of Calahorra reported to the Crown that 'los ministros [*de las iglesias*] son inhábiles y de poca virtud y ejemplo, y no pueden enseñar a los feligreses lo que han de menester para salvarse y viven como bárbaros e infieles, sin saber las oraciones ni persignarse' (Domínguez Ortiz, *Las Clases Privilegiadas*, p. 252). The Alpujarras mountains outside Granada, twice the scene of *morisco* uprisings, remained a pastoral 'no man's land' well into the seventeenth century and its inhabitants essentially ignorant of the faith.[14] But modern research indicates that there was an improvement in the educational level of those priests serving in areas close to major centres of learning and where royal rights of presentation were operative. For example, a survey of the backgrounds of ninety priests who held livings in the Archdiocese of Toledo between 1590 and 1660 reveals that 53 per cent had graduated at licenciate level and 15 per cent at doctoral level. A similar phenomenon is recorded in the diocese of Cuenca.[15]

In fact, it was the lesser, supernumerary levels of the secular branch of the clerical estate that expanded most rapidly and where the potential for opportunism was greatest. Although the statistical evidence still remains patchy, the number of assistant priests, chaplains, prebendaries, and minor beneficiaries (without care of souls) in Castile is likely to have grown at least three times during the course of the seventeenth century (from an estimated figure

[13] Henry Kamen, *The Phoenix and the Flame. Catalonia and the Counter-Reformation* (New Haven: Yale UP, 1993), pp. 162–3.

[14] Fernand Braudel, *The Mediterranean and the Mediterranean World in the Age of Philip II* (London: Harper Collins, 1972), I, p. 35.

[15] Sara T. Nalle, *God in La Mancha. Religious Reform and the People of Cuenca, 1500–1650* (Baltimore: Johns Hopkins UP, 1992), pp. 96–103; Helen Rawlings, *Church, Religion and Society*, pp. 67–73.

of 15,000 to one of 45,000), after which it levelled off (Domínguez Ortiz, *Las Clases Privilegiadas*, p. 206). The majority of these simple benefice holders, although classified as clergy, were either unordained or merely tonsured clerics, who exercised a part-time, non- or semi-professional clerical function (for which they generally received a meagre recompense) alongside a lay one. Simple benefice holders, the majority of whom were appointed by lay patrons, gained a reputation – difficult to substantiate from the data available, but widely accepted by contemporaries – for being of limited talent and questionable vocation. At the same time there is some, albeit fragmented, evidence to suggest that the limited opportunities for promotion into the middle ranks of the Spanish Church served to raise the social and academic calibre of recruitment to positions of lower status and thus the prestige they conferred. Many *arbitristas*, Sancho de Moncada, Jerónimo de Ceballos and Pedro Fernández de Navarrete among them – professionals in their own right – were themselves part of this supernumerary expanding branch of the clerical estate. There was a common misunderstanding among contemporaries of the difference between a simple tonsured cleric and a priest who had risen through the official career structure of the Church to acquire a benefice with care of souls, leading to a distortion of what each category actually constituted in terms of size.

Some of the expansion in the number of minor benefice holders derived from the Catholic Church's promotion of intercessory prayer for the dead as a means of facilitating the passage of the soul through purgatory, in contrast to the Protestant Church's rejection of its value. As the mortality rate rose in early seventeenth-century Spain, it prompted more and more money to be spent by the surviving population on 'heavenly protection'. In Toledo, requests for devotional masses rose almost fourfold over half a century, from 106 per testator in the period 1575–1600 to 389 per testator in the period 1601–25.[16] Madrid witnessed a significant multiplication of these figures, an average 500 masses requested via the wills of deceased *madrileños* in the 1570s rising to 777 in the 1590s.[17] The setting up of private chapels to honour the memory of the dead, and the dramatic increase in the number of post-mortem masses being requested, resulted in the endowment of hundreds of chaplaincies to deliver the pious legacies of testators and their families. Sizeable bequests for perpetual masses from members of the élite could ensure a respectable living for some members of the lesser clergy. Lay devotional fervour, generated in response to the Church's teachings and set against the background of the fragility of the times, thus bore considerable responsibility for financing the growth of the clerical estate.

[16] Fernando Martínez Gil, *Muerte y Sociedad en la España de los Austrias* (Madrid: Siglo Veintiuno, 1993), pp. 547–8.

[17] Carlos Eire, *From Madrid to Purgatory. The Art and Craft of Dying in Sixteenth-Century Spain* (Cambridge: CUP, 1995), pp. 178, 186.

The vast expansion in size of the lesser ranks of the secular clergy in late sixteenth-century Spain was accompanied by a parallel growth in membership of the religious orders as they underwent reform and renewal. There were a total of 41,066 regular clergy in Castile in 1591. Over half were concentrated in the major towns of southern and central Castile where favourable economic circumstances encouraged charity and patronage, so essential to their survival. Seven of the most heavily populated Castilian cities housed a total of 9,500 regular clergy and where they outnumbered secular clergy by a ratio approaching 3:1 (see Table 2). It was in urban settlements such as these that early modern Spain acquired the reputation for being excessively clericalized, a false impression created by the uneven distribution of the religious orders throughout the peninsula as a whole. While major cities such as Toledo, Seville, Córdoba, Granada, Valladolid, Salamanca, and Madrid were overpopulated with religious, their presence was less prominent in medium-sized villages and negligible in very small ones. The much-criticized growth of the regular clergy to which contemporaries referred needs to be set within the context of these trends. It was essentially an urban phenomenon resulting from the establishment of new and reformed orders in major towns in the post-Tridentine period.

Table 2. Castilian towns housing over 1,000 religious in 1591

Town	Number of regular clergy	Number of secular clergy	Number of families
Toledo	1,942	793	10,933
Seville	1,666	1,047	18,000
Córdoba	1,505	313	6,257
Granada	1,207	450*	8,200
Valladolid	1,140	350	8,112
Salamanca	1,028	161	4,403
Madrid	1,011	418	14,000

Sources: Eduardo García España and Annie Molinié-Bertrand (eds), Censo de Castilla de 1591: Estudio Analítico (Madrid: Instituto Nacional de Estadística, 1986), pp. 736–7; Felipe Ruiz Martín, 'Demografía Eclesiástica', DHEE, II, p. 717. * Estimated figure.

Madrid provides a prime example of this phenomenon. The re-establishment of the Court in Madrid in 1606 profoundly affected its development. One of the key features of its growth was the foundation of religious houses in the city by prominent members of the nobility, as well as the Crown itself, as a means of further enhancing their status in society and of ensuring their place in heaven. At the end of the sixteenth century, as

Philip III succeeded to the Spanish throne, Madrid had a population of between 70,000 and 80,000 inhabitants, including some 1,000 friars and nuns housed in a total of eighteen communities. Both the new King and the Duke of Lerma, his powerful favourite, were renowned patrons of the orders, notably the Capuchins – a reformed branch of Franciscan friars – who first established themselves in the capital in 1609 and whose influence subsequently spread rapidly through Castile and Andalusia. A total of twelve new religious houses (six convents and six monasteries) were founded in Madrid between 1606 and 1618 (the period immediately following the revival of its status as capital). By the end of Philip III's reign, Madrid's lay population had doubled to 150,000, it provided livings for 1,000 secular clergy, and the number of friars and nuns inhabiting the capital had risen to 2,500.[18] It is surely significant that early seventeenth-century Madrid, where close on one in every forty of its inhabitants belonged to the clerical estate, should be the backdrop for much of the anti-clerical literature being written at the time.

Via their representatives at the Castilian *Cortes*, urban communities regularly voiced their concerns as to the excessive growth in the number of religious houses and the burden they placed on already impoverished citizens. The 1607 *Cortes*, held in Madrid, called upon the Crown to prohibit new religious foundations, especially those of mendicant rule, heavily dependent on charity, for the next ten years:

> Se han aumentado y aumentan cada día tanto los monasterios, mayormente de las Órdenes mendicantes, que padecen mucha necesidad y los naturales de estos reinos no podellos socorrer como quisieran; suplicamos a V.M. mande por diez años no se dé licencia para fundar monasterio ninguno de nuevo.[19]

But the practice continued. The attempt by the 1621 *Cortes* to link the concession of the regular fiscal subsidy known as the *servicio* to a restraint being placed on the licensing of new monasteries failed, and the deliberations of the 1633 session made it clear that dispensations were still being granted for new foundations and the consequences for the wealth of the nation ignored:

---

[18] Gil González Dávila, *Teatro de las Grandezas de la Villa de Madrid* (Madrid: Publicaciones Abella, 1986), pp. 234–99; José Antonio Álvarez y Baena, *Compendio Histórico de las Grandezas de la Coronada Villa de Madrid* (Madrid: El Museo Universal, 1985), pp. 98–177; María F. Carbajo Isla, *La Población de la Villa de Madrid: desde finales del siglo XVI hasta mediados del siglo XIX* (Madrid: Siglo Veintiuno, 1987), ch. 6.

[19] *Actas de las Cortes de Castilla*, 60 vols (Madrid: Real Academia de la Historia, 1877–1974), XXVI, pp. 280–1.

> Las vecindades de los eclesiásticos así seculares como regulares se
> aumentan continuamente con fundaciones yglessias capellanías y obras
> pías a que se aplican los bienes rayces juros zenssos y demás rentas y de
> mejor situación y calidad y al mesmo passo se va menoscavando la
> población y los caudales de los seglares que son los que sustentan el pesso
> de esta Monarquía en la paz y en la Guerra y callan reducidos a suma y no
> creíble miseria.[20]

In spite of such widespread criticisms, echoing those of the *arbitristas*, a
policy of religious protectionism, supported by the Crown and legitimized by
the intensely pious nature of public life, prevailed against the prudent advice
of observers. New foundations of reformed habit, however genuine their
goals, continued to emerge, absorbing money and potential manpower, until
at least the end of the seventeenth century, by which time their number had
well surpassed the spiritual needs of society.

The temporal wealth of the Spanish Church was commonly regarded as
being excessive by early seventeenth-century observers, providing a sharp
contrast with the economic crisis afflicting the State. It was reported to
Philip IV at the beginning of his reign that, 'El brazo eclesiástico, que puede
considerarse por la piedad de la religión por el primero, [. . .] es sin duda hoy
el más poderoso en riqueza, rentas y posesiones. Y temo no solamente que es
el más rico, sino que ha de reducir y traer a sí toda la sustancia destos
reinos.'[21] In 1630, the fixed wealth of the Castilian Church (derived mainly
from its ownership of land, its property and financial investments, as well as
its material possessions) stood at some ten million ducats, while its regular
annual income (as much as 75–80 per cent of which came from its tithe entitlement) averaged just under a million ducats.

The traditional sources of regular ecclesiastical income in the kingdom of
Castile, which had more than doubled in value during the course of the
sixteenth century (rising from 392,000 ducats c. 1530 to 981,000 ducats
c. 1590), declined only marginally in worth in early seventeenth-century
Spain (falling to 967,000 ducats c. 1630). The Castilian Church managed to
survive the acute economic crisis that cut across the turn of century, with any
losses soon being recovered. By 1665 its annual regular income has risen to
over one million ducats. How is this resilience to be explained? Two crucial
factors had a bearing on the rental income of the Church: agricultural
production and price inflation. Both directly affected the size and value of
the tithe – a 10 per cent tax on the agricultural product – worth in the region
of nine million ducats in early seventeenth-century Spain. Approximately

---

[20] *Actas*, LIV (*Cortes* of Madrid, 1633), p. 238.

[21] J.H. Elliott and José F. de la Peña, eds, *Memoriales y Cartas del Conde-Duque de
Olivares*, I, *Política Interior, 1621 a 1627* (Madrid: Alfaguara, 1978), doc. IV: *Gran Memorial*,
25 XII 1624, pp. 49–100 (p. 51).

half of the proceeds of the tithe was retained by the Church and principally went to pay for the upkeep of senior (and some lesser) clergy, with the remaining percentage being divided between the Crown and lay beneficiaries.

Between c. 1580 and 1630, Castilian cereal production (especially that of wheat and barley) fell by an average of 40 per cent in the kingdom as a direct result of poor harvests, adverse weather conditions and depopulation, all of which prompted an acute agrarian crisis with the severest repercussions being felt in Old Castile.[22] The grain price index reached its peak between 1598 and 1601 while monetary inflation soared to its highest rate between 1615 and 1630, following the debasement in the value of the coinage. Using episcopal rents as a reliable source of data that can be charted over an extended period of time, it is possible to analyse the effects of these fluctuating economic circumstances on the regular income of two Castilian dioceses, Segovia in Old Castile and Seville in Andalusia.[23]

Over the period 1630–39, bread tithes in the region of Segovia fell to 30 per cent below their quantity in 1590–99, with catastrophic consequences for the rental income of the bishopric. Segovia's diocesan rents simultaneously plummeted by 50 per cent (falling from 34,000 ducats in 1590 to 17,600 ducats in 1630), a decline partly attributable to the reduction in the rent levied on the propertied assets of the cathedral chapter, which fell by 30 per cent during the first half of the seventeenth century (see Table 3). Over the same period, the population of the city of Segovia fell by 60 per cent from 5,000 to 3,000 households (Braudel, I, p. 324). A recovery began in the 1640s. By the mid-1660s tithe returns had regained, if not surpassed, their level in the 1590s while the value of Segovia's diocesan rents steadily rose.

It was mid-century before crisis overtook the more densely populated and fertile region of Andalusia in the south. Here a series of poor harvests and a rampant rise in wheat prices followed in the wake of the second great plague (1647–52) in which around half a million lost their lives. The wheat tithe of the Sevillian archbishopric fell by 37.5 per cent, from 120,000 *fanegas* in 1640 to 75,000 *fanegas* in 1645–50 but without this adversely affecting the local church's income, which rose from 88,000 to 100,000 ducats over this period.[24] How can we explain this anomaly? Sevillian wheat prices plummeted to around 700 *maravedis* per *fanega* in 1650 but soared dramatically

---

[22] Ángel García Sanz, 'Castile 1580–1650: economic crisis and the policy of reform', in *The Castilian Crisis of the Seventeenth Century*, eds I.A.A. Thompson and B. Yun (Cambridge: CUP, 1995), pp. 13–31.

[23] AHN Consejos Suprimidos, legs 15220–15293; Antonio Domínguez Ortiz, 'Las rentas de los prelados de Castilla en el siglo XVII', in *Estudios de historia económica y social de España* (Granada: Universidad de Granada, 1987), pp. 223–60.

[24] Ángel García Sanz, 'El sector agrario durante el siglo XVII: depresión y reajustes', in *Historia de España Menéndez y Pidal*, XXIII (Madrid: Espasa Calpe, 1989), pp. 161–235 (pp. 171–2).

Table 3. The size of the Segovian tithe set against diocesan income, 1590–
1659 (calculated in *fanegas* [a] of cereal production and ducats [b] per
annum)

Year	Size of tithe [a]	Index 1590–99	Diocesan income [b]	Index 1590–99
1590–99	3,104	100	34,000	100
1600–09	2,910	93.7		
1610–19	2,869	92.4	20,600	60.5
1620–29	3,401	109.5		
1630–39	2,198	70.8	17,600	51.7
1640–49	2,934	94.5		
1650–59	2,915	93.9		
1660–69	3,326	107	25,000	73.5

Source: Tithe figures taken from Ángel García Sanz, 'El sector agrario durante el siglo XVII:
depresión y reajustes', in *Historia de España Menéndez y Pidal*, XXIII (Madrid: Espasa Calpe,
1989), pp. 166–7. I have used a different index from that used by García Sanz to equate the level
of diocesan income in conjunction with tithe returns.
Notes: (a) a *fanega* was a measure of bulk, equivalent to 1.6 bushels; (b) a ducat (*ducado*) was a
unit of account, equivalent to 375 *maravedís*.

to 3,400 *maravedis* per *fanega* in 1652 as a result of the scarcity of supply.
Price inflation and monetary devaluation, both of which crippled the
consumer, paradoxically worked in the Church's favour. It became a direct
beneficiary of the higher resale value of wheat – a vital consumer commodity
– at a time of scarcity of supply and currency instability. In 1652 Friar Pedro
de Tapia, who had transferred from the bishopric of Sigüenza to Córdoba in
1649 and was about to take up office in Seville, pointed out in a letter to the
President of the Council of Castile that while bishops in Old Castile were in
the habit of only claiming half their grain entitlement during periods of
famine, in Andalusia this was not the case. He condemned the practice and
gave his full support to the popular disturbances that arose in the region motivated by the rising cost of bread. [25]

When considering criticism of the excessive wealth enjoyed by clergymen,
we should not forget that the Spanish Church's capacity to ride out the relatively short-term economic crisis contrasted with its long-term battle to
evade the fiscal burden. The Crown had a direct interest in encouraging the
acquisition of wealth by members of the ecclesiastical estate. Had it not been
able to extract a number of taxes and subsidies from clerical incomes with
papal approval, its own revenues would have been considerably depleted. At

[25] Antonio Domínguez Ortiz, *Alteraciones Andaluzas* (Madrid: Narcea, 1973), pp.
191–3.

the beginning of the reign of Philip IV, the Crown was in receipt of over 3.6 million ducats a year from the Church (approximately a third of its overall income). Alongside ordinary fiscal deductions, heavy pension charges (worth around 250,000 ducats annually to the Crown) were a considerable burden for some prelates. Although destined as rewards for long-serving churchmen, in practice they frequently fell to the benefit of those in political life. In 1615, the bishop of Zamora complained that 'la renta de este obispado es más para pensionarios que para mí'.[26] Pension claims and royal subsidies were now depriving him of almost a half of his diocesan income, which had already fallen by 33 per cent (from 24,400 ducats in 1590 to 16,800 in 1615) as a result of the reduction in value of the bread tithe. He was left with under 10,000 when all deductions had been made (see Table 4). His was not a lone voice. Although the majority of churchmen lived much more comfortably than the mass of the population, the demands on their incomes and the fluctuation in the real value of the latter were far greater than contemporaries acknowledged.

Table 4. Examples of direct deductions from episcopal incomes (in ducats per annum)

Bishopric	Year(s)	Gross income	Pension	Subsidio + Excusado	Residual income
Ciudad Rodrigo	1598–1600	8,956	810	730	7,416
León	1602–06	13,400	3,400	2,800	7,200
Segovia	1607–11	20,970	5,650	3,825	11,495
Burgos	1612	40,000	8,500	6,000	25,500
Zamora	1612–14	16,800	4,200	3,250*	9,350

Sources: AGS Estado, Patronato Eclesiástico, legs 135, 136; AHN, Consejos Suprimidos, leg. 15215. * Estimated figure.
Note: The *Subsidio* and *Excusado* were regular taxes levied on clerical incomes with papal sanction.

The Spanish Church survived the criticisms it was subjected to by contemporaries at the beginning of the seventeenth century – some of which were ill-founded as we have seen – by virtue of its extensive spiritual and ideological power base in society. Although the traditional sources of ecclesiastical income were declining in face value, there was an increase in the quantity of money, goods, property, and real estate being bequeathed and donated to the Church by private benefactors. Jerónimo de Ceballos advised

[26] AHN Consejos Suprimidos, leg. 15214, 17 February 1615 (Bishop of Zamora to the Cámara de Castilla).

the readers of his *Arte Real* in 1623: 'Hagan la cuenta de los juros que están incorporados en las Religiones, véanse por libros de las contribuciones del Subsidio y Excusado, las heredades, casas, tierras, dehesas y tributos que poseen, que se hallará que es mucho más de lo que está fuera del comercio temporal' (cited by Domínguez Ortiz, *Las Clases Privilegiadas*, p. 360). Despite the rigours of the economic crisis, there were still sufficient resources available within society to maintain the Church in the traditional opulence and splendour that was so often commented on by early seventeenth-century observers. The need to secure one's place in heaven by one's actions on earth – a fundamental message of the Counter-Reformation Church – led to a heavy investment, both human and material (via the endowment of chapels and remuneration of clergy to deliver anniversary masses), in the least productive sector of society and the perpetuation of the social and economic imbalance this created. By joining the lesser ranks of the ecclesiastical estate or by making a devout bequest in his will, the average Spaniard, notwithstanding the strength of his commitment to Catholicism, was taking out a form of religious insurance policy. While the contradictions inherent in the combination of the Church's spiritual role with its accumulation of temporal wealth alongside its over-recruitment of ill-prepared lesser clergy were readily identifiable – if somewhat exaggerated – by contemporaries, the intensely pious nature of public life seemed to justify and legitimize these anomalies, effectively rendering the arguments of the *arbitristas* null and void.

Law and Disorder: Anti-Gypsy Legislation and its Failures in Seventeenth-Century Spain

RICHARD J. PYM

Anyone reviewing the lengthy catalogue of laws passed against gypsies in pre-Bourbon Spain is likely quickly to conclude that their frequent reiteration or reformulation over two centuries, usually with increased restrictions and penalties, speaks eloquently enough of their failure.[1] In fact, had the Crown ever come close to achieving its objectives of enforced sedentarization or expulsion, by the middle of the seventeenth century there would hardly have remained in Spain a footloose gypsy against whom to legislate. But remain they did, and complaints about their criminality, irreligion and reputedly scandalous lives continued much as before well into the eighteenth century and beyond. This is not to suggest for a moment that the gypsies were not persecuted. They were. The privations endured by those sent off to serve as *forzados* in Spain's Mediterranean galley squadrons or to toil in the fearsome mercury mines at Almadén are not to be underestimated. But most were not sent, notwithstanding orders like the one prepared in conditions of great secrecy and issued in December 1639, which had demanded that *all* able-bodied gypsy males be put to the oar.[2]

In fact, it is clear that laws designed to control Spain's gypsies were not, or could not be enforced to anything like the extent desired by the legislators. The difficulties encountered by the Crown in its attempts to enforce its will, to translate its nominal authority into the effective *exercise* of power, have been the subject of a number of studies over recent years.[3] It is in this context that this chapter will focus specifically on anti-gypsy laws promulgated in the seventeenth century and explore the reasons for what was recognized even by contemporaries as their inefficacy. What emerges is a picture of

---

[1]   Some two dozen such laws (or reiterations thereof) were promulgated over this period.

[2]   José de Pellicer, *Avisos históricos* (Madrid: Taurus, 1965), p. 56.

[3]   See for example I.A.A. Thompson, 'Castile', in *Absolutism in Seventeenth-Century Europe*, ed. John Miller (London: Macmillan, 1990), pp. 69–98 and Ruth Mackay, *The Limits of Royal Authority: Resistance and Obedience in Seventeenth-Century Castile* (Cambridge: CUP, 1999).

early modern Spain in which, far though the royal writ was held imperiously to run, the reality at a local level was that demands from the centre were quite often resisted or, one way or another, frustrated. True, the notion that the King represented the embodiment and guarantee of law and justice was one to which most Spaniards readily, even fervently subscribed – at least in theory. Diego Saavedra Fajardo put it thus: 'Ca así como yaze el alma en el corazón del ome, e por ella vive el cuerpo, e se mantiene, así en el rey yaze la justicia, que es vida e mantenimiento del pueblo y de su señorío.'[4] But while theory and practice continued locally to enjoy a hopeful *modus vivendi* of sorts, the match, unsurprisingly, was ever less than perfect. The fact was that various forms of reluctance, resistance, or simple inability to comply with the Crown's wishes were common, a fact of life at every level of society, while wrangles over jurisdictional competence, endemic corruption, and interminable appeals procedures also continually bedevilled efforts to enforce the law.

But there was another issue, too, which, almost from the outset, was to have fundamental implications for the way anti-gypsy legislation developed in Spain and elsewhere. Not only did the Habsburg regime repeatedly legislate to sedentarize, assimilate and control Spain's gypsies; in the seventeenth century it also sought, in more than one sense, to legislate them away altogether. Central here is the question of precisely who or what the gypsies were understood to be.

Spain's first piece of legislation against gypsies pre-dates the Habsburgs. The Catholic Monarchs' ordinance of 1499 gave the 'Egipcianos' – for so they had announced themselves on their arrival in the peninsula in 1425 – sixty days either to take up settled residence and a recognized trade or find a master to serve.[5] The ordinance laments not just the harm done to their Majesties' subjects by gypsy beggars, fraudsters, and thieves, but also the 'mal exemplo' represented by this idle, wandering people.[6] Forty years later, Charles I confirmed this original legislation as he had done twice before in 1525 and 1528, adding now that any gypsy male aged between twenty and fifty found without a trade or a master was to be sent to the galleys for six years. Gypsy women were to be flogged, though the ordinance then added

---

[4] *Empresas políticas* [1643], ed. Sagrario López (Madrid: Cátedra, 1999), p. 359. Even Sancho Panza reminds Don Quijote in the *galeotes* episode of 'la justicia, que es el mesmo rey' (*Don Quijote*, I (Madrid: Castalia, 1978), p. 266).

[5] While fifteenth-century Castilian society cannot be described as entirely sedentary, most people lived at least relatively settled lives bound up in various cycles of production. The gypsies, though, constantly on the move, produced little or nothing of their own, and within seventy-five years of their arrival had come to be perceived as almost entirely reliant on predation of one form or another.

[6] Faustino Gil Ayuso (ed.), *Noticia bibliográfica de textos y disposiciones legales de Castilla impresos en los siglos XVI y XVII* (Madrid: S. Aguirre, 1935), p. 401.

distrustfully, 'y aunque no lo sean, si anduvieren en hábito de gitanas, hayan la pena de azotes en la ley precedente contenida'.[7]

Such suspicions were not confined to Spain. Nine years earlier in Germany, Albert Krantz had claimed of the gypsies in his widely read *Saxonia* that they accepted into their companies other men or women who wished to join them.[8] In England in 1554, the authorities' introduction of the death penalty for 'Egyptians' who refused to leave the country was met by indignant rejoinders from the latter that they were in fact born and bred Englishmen. This prompted a more judiciously worded extension of the death penalty in 1562 to those found 'in any company or fellowship of vaga-bonds, commonly called, or calling themselves Egyptians', as well as any persons passing themselves off as Egyptians by 'counterfeiting, transforming or disguising themselves by their apparel, speech or other behaviour'.[9] Half a century later, a pamphlet of 1610 claimed that such groups even resorted to 'causing their faces to be made blacke, as if they were Egyptians'.[10]

In Spain, a similarly extravagant claim appeared in the vitriolic *Discurso contra los gitanos* written in 1631 by Juan de Quiñones, an *alcalde de casa y corte*. Typically derivative and salted liberally with demonizing myth, as anti-gypsy tracts invariably were, it is nevertheless worth quoting for the now essentially deracialized view it offers of Spain's gypsies:

> Llamallos gitanos más es porque los imitan en el torpe modo de vivir que por ser sus descendientes. Y así esta vil canalla no es otra cosa que hombres y mujeres huidos por delitos o deudas, gente amotinada y facinerosa que no pudiendo estar en los lugares donde son conocidos, se retiran a los montes o lugares de poca vecindad, y escondidos, para ocultarse. [. . .] sin duda son nacidos y criados en estos Reinos, si bien entre ellos andaran otros de otras naciones, de que se componga esta secta del gitanismo, pues admiten a ella cada día la gente ociosa, perdida, y rematada, a quien con facilidad enseñan su idioma.[11]

---

[7]   *Novísima recopilación de las leyes de España,* 4 vols (Paris: Mégico, 1831), III, ley 13, tít. 11, libro 8.

[8]   Albert Krantz, *Rerum Germanicarum historici clariss. Saxonia* (Frankfurt am Main: Andreas Wechel, 1580 [1520]), p. 303.

[9]   In Spain, a royal ordinance of 1566 designed to curb the growing problem of vaga-bondage expressly stipulated that gypsies were to be considered vagabonds for the purposes of the law (*Pragmática de los vagamundos y gadrones*). A later, similar pragmatic (AHN, Consejos, leg. 51442, doc. 6) of 15 June 1643, did not mention gypsies specifically; but it was clearly understood to refer to them by the Professor of Law and Dean of the Univer-sity of Salamanca, Pedro de Villalobos, as he made clear in his *Discursos jurídicos políticos en razón de que a los gitanos vandoleros de estos tiempos no les vale la Iglesia para su inmunidad* (Salamanca: Diego de Cossío, 1644). Copy consulted AHNT Nobleza, Osuna, caja 4248, doc. 4.

[10]   Judith Okely, *The Traveller-Gypsies* (Cambridge: CUP, 1983), p. 4.

[11]   Madrid: Juan González, 1631 (copy consulted BNM R/31436). For a fuller account of the curiously prominent place occupied by gypsies in the early seventeenth-century

Several of Quiñones's phrases are repeated verbatim from the *arbitrista* Sancho de Moncada's 1619 *Restauración política de España*, which itself had borrowed heavily from Pedro de Salazar de Mendoza's *Memorial de el hecho de los gitanos*, written a year or so earlier. In fact, by the time Quiñones wrote his diatribe, the idea that Spain's gypsies amounted to little more than a ragged agglomeration of the criminal dregs of Spanish society had become common currency in official circles. It had even been incorporated into policy over a decade earlier in a royal decree issued at Belem in Portugal on 28 June 1619. This represented the culmination of a debate that can be traced back at least as far as the *Cortes* of Valladolid of 7 July 1603, which discussed a report addressed to Philip III on the gypsies' excesses in Castile. The report noted the failure of previous legislation 'en que se prohíbe no vivan ni hablen como gitanos los que falsamente dicen serlo, como los que lo son'. It offered no reasons for this failure, and went on to recommend expulsion, adding optimistically, 'porque demás de quitar este abuso de gitanos, muchos que se valen del nombre para ejecutar sus malas inclinaciones, se abstendrán dél por no dejar su natural'.[12] At this stage, then, some distinction was still being drawn between true and false gypsies. No doubt there were reasons why some may have found it convenient or necessary to pass themselves off as gypsies. Such a stratagem may even have had a certain deterrent value for those with reason to fear the law. Numerous documents attest to the reluctance of local justices, who were invariably short of resources, to undertake the always difficult and frequently dangerous pursuit of gypsies. The *Cortes* of Madrid of 8 November 1610 were presented with a report, which noted that:

> Ha venido la vida licenciosa de esta gente a tanta rotura, que andan compañías enteras de hombres y mujeres, todos con armas y escopetas, y llegan a los lugares y les dan lo que piden por excusar sus violencias, y quando se tiene noticia de ellos y se quiere hacer alguna prevención para castigarlos, son gente tan astuta y montaraz, que jamás se puede dar con ellos, y quando se da, se resisten y han hecho muchas muertes, y luego dejan las mujeres y ellos huyen, porque son tan sueltos que no puede nadie seguirlos.[13]

Spanish imaginary, see my article 'The Pariah Within: Early Modern Spain's Gypsies', *Journal of Romance Studies*, 4:2 (2004), 21–35.

[12] *Actas de las Cortes de Castilla* [henceforth *Actas*], 60 vols (Madrid: Real Academia de la Historia, 1877–1974), XXI, 1902, p. 482.

[13] *Actas*, XXVI, 1902, p. 164. A sign of the times, it also noted of the gypsies that 'es tan mala gente, que sin comparación exceden a los moriscos, porque en no ser cristianos les imitan y en robos les ganan'. The report demanded that 'se provea cómo este nombre y habla de gitanos se quite en estos reinos' and recommended expulsion or death for those who refused to accept sedentarization.

On 16 October 1638, one of the witnesses called before the *alcalde mayor* Juan García de Córdoba to give evidence relating to the theft by gypsies of livestock in the village of Retortillo near Soria reported that 'se dice vienen tan armados de escopetas y pistolas que las justicias de villas cortas no se atreven a remediallos sin convocatoria de otras justicias'.[14] That same year, in Coruña del Conde, north-west of Aranda del Duero, an *alcalde*, ordered by the King to apprehend a group of gypsies accused of a litany of crimes in the area, put the problem more succinctly: he just replied, 'Venga el Señor Almirante de Castilla a prenderlos, porque yo no me atrevo.'[15]

But by 1610 the official view of Spain's gypsies, of whether to define them in racial or behavioural terms, had already begun to change. Others from what the social historian Antonio Domínguez Ortiz described as 'the oppressed classes of society – fugitive slaves, *moriscos*, even Christians wanted by the law, criminals, adventurers and vagabonds' had long been suspected, not without a degree of paranoia, of having joined up with gypsy groups.[16] When the *Cortes* of Madrid of 24 December 1610 once again raised the question of what was to be done about the gypsies, delegates demanded not just the prohibition of their dress, language, and unregulated way of life – they are described as 'amancebados y sin ser cristianos más que en el nombre' – but also of the very word 'gitano'; and it added by way of justification the telling phrase, 'pues no lo son de nación'. Gypsies should not be allowed to deal in livestock, 'ni en otras cosas semejantes que usan', while serious penalties should be reserved for those justices who failed to enforce the law.[17]

By now, other more pressing matters had begun to occupy the attention of the authorities, specifically the expulsions from 1609 onwards of Spain's *moriscos*. But the Duke of Lerma still instructed the Council of State in 1610 to explore the possibility of expelling the gypsies, too, even though it was suspected that such a move would impose a greater strain on resources than had thus far proven necessary with the *moriscos*. The idea was that the task would be entrusted to the Count of Salazar, the man already charged with overall responsibility for the expulsions of the *moriscos*:

[14] AHN Consejos, leg. 51060.

[15] Teresa deSan Román, *La diferencia inquietante: Viejas y nuevas estrategias culturales de los gitanos* (Madrid: Siglo Veintiuno, 1997), p. 30.

[16] Antonio Domínguez Ortiz, *The Golden Age of Spain: 1516–1659* (London: Weidenfeld & Nicolson, 1971), p. 165. An interesting later example from 1680 is provided by the case of Francisco de la Puente Montecillo Miranda, an army deserter who had escaped when the ship transporting him to prison in North Africa was forced by a storm to return to Cartagena. Subsequently gaoled in Valladolid because, the accusation went, 'había andado con gitanos y personas de mal vivir, con pistolas y armas, robando y maltratando a los pasageros que encontraban', he was ordered to be returned to Madrid and thence to Orán, the destination originally intended for him (ARCV Pleitos criminales, caja 3320002).

[17] *Actas*, XXVI, 1902, pp. 291–2.

> Su Majestad ha entendido que en España hay mucha cantidad de Gitanos y particularmente aquí en Castilla, y por ser gente que vive sin fe y sin sacramentos y que sólo tratan de hurtar, está resuelto de que sean expelidos de España y manda que se trate en la sala del Gobierno la forma de la execución desto y se le avise de lo que pareciere, o si sería bien cometérselo al Conde de Salazar para que los vaya echando como a los moriscos, aunque con éstos será necesario usar de mayor rigor por ser gente incorregible y que su vivienda es en el campo.[18]

The Council argued that just as had happened in the case of the *moriscos*, it alone should be charged with responsibility for the matter, since it was assumed that the involvement of other, local tribunals would merely be a recipe for failure. In fact, a decision was taken in July the following year that such expulsions should go ahead, but only after the last *moriscos* had left the region of Murcia.[19] Nonetheless, it was actually not until almost a decade later, amid a continuing chorus of complaints from the *Cortes* and *arbitristas* alike, that the legislative spotlight really turned once again to what it was hoped would be a lasting solution to the gypsy question.

The decree that Philip III issued from Belem in June 1619, to which we now return, represented more than just another sedentarization or expulsion order. In the light of previous failures, physical expulsion of those refusing to settle must, after all, have seemed a somewhat unrealistic aim even to those framing the order, though they clearly considered the threat worthy of reiteration. But they also wanted to expel an idea. The order represented an attempt officially to deracialize Spain's gypsies and consign the very word *gitano* to oblivion once and for all. In so doing, the decree sought to insure itself to some degree against failure. If this latest attempt to rid the nation of its wandering gypsies via forced sedentarization and assimilation were to come to nothing, then what could not be achieved in reality would be achieved, in one sense at least, via language. It would be achieved, that is to say, via the symbolic erasure of notions of *gitano* identity conceived in terms of racial difference. With the expulsions of the *moriscos* still relatively fresh in Spaniards' minds, the political expediency of removing at the stroke of a pen another 'foreign' contagion threatening the body of the state would hardly have gone unappreciated. The order's tacit appeal to the linguistic equivalence of *gitano* and *egipciano*, terms used almost interchangeably until late

---

[18] AGS Estado, leg. 228, 7 August 1610.

[19] In a letter of 23 July 1611 to Philip III, the Council of State noted that 'la experiencia muestra que por el bien público conviene descartarlos destos Reynos, y que la execución sea por vía de este Consejo, pues de otra manera no tendrá efecto'. A second letter dated 28 August reiterates the point: 'desde luego representa el Consejo a V. Mg. que el haberse hecho tan felizmente la [expulsión] de los Moriscos, ha sido por correr por este Consejo, y no por otros Tribunales y que convendrá que sea así ésta de los Gitanos' (AGS Estado, leg. 4126).

in the seventeenth century, allowed it quite reasonably to revive the phrase used of the gypsies in the *Cortes* of 1610 and repeated at those of Madrid on 30 July 1618, 'pues no lo son de nación'. The word 'nación', of course, combines the notions not just of common descent, but also, etymologically, of birth. Had not these people been in Spain now for over two hundred years? Born and bred there, how could they be considered anything other than Spaniards, albeit of the worst sort? Accusing them of murder and theft, especially the theft of livestock belonging to the poor, the decree ordered all those failing to take up settled residence in towns of at least a thousand households to leave Spain.[20] Any returning thereafter would incur the death penalty. All of this had been proposed at the *Cortes* of Madrid the previous year, though not without opposition. In the event, fifteen delegates voted for the proposal as it stood, while six voted for less draconian penalties.[21]

But while this attempt to legislate away Spain's gypsies via expulsion or assimilation further encouraged the gradual process of sedentarization that had been going on for over a century, it had little effect in terms of curbing the gypsies' illegal activities or their recalcitrant determination to continue to be different. On 8 May 1633, a pragmatic issued by Philip IV sought once again to 'estirpar de todo punto el nombre de Gitanos'. It asserted once again that those calling themselves gypsies (so went the formula typically employed) 'no lo son ni por origen, ni por naturaleza'; and it demanded that they dress, speak, and take up the same occupations as other Spaniards. Henceforth, it continued, 'ni en danzas, ni en otro acto alguno se permita acción, ni representación, trage, ni nombre de Gitanos'. This last prohibition may have had some effect in the short term, but it did not last. Indeed, four years later, even the palace saw fit to contract the services of gypsy entertainers (San Román, p. 30), and gypsies continued subsequently to dance in Corpus Christi processions across Spain just as they had been doing since the fifteenth century.[22] The pragmatic also grants permission for all justices, 'ansí Realengas como de Señorío y Abadengo', to continue the pursuit of gypsies across neighbouring jurisdictions. But the frustration is evident as it

---

[20] *Cédula de SM tiene por bien, y manda, salgan del Reyno dentro de seis meses los Gitanos, que andan vagando por él*, BNM MS 13120. A much later *consulta* of 1749 makes it clear that the oft-repeated insistence that gypsies should take up residence only in larger towns had been 'con reflexión a que fuesen los principales del Reyno donde las justicias tubiesen fuerza bastante para corregirles y ellos en que ocuparse y ganar la vida' (AHNT Nobleza, Osuna, caja 4256, lib. 3, doc. 13).

[21] *Actas*, XXXII, 1902, pp. 118–19.

[22] The city of Cádiz, for example, contracted gypsy dancers for this purpose in 1664 (Mercedes Agulló y Cobo, 'Primera entrega documental sobre teatro en Andalucía', in *En torno al teatro del Siglio de Oro: Actas Jornados XII–XIII* (Almeria: Instituto de Estudios Almerienses, Disputación de Almeria, 1996), p. 124), though the earliest example of which I am aware was at Guadalajara in 1488 (Luis Astrana Marín, ed., *Vida ejemplar y heroica de Miguel de Cervantes Saavedra*, 7 vols (Madrid: Reus, 1948–58), I, 129).

adds, 'y mandamos a los de nuestro Consejo, Audiencias, y Chancillerías, castiguen gravamente a las justicias y juezes que tuvieren en esto alguna omisión, y no salieren a la prisión de los dichos delinquentes'. The pragmatic is interesting, too, because it reveals that such sedentarization as had already occurred had merely led to the formation of *gitanerías*, gypsy *barrios*, and had thus failed to achieve the desired effect of diluting the gypsies' sense of group identity or, indeed, their physical strength in numbers. With little thought for the practicalities involved, it now attempted belatedly to undo the damage: 'salgan los susodichos de los barrios en que viven con nombre de gitanos, y que se dividan y mezclen entre los demás vecinos, y no hagan juntas en público, ni en secreto'.[23]

Most of the central provisions of the 1633 pragmatic reflected the recommendations of a *consulta* of March that year on the continuing depredations suffered by the *Mesta* at the hands of gypsies.[24] This had claimed that sedentarization had actually encouraged precisely the opposite of the effect intended:

> antes con avérseles dado vecindades, se an conservado en su mal modo de vivir y a título de nación se congregan y discurren por diferentes partes destos Reynos invadiendo los lugares con tan gran superioridad y pavor de los abitadores que unos desamparan sus casas, otros tienen a buena suerte el albergarlos y contribuirles por que les reserven alguna parte con que sustentarse, y como las necesidades an crecido tanto se tiene por cierto se les va agregando mucha gente facinerosa con que si no se pone remedio podría este daño venir a estado que no fuese posible el dársele sino a costa de mucha sangre y dinero.[25]

Similar claims are made in a fascinating letter of 23 May 1674 addressed to the Queen Regent Mariana and written from Porcuna, Jaén, by one Manuel de Montillo, a priest and lawyer. Its contents relate to the period of forty years that Montillo had already spent in Andalusia. In it he complains about 'la poca o ninguna obserbancia de las leyes promulgadas en estos reinos contra gitanos desde el tiempo de los señores Reyes Católicos hasta Su Magestad'. Accusing the gypsies of being thieves, highwaymen, and even paid assassins, he nevertheless observes ruefully that 'no les falta[n] patrones y rogadores'. The letter merits quotation at length:

---

[23] *Pragmática que su Magestad manda se promulgue en razón de los gitanos que andan por el Reino, y otras cosas* (Madrid: Viuda de Juan González, 1633).

[24] Of medieval origin, the Mesta was the umbrella organization of Spain's sheep-owners. It was responsible for managing and, through its peripatetic *alcaldes entregadores*, policing the practice of transhumance, as flocks moved over great distances from winter to summer pasture and back. By 1633 it was a shadow of its former, powerful self, though one still clearly capable of exercising some influence.

[25] AHN Consejos, leg. 7133, Mesta.

Cometiendo cada día en estos Reinos dichos gitanos tantos y tan enormes delitos he bisto que de quarenta años a esta parte, no se a ahorcado ninguno y pocos a las galeras quando por las leyes y por gitanos están todos condenados a ellas, y de aquí a nacido que este linaje de gente en este tiempo se a hecho y se está haciendo mui balida y fuerte, entre ellos mismos y otras ayudas, con mucha multiplicación, porque como huelgan y se mezclan unos con otros en matrimonios o sin ellos, y como quieren, an crecido demasiadamente, pues no ay lugar que en el y en sus campos no esté poblado con gitanos que se deben de aber retirado de otras partes, y muchos lugares de corta becindad los temen, y los tienen sugetados y acobardados, con quadrillas de cinquenta y cien gitanos que se ayudan unas a otras, y muchos dellos los que son más hombres tienen a sus caballos alistados con frenos y espuelas, carabinas dobles y arcabuçes como soldados de a caballo, de que usan así para sus robos como para librarse de los riesgos.[26]

Montillo's letter also indicates that there were exceptions to the gypsies' normal practice of endogamy, especially perhaps in Andalusia. He notes grimly that

los vasallos de VM por temores y miedos y por guardar sus bidas se hacen amigos con ellos y aun mugeres se incorporan y agregan y otros hombres de mal bibir a las chusmas y conpañías de gitanos y se casan con ellos.

It is not possible at this remove to quantify mixed marriages between gypsies and non-gypsies, given that no census figures are available for the seventeenth century.[27] But there is no question that there were exceptions to the general endogamy of gypsy lineages. In 1611, to take one example, the *Consejo* received a request that a gypsy woman, Catalina Pérez, married to Juan Bautista, an Old Christian water-carrier, should not be forced to leave Madrid and work the land, as repeated *autos* had demanded in response to petitions by the *alcaldes de casa y corte*.[28] Of course, the picture varied from one locality to another. As María Helena Sánchez Ortega has observed, the Inquisition's own records make it abundantly clear that relations between gypsy and non-gypsy, while deeply hostile in some villages, were nonetheless excellent in others.[29] Frequent, too, were claims that there was no

[26] AHN Consejos, Cámara de Castilla, leg. 51442, fol. 6.

[27] Sadly, the results of the census of gypsies ordered by Charles II in June 1695 have been lost.

[28] AHN Consejo de Castilla, Sala de Alcaldes de Casa y Corte, fol. 33. Some figures do become available in the 1783 census of gypsies ordered by Charles III. Here it is interesting to note that, while endogamy continued to be the normal practice, one in eight gypsy families in Utrera, admittedly an untypical case, was of mixed blood; see Torcuato Pérez de Guzmán, *Los gitanos herreros de Sevilla* (Sevilla: Ayuntamiento, 1982), p. 90.

[29] María Helena Sánchez Ortega, *La Inquisición y los gitanos* (Madrid: Taurus, 1988), p. 132.

shortage of ordinary people prepared to receive stolen goods from the gypsies or, indeed, to offer them protection. Several villagers called as witnesses in the case of the stolen horses and mules of Retortillo, cited earlier, claimed, for example, that the animals would be taken to other, distant villages where the gypsies would take advantage of their 'muchos receptadores y encubridores' in order to trade their ill-gotten gains.[30]

That the gypsies enjoyed some sympathy and/or support in certain quarters is further evidenced in a letter to Philip IV of 19 November 1639 from the *junta de galeotes, esclavos, y gitanos*.[31] It reported that the Protonotary of Aragon, Gerónimo de Villanueva, one of the co-signatories to the letter, had raised the urgent need to man and arm Spain's seriously under-resourced Mediterranean galleys, the first line of defence for the nation's threatened eastern and south-eastern coasts. Gypsies had long been regarded as obvious candidates to man the oars as *forzados*. Of an earlier ordinance that had instructed that gypsy males be sent to the galleys, it noted that, 'o por la falta del secreto, o por la floxedad o omisión de las justicias aquella diligencia se desbaneció, y sólo sirvió de que muchos de los gitanos se pasasen a Francia, y otros se fuesen a los montes'.[32] But leaks, laxity, or dereliction of duty on the part of the authorities at a local level, the gypsies' long-practised mobility, and Spain's distinctly policing-resistant terrain were not the only obstacles to be overcome. The letter goes on frustratedly to lament the gypsies' habitual abuse of Church sanctuary, the unconscionable delays in the hearing of appeals at a time when the government was desperate to see convicted gypsies (and others) sent as quickly as possible to the galleys, and, not least, the corruption of galley captains, gaolers, and justices alike. In fact, appeals could take up to six years, by which time many prisoners either escaped or became unfit for galley service; and it was also reported that prisoners in Granada sentenced to the galleys were able to buy their way out of gaol.[33]

Against this background, the Crown had earlier that year recalled and strengthened legislation first passed under Philip II in 1566, which had demanded that the sentences of those condemned for serious crimes be

---

[30] AHN Consejos, leg. 51060.

[31] AGS Guerra Antigua, leg. 3173.

[32] I take this previous ordinance to be the one promulgated in 1635, which ordered all gypsy males between twenty and fifty years old to be sent to the galleys (Bernard Leblon, *Los gitanos de España* (Barcelona: Gedisa, 2001), p. 117). The tactic of retreat to mountainous areas is mentioned in a 1705 pragmatic. It notes of the gypsies that 'hazen sus ranchos en las llanuras inmediatas a las montañas, donde se recogen quando se intenta prenderlos, passándose de ellas a otros parages a cometer los mismos insultos' (AHN Consejos, lib. 1290, fols 260–264). One recalls, too, that Cervantes's gypsies in *La gitanilla* 'tenían determinado irse a los montes de Toledo y desde allí correr y garramar toda la tierra circunvecina' (Madrid: Castalia, 1982, p. 124).

[33] David Goodman, *Spanish Naval Power, 1589–1665* (Cambridge: CUP, 1997), p. 217.

commuted wherever possible to galley service.[34] This included even the death sentence. And the Council of State had demanded in February that appeals by convicted gypsies and bandits still outstanding in the *Chancillerías* be remitted to it for urgent resolution. A commission was, for example, issued to Enrique de Salimar, the *alcalde del crimen* of the Valladolid *Chancillería*, to apprehend the 'muchos gitanos y vandoleros' who were plaguing the area. Claiming that they were responsible for 'muchas muertes, hurtos y robos y salteamientos', it goes on to insist that any appeals that might legitimately be lodged by those sentenced for these crimes should indeed be heard, but only 'ante los de nuestro Consejo y no en otra parte ni tribunal alguno'.[35]

But resistance continued, even at the highest levels. The *junta de galeotes'* letter goes on to note that 'en algunos lugares de Señorío son acogidos y defendidos muchos gitanos de los mismos señores y sus criados'. A little later, it describes the experience of Pedro de Amezqueta, an *alcalde de casa y corte* and the Crown's *juez de comisión* or special commissioner in Andalusia and Murcia with special responsibility for ensuring that eligible convicts were sent to the galleys.[36] Asked to investigate and expedite suitable cases pending in the courts, he had travelled to Andalusia, where, the letter notes, he spent three days going from place to place, 'haviendo obrado con gran resistancia de algunos señores y aun de las mismas justicias'.[37] In La Mancha, too, gypsies enjoyed seigniorial protection in some areas, as the *alcalde mayor* Juan Hurtado, charged with ensuring that the laws against gypsies were enforced, discovered when he travelled in 1633 through lands owned by the Military Order of Santiago and the Marquis of Villena (Leblon, p. 93).

Such resistance continued throughout the seventeenth century and was acknowledged in a royal decree issued in 1673 and in two later ordinances promulgated in 1692 and 1695. The decree issued on 27 July 1673, once again demanded that all male gypsies of over twelve years of age found in the company of non-sedentarized groups be sent to the galleys. But it also observed of the gypsies in general that 'este género de gentes tenía amparo y refugio en hombres poderosos que los receptaban y protegían'.[38] The royal ordinance issued on 20 November 1692 once again reiterated the provisions

---

34 AGS Registro del Sello, 9 February 1639. Philip II had originally issued this order in his 1566 *Pragmática de los vagamundos y ladrones.*

35 AGS Registro del Sello, 16 February 1639.

36 The letter notes that Amezqueta had one year earlier sent four hundred men to the galleys. Given that vagabonds, healthy beggars, bigamists, perjurors, blasphemers, procurers, homosexual men, donated slaves and any man resisting arrest could also be sent to the galleys, it is unlikely that more than a small proportion of this number were gypsies.

37 AGS Guerra Antigua, leg. 3173.

38 José Capdevila y Orozco, *Errantes y expulsados: normativas jurídicas contra gitanos, judíos, y moriscos* (Córdoba: Francisco Baena, 1991), p. 53.

of earlier legislation. But it included the observation that the failure to enforce the laws promulgated by Charles II's predecessors should be attributed to 'la floxedad de las justicias a quienes ha tocado la execución y cumplimiento de las dichas leyes, cuya omisión debía ser castigada con la severidad que pide la importancia del fin a que se promulgaron'.[39] Tightening significantly the procedures henceforth to be followed, it went on to insist that any such failure on the part of the justices in the future would be treated as an impeachable offence. Moreover, those found to be in dereliction of their duty to apprehend gypsy criminals would also be required to make good from their own pockets any damage resulting from the latter's delinquent behaviour.

Finally, a royal ordinance issued by Charles II in Madrid on 12 June 1695 offered any member of a gypsy band caught in open country with firearms, and therefore automatically subject to the death penalty, a pardon, provided, that is, that he deliver at least one of his confederates to the authorities. And in a further indication of the frustration felt by the authorities in Madrid, it took aim at nobles and commoners alike, adding, 'entendemos que la permanencia de los gitanos en estos Reynos ha dependido del favor, protección, y ayuda que han hallado en personas de diferentes estados'. The ordinance went on to stipulate the severe penalties to be applied to such individuals: 'incurra siendo noble en la pena de seis mil ducados aplicados a nuestra Cámara y gastos de justicia por mitad; y siendo plebeyo en la de diez años de galeras'. Meanwhile, any local justices failing to comply with the provisions of the new ordinance were to be removed and debarred from office in perpetuity, while half their assets were to be confiscated and used to defray the crown's expenses. Some were clearly suspected of harbouring gypsies, as the ordinance continues, 'ordenamos que qualquiera de las dichas justicias que tenga noticia de que otra tolera y permite en el distrito de su jurisdicción gitanos que no estén avecindados [. . .] deba recibir sobre esto información y remitirla al Consejo o a la Chancillería y Audiencia de su distrito, para que se vea y juzgue según derecho'.[40]

There were a variety of reasons, not always edifying, why people from such a wide cross-section of Spanish society should have sought to protect, assist, or simply turn a blind eye to the gypsies. One factor was certainly the jealous reassertion by elements of the nobility of their seigniorial jurisdictions, this, of course, against a background in which power was still effectively a matter of consent, of continuing negotiation between the King, his councils, the aristocracy, and even, *de facto*, lesser officials (Mackay, p. 66; Thompson, pp. 93–4). It is clear, too, that a low-level 'black economy' based on the sale or barter of stolen goods operated sporadically in certain areas in ways that tended to favour the gypsies. Then again, fear of revenge, bolstered

---

[39] AHN Consejos, lib. 1474, no. 188.
[40] AHN Consejos, leg. 51442, fol. 6.

by a lack of confidence in the authorities' ability to uphold the law, must have played its part. And it seems likely, too, that laws which typically vilified all gypsies, which sought to carry off their menfolk or deprive them of their traditional occupations, and which too often signally failed to distinguish between criminal elements and those who lived less scandalous lives, may well have elicited a certain sympathy for the latter among at least some of their non-gypsy neighbours.

But for all the protection afforded them here and there, gypsy men still lived under the real threat of condemnation to the galleys. Eleven of them, to take one example, were sentenced, along with two slaves, to four years at the oar in Madrid early in 1639. A letter of 16 March instructed the *alguacil* Martín de Cuéllar to escort them from the capital to Toledo. From there, having been handed over to the *alcalde* of that city's gaol, they were to be escorted to the galley ports. But the letter also insisted that the group be accompanied by the royal notary Mateo de Vitoria. It was to be his job not just to certify that the prisoners' heads, whiskers and beards were shaved clean, but also to ensure that the one *real* per day issued for the sustenance of each prisoner was actually spent by their guards on the food for which it was intended.[41] Even more worrying for the authorities, however, was the fact that it was difficult to guarantee that such prisoners would ever even reach the southern and south-eastern coasts to begin their sentences. Indeed, the special commissioner Pedro de Amezqueta, mentioned earlier, was ordered by Philip IV in a letter of 23 March that same year, 1639, to investigate the escapes over the winter of 'cantidad de galeotes' from gaols in Córdoba, Málaga, Jaca, and the towns of Vilches and Mengíbar in the province of Jaén.[42] And there were clearly suspicions in Madrid, to put it no more strongly than that, that these cases were not unique, since the letter also asks Amezqueta to report back not just on these escapes, but also on 'las demás que vereficáredes en las partes donde anduviéredes'. The open road, too, could present its opportunities, as Pellicer reported. On 15 September 1643 he wrote, 'enviando una sarta de galeotes desde la cárcel de Toledo, se pudieron rebelar en el camino y, matando los comisarios, todos se pusieron en libertad'.[43]

Meanwhile, some gypsies adopted another stratagem in an attempt to insulate themselves against the worsening civil climate. In a letter of 8 April 1639, Gaspar de Bracamonte, a member of the *Consejo*, informed the *Junta de Execución* of an offer he had received from one Sebastián Maldonado, a gypsy from Cazorla, a man 'muy conocido en aquella tierra y de buen crédito'. Maldonado had offered to raise two hundred men 'de su nación' to

---

[41] AGS Registro del Sello, March 1639.
[42] AGS Registro del Sello, March 1639.
[43] *Avisos históricos* (Madrid: Taurus, 1965), p. 198.

serve the King as soldiers.[44] What the letter does *not* say is that in that capacity they would likely benefit from the not insignificant measure of protection afforded by the *fuero militar*, the source of regular jurisdictional disputes between civil and military authorities in which the latter could usually be guaranteed to prevail.[45] Two days later, in another letter of 10 April that same year, the Count of Salvatierra relayed to the *junta de coronelías* a virtually identical offer made to him by a gypsy from Triana, Sebastián de Soto.[46] Maldonado had claimed to be the grandson of a captain who had served in the war in the Alpujarras, while de Soto declared that he had served both in the army in Flanders and in the navy. Both letters stressed the gypsies' physical endurance when exposed to the elements in open country; both, noted their experience with firearms; and both observed, by way of further encouragement, that this proposal might be a way of ridding Spain of them for good. But the gypsies' offers were not unconditional. De Soto demanded that he be made a captain, while Lázaro and Simón de Soto were be appointed ensign and sergeant, respectively. Maldonado insisted that if he recruited other gypsies, 'V. Magestad ha de dar su palabra Real de no servirse dellos para otro efeto que para el exercicio militar de la guerra'. Forced service at the oar could not, of course, conceivably be represented in such honourable terms. Indeed, later that year, the *junta de galeotes, esclavos, y gitanos* suggested that prisoners guilty of crimes not automatically meriting a term in the galleys might nevertheless be offered some remission of sentence in return for volunteering to serve for a fixed term; but it added that they would only do so 'con sueldo y ración de buena boya, y con declaración que este servicio no ofenda su onor y reputación'.[47] As it was, the fate of Maldonado and de Soto's offers is summed up by a laconic marginal note in a different hand on the second of them. It simply reads, 'no conviene admitir esta propuesta'. A similar tactic was employed as a desperate last resort by gypsies attempting to avoid arrest in Madrid in March 1639. The crown's Special Commissioner, Juan García de Córdoba, mentioned earlier, had been pursuing the gypsies 'Pitocho', 'el Valiente', Salazar, and Juan González, all of them accused of highway robbery. He was presented with numerous obstacles in the villages he visited, including a *juez eclesiástico* who excommunicated him and various forms of obstruction by local people, some of whom had dealt in the stolen goods. When he eventually closed in on the fugitives in Madrid, he noted that, 'yo los e visto [. . .]

---

[44] AGS Guerra Antigua, leg. 1256.

[45] J.H. Elliott, *Imperial Spain 1469–1716* (London: Edward Arnold, 1963), p. 295. In Calderón's *El alcalde de Zalamea*, which explores just such a jurisdictional dispute, the *dénouement* pointedly favours civil authority and is endorsed by no less a figure than Philip II.

[46] AGS Guerra Antigua, leg. 1261.

[47] AGS Guerra Antigua, leg. 3173, 19 November 1639.

en esta Corte en traje de soldados'.[48] As it was, such abuses had by that time already come to the attention of the King and moves were afoot by March effectively to suspend the *fuero militar* in the capital, though the royal order to that effect was not issued until 16 August that year (Mackay, p. 41).

Given that the 1639 order now required *all* gypsy males to be put to the oar, the sparse data available suggest that failure to enforce the law or successful evasion thereof were widespread. The galley musters at Cartagena, where many of those convicted were sent for embarcation, show that 141 men, about 13 per cent of those who arrived there between 1639 and 1641, were gypsies (Goodman, pp. 217–20). While this doubtless represented an increase on those apprehended previously, it was clearly a very long way from the clean sweep that had been demanded by the legislators in Madrid. No figures are available for Puerto de Santa María, the other main point of embarcation for *galeotes*. But some idea of what this number represented in comparative terms may perhaps be gleaned from the fact that when some sixty years earlier in the late 1570s, the Marquis of Santa Cruz, responding to a request by Philip II, ordered the *veedor y contador de galeras* to report on how many Gypsies were currently serving in the galleys, he was informed that there were fifty-nine. Of these, twenty-seven had been sentenced to six years at the oar. The sentences of the remaining thirty-two were not specified.[49]

The role of the Church as protector of gypsies was also condemned by the *Junta de galeotes, esclavos, y gitanos*. In fact, as early as 1566, an ordinance had ordered the justices to ignore claims by gypsies to ecclesiastical sanctuary.[50] Nonetheless, the frequent jurisdictional disputes involving gypsies between the lay and religious authorities continued until well into the eighteenth century, when, in 1748, an agreement that saved face all round was finally reached with Rome. Henceforth, gypsies could be removed from the churches where they had claimed sanctuary and taken to others within the perimeters of penal colonies.[51] Ostensibly lacking any specific religious tradition of their own, some gypsies, especially those who had accepted *vecindades*, nominally accepted Christianity, even if only to the extent of baptising their children. Spurred on as it was by such small successes, the Church's attempts to shelter these wayward people from the civil authorities doubtless reflected a parallel urge, as infantilizing as it was didactic, to save them from themselves, too. It is true that the Inquisition did summon gypsies

---

[48] AHN Consejos, leg. 51060, 'Quaderno de autos generales'.

[49] AGS Guerra y Marina, leg. 88, fol. 359.

[50] *Pragmática que su Magestad manda que se imprima. Sobre los Vagamundos, Ladrones, Blasphemos, Rufianes* . . . (Alcalá de Henares: En casa de Juan de Villanueva, 1566). Copy consulted BNM R/14090 (26).

[51] María Helena Sánchez Ortega, *Los gitanos españoles: el período borbónico* (Barcelona: Castellote, 1977), p. 261.

before it on numerous occasions, typically on charges ranging from blasphemy and superstition to sorcery, and quite often as a result of denunciations by non-gypsy neighbours with whom the accused had been in dispute. Yet despite a number of notable exceptions, it tended on the whole to hand down only light or token sentences, perhaps requiring the accused to attend a mass or two to atone for what were more often than not misdemeanours fuelled by abuse by non-gypsies, alcohol or simply the need to make enough money, albeit via deception, in order to subsist.

As the century drew to a close, however, Charles II's ministers began to take a much less tolerant view, and one detects the first, ominous signs of a new determination to see the gypsy problem finally brought under control. The ordinance of 1692, referred to earlier, had continued to take the line adopted in 1619, insisting loftily that 'jamás se ha entendido que en estos nuestros Reynos hubiese verdaderos Gitanos'. It had introduced new and tighter measures, including detailed reporting procedures, designed to ensure compliance. Three years later, the lengthy ordinance of 1695 tightened the noose even further. It set the scene for a new century, which would not only see the most fearsome crackdown visited on Spain's gypsies with the general round-up of 1749, but which, paradoxically, would also eventually give way in 1783 under the 'enlightened despotism' of Charles III to at least a kind of reform and repeal of much of the repressive legislation of the past.

Diego Hurtado de Mendoza and the Jewess of Venice: Tolerance, Interfaith Sexuality and *Converso* Culture

ALEXANDER SAMSON

Four years before being made responsible for the opening sessions of the Council of Trent in 1545, the Imperial ambassador, Diego Hurtado de Mendoza had spent the summer frolicking with his Jewish lover on Murano, island retreat of the Venetian patriciate. While this may seem surprising, the letters he wrote back to the imperial secretariat, detailing his affair, are even more so, casting a fascinating light on the possibility of tolerant religious and sexual attitudes in the Spain of the early 1540s. A consideration of these letters calls into question the consecrated picture of *conversos* as a largely endogamous group.[1] Research on Toledo has suggested that all the children in certain *converso* families married into other families with similarly recognizable *converso* surnames.[2] It has also been convincingly argued that the *estatutos de limpieza de sangre*, which excluded the descendants of Jews from municipal office, military orders and various areas of the Church 'drove the *conversos* to become, in a fairly high degree, an endogamous group holding itself apart from the Old Christians, and forming its own associations and clubs'.[3] Sexual relations between men and women of different religion or ethnicity certainly attracted harsh condemnation in the early modern period from certain quarters, and concerns about the possibility of liaisons between

---

[1] The literature on the *conversos* is ample. Some of the most distinguished contributions include: Cecil Roth, *A History of the Marranos* (Philadelphia: The Jewish Publication Society, 1932); Antonio Domínguez Ortiz, *Los conversos de origen judío después de la expulsión* (Madrid: CSIC, 1955); Julio Caro Baroja, *Los judíos en la España moderna y contemporánea* (Madrid: Ariel, 1961); Haim Beinart, *Los conversos ante el Tribunal de la Inquisición* (Barcelona: Riopiedras, 1983); Juan Blázquez Miguel, *Inquisición y criptojudaísmo* (Madrid: Kaydeda, 1988); and Benzion Netanyahu, *The Origins of the Inquisition in 15th Century Spain* (New York: Random House, 1995).

[2] See Linda Martz's article 'Pure Blood Statutes in Sixteenth Century Toledo: Implementation as Opposed to Adoption', *Sefarad*, 54 (1994), 83–106.

[3] Brian Pullan, *The Jews of Europe and the Inquisition of Venice, 1550–1670* (Oxford: Basil Blackwell, 1983), p. 205.

Jews and Christians found frequent expression in a rash of legislation imposing the wearing of a distinguishing mark or badge on Jews that stretched back to the Fourth Lateran Council of 1215 – the first of innumerable attempts to enforce prohibitions designed to make religious difference visible: 'et omni tempore qualitate habitus publice ab aliis populis distinguantur' ('and that at all times they might be distinguishable from the rest of the population by some aspect of their dress').[4] Despite the obvious anti-Semitism of certain sectors of Spanish society this is not the whole story. This chapter suggests that at least in the first half of the sixteenth century, interfaith and interracial marriages were a far more common and widely accepted occurrence in Spain than has previously been thought.

One reason for suspecting that this might be the case is the heterogeneous religious world of the seventeenth-century Spanish Netherlands, where relationships between Catholics and Protestants, Lutherans or Calvinists, were commonplace. Often, far from being seen in an entirely negative way, they were viewed as important opportunities to win new converts, to gain an entrée into families traditionally of another sectarian persuasion. Despite attempts to secure conversion, relationships frequently proved stronger than religious conviction and the cohabitation of different confessions and faiths under one roof took place. Within such households a variety of arrangements could govern this *convivencia* of different religious faiths – sometimes all the children would follow just one of the parents' religious faiths. However, more often than not, some would follow one confession and others another, with male children brought up in the faith of their father and females that of their mother. Interfaith marriage could be viewed as a problem and an opportunity. In Habsburg Spain, dynasticism and the encounter with the New World among other factors created a need for other ways of viewing interfaith and interracial relationships. When Philip II offered to marry Elizabeth I even before the death of his then wife Mary Tudor, there was almost certainly an expectation that given time she would convert, or at the very least tolerate the Catholic reforms of the previous regime. Similarly, Henrietta Maria's marriage to Charles I in 1625, according to some of his subjects, compromised and poisoned the monarch's attitude towards the true faith, leading to an unacceptably tolerant attitude towards Catholic powers bent on eradicating Protestantism. This was a major factor in Charles's problematic relationship with Parliament. Anxieties about the proposed Spanish match for him in 1623 had surfaced in a number of fictional representations of interfaith marriages. A courtship between a Catholic Italian merchant Vitelli and a Muslim Ottoman princess Donusa in Philip Massinger's *The Renegado*, it has been argued, functioned as a displaced meditation on the proposed

---

[4]   Cited in Solomon Grayzel, *The Church and the Jews in the XIIIth Century* (New York: Hermon Press, 1966), pp. 308–9.

marriage between the Prince of Wales and the Infanta, underlining the dangers of entering into relationships with women of other religions.[5] Transgressive sexual attraction across religious divisions was also a recurring theme in the work of Cervantes from his play *Los baños de Argel* to the interpolated novella, the 'Captive's Tale', and the espousal of Zoraida and Ruy Pérez de Viedma in *Don Quijote*.

Instructions issued by the Spanish Crown in 1516 to govern sexual behaviour in their Latin American colonies advised the *conquistadores* to marry the daughters of *caciques* 'para que pronto todos los caciques sean españoles'.[6] Racial mixing could be transformative as well as transmissive. There is a clear echo of this idea in Lope de Vega's play *El nuevo mundo descubierto por Cristóbal Colón*, which was sponsored by the son of the man it celebrated, García Hurtado de Mendoza. Lope had a long-standing association with the family, and his sponsor became the godfather of his son Lopito. Here, in a projection of Spanish colonial fantasies, the *indiana* Tacuana argues that such transformation was what her people desired, now they were a subject people, through her liberation from the tyrannical and rough embrace of her Araucanian lover:

> Tacuana: y volváis a vuestras patrias,
> y que vuestros hijos pobres
> jueguen ricos al tejuelo
> con el oro de estos montes,
> o los traigáis a casar
> con nuestras hijas, adonde
> mezclándose nuestra sangre
> seamos todos españoles.
> Que me libréis del tirano
> cacique, bárbaro, y torpe,
> que aquí me tiene cautiva
> entre sus brazos disformes[7]

The implicit condemnation of the exploitative figure of the *nouveau riche indiano*, those adventurers who returned to Spain from the New World to squander their riches on illicit activities such as gambling, is contrasted with the utopian possibility of assimilation through marriage and the transformation of the indigenous (female) population into Spaniards. Diego Hurtado de

---

5   On this, see the forthcoming chapter by Claire Jowitt, ' "I am another woman": The Spanish and French Matches in Massinger's *The Renegado* (1624) and *The Unnatural Combat* (1624–5)', in Alexander Samson (ed.), *The Spanish Match: Prince Charles' Journey to Madrid, 1623* (Basingstoke: Ashgate, 2006).

6   Bartolomé Bennassar, *La América española y la América portuguesa siglos XVI–XVIII*, 3rd edn (Madrid: Akal, 1996), p. 206.

7   Lope de Vega Carpio, *El nuevo mundo descubierto por Cristóbal Colón*, ed. Robert M. Shannon (New York: Peter Lang, 2001), p. 234, ll. 2188–99.

Mendoza had grown up in the multicultural environment of Granada, surrounded by *morisco* and *converso* retainers, whose acceptance was confirmed and cemented by marital alliances. The Mendoza family shared the precincts of the Generalife with the ex-*alcalde* of the Nasirid dynasty, Ben Omar. Rechristened Alonso de Granada y Venegas, he married María de Mendoza, a cousin of Diego's father Íñigo López de Mendoza, second Count of Tendilla, who had been appointed governor of the city after its fall in 1492. Towards the end of his life, on his enforced return to Granada, Diego described Omar's son in a letter as a *compañero*.[8] On his mother Francisca Pacheco's side Diego was descended from both Jewish and Moorish ancestors, a descent shared with the Ponce de León, Aguilar, and Alba families, as well as Fernando de Aragón (his great aunt Juana Enríquez was Fernando's mother). He probably spent at least some of his childhood at the Alhambra palace in the company of his sister María Pacheco, who married Juan de Padilla, the *converso* leader of the *comuneros* revolt. He later visited her in exile in Portugal in 1530.[9]

The first man to be arrested and accused in the notorious case of the 'Santo Niño de la Guardia', the *converso* Jucé Franco, testified that his brother Alonso Franco had said to him: 'Ved qué trabajo tenemos nosotros, los que somos casados con mugeres cristianas viejas, que aunque querríamos circuncidar nuestros fijos, non lo osamos faser por cavsa dellas.'[10] The symbolic power of this incident, argued by some to have been crucial in paving the way for the expulsion, lay precisely in that it uncovered a threat from *conversos* of contaminating and undermining the imperviousness of Christian religious practices and communities. The crypto-Jew and Judaizer were disturbing and menacing symbols of the instability and porousness of Catholic identities. Evidence in Mexico as late as the seventeenth century demonstrates that 98 per cent of men brought before the Inquisition for judaizing had been circumcised.[11] The *converso* chronicler Hernando del Pulgar described the situation in Andalusia in the second half of the fifteenth

---

8 Ángel González Palencia y Eugenio Mele, *Vida y obras de Don Diego Hurtado de Mendoza* [henceforth *Vida y obras*], 3 vols (Madrid: Instituto de Valencia Don Juan, 1941–3), III, p. 458.

9 The details in this paragraph are well-known: see the biography of Mendoza by Erika Spivakovsky, *Son of the Alhambra: Don Diego Hurtado de Mendoza, 1504–1575* (Austin: University of Texas Press, 1970), esp. chs 1–3. There is a biography of Diego's brother: Arthur Aiton, *Antonio de Mendoza: First Viceroy of New Spain* (Durham: Duke UP, 1927) and, on the family, see Helen Nader, *The Mendoza Family in the Spanish Renaissance, 1350–1550* (New Brunswick: Rutgers UP, 1979).

10 Fidel Fita, 'La verdad sobre el martirio del santo niño de la guardia, o sea el proceso y quema (16 noviembre, 1491) del judío Jucé Franco en Ávila', *Boletín de la Real Academia de la Historia*, 11 (1887), 6–160 (p. 45).

11 See David Gittlitz, *Secrecy and Deceit: The Religion of the Crypto-Jews* (Philadelphia: The Jewish Publication Society, 1996), p. 81.

century in terms reminiscent of the situation in the Low Countries in the seventeenth century:

> E aunque guardavan el sábado y ayunaban algunos ayunos de los judíos, pero no guardaban todos los sábados, ni ayunaban todos los ayunos, e sy façían un rito no façían otro, de manera que en la una y en la otra ley prevaricavan. E fallóse en algunas casas el marido guardar algunas çeremonias judaycas, e la mujer ser buena cristiana; e el un hijo e hija ser buen cristiano, e otro tener opinión judayca. E dentro de una casa aver diversidad de creençias, y encubrirse unos de otros.[12]

Pulgar testified to the fact that diversity of religious practice and belief was often to be found in one and the same household where an interfaith marriage had taken place, whether this was witting or not. The picture of households within which there was a multiplicity of different beliefs, practices and opinions, some of which were kept secret even from other members of the same family, suggests that interracial marriage and heterogeneity of religious practice and belief in early modern Spain was more common and tolerated than has been thought. The religious and sectarian differences dramatized here only became starkly defined and divisive in the wake of the re-examination forced upon Catholic Europe by a period of unprecedented religious ferment whose most prominent symptom was the Reformation, although the expulsion was another. It is easy to read the increasing pressure towards cultural and religious uniformity of post-Tridentine Catholicism back into the period before Trent.

In a letter to Diego Hurtado de Mendoza's great-uncle, Cardenal Mendoza, Archbishop of Seville, about the intensified persecution of the *moriscos*, the tolerant Pulgar again referred to the social problems created by the expulsion and compulsory baptisms of both Jews and Muslims:

> Pero como los viejos sean allí tan malos Christianos los nuevos son tan buenos Judíos sin duda señor creo que mozas Doncellas de diez a veinte años hay en el andalucía diez mill niñas que dende que nacieron nunca de sus casas salieron ni oyeron ni supieron otra doctrina sino la que vieron hazer a sus Padres de sus Puertas adentro. Quemar todos estos sería cossa cruellissíma y aun difícil de hazer Porque se absentarían con desesperación a lugares donde no se esperase dellos coreptión jamás.[13]

The sympathetic second Count of Tendilla, the Cardinal's nephew, had

---

[12] Hernando de Pulgar, *Crónica de los Reyes Católicos*, ed. Juan de la Mata Carriazo (Madrid: Espasa Calpe, 1943), II, p. 210. See analysis of Pulgar by Cantera Burgos, 'Hernando del Pulgar and the *conversos*', *Sefarad*, 4 (1944), 296–348.

[13] BNM MS 1517, fol. 4. See also E. Meneses García (ed.), *Correspondencia del Conde de Tendilla, 1508–1513*, 2 vols (Madrid: Real Academia de la Historia, 1973–4).

vigorously opposed the operation of the Inquisition in Granada as well as the policy towards the *moriscos* in Andalusia. Pulgar called into question the terms *cristiano nuevo* and *viejo*, by asserting that the former could still be described as good Jews, while the latter were poor Christians. The problem was how to penetrate behind closed doors to deal with ethnic and cultural diversity at the level of the household, the irreducible 'doctrina' of the 'puertas adentro'. Again the task of cultural assimilation is seen exclusively in relation to (unmarried) females, 'mozas Doncellas de diez a veinte años'. Initial tolerant solutions to these problems eventually gave way to more violent and radical solutions. The settlement of 1526, which permitted a whole range of Moorish cultural practices to continue, finally lapsed in 1566 with the *pragmática* of Philip II that sparked off the Alpujarras revolt, one of whose most hated conditions was that the *moriscos* kept their doors open, precisely to counter the problem of the 'puertas adentro'. The rebel leader Aben Xahuar as dramatized by Diego Hurtado de Mendoza in his *Guerra de Granada* complains bitterly that this injunction for them to have doors and windows open renders them 'sujetos de ladrones, de malhechores, de atrevidos y desvergonzados adúlteros'.[14] His representation of the revolt is another suggestive piece of evidence for the tolerance of his attitudes, although this interpretation is not without its problems, as we will see below.

In a letter to his intimate friend and colleague the Bishop of Arras, Antoine Perrenot de Granvelle, from Rome in 1548, writing in his capacity as Imperial ambassador, Diego Hurtado de Mendoza wrote: 'y esto hablo como philosopho y como moro de Granada, o como marrano'.[15] A verse portrait of him, which circulated in Siena around 1552, where he had been placed in charge of the military garrison, described him similarly as 'Diego Urtado Mendozza, arcimarrano'.[16] Bernardo Blanco-González has suggested that this was a direct reference to 'los amores de don Diego con una judía de Venecia' and that his brief posting to London in 1536 had owed much to his notorious antecedents.[17] His relativization of religious identities had its roots in his background, awareness of his origins and active engagement with other cultures. In his account of the history of the city of Granada he asserted, 'será lo que hallé en los libros arábigos de la tierra, y los de Muley Hacen rey de Túnez, y lo que hasta hoy queda en la memoria de los hombres' (*Guerra de*

[14] Diego Hurtado de Mendoza, *Guerra de Granada*, ed. Bernardo Blanco-González (Madrid: Castalia, 1970), p. 118.

[15] Alberto Vázquez and R. Selden Rose (eds), *Algunas Cartas de Don Diego Hurtado de Mendoza escritas 1538–1552* [henceforth *Algunas cartas*] (New Haven: Yale UP, 1935), p. 119.

[16] From Alessandro di Girolamo Sozzini, 'Il succeso delle rivoluzioni della cita di Siena, d'imperiale franzese, e di franzese imperiale, scrito da . . . gentiluomo senese' (Siena, 1577), repr. in *Archivio storico italiano*, II (1842), p. 456, doc. XIV. Cited in *Guerra de Granada*, p. 19.

[17] See his introduction to *Guerra de Granada*.

Granada, p. 96). He had met Muley Hasen, when he accompanied the Emperor Charles V in the conquest of Tunis in 1535. After he was deposed and blinded by his son, he again met the King of Tunis in Rome in 1548. His library, as well as printed books, included 32 Hebrew and 255 Arabic manuscripts. It came under the scrutiny of the Inquisition after his evidence at the trial of Bartolomé Carranza, at which point Luther's prologue to the first printing of the Koran was probably torn out.[18] In 1539 he was despatched to Venice to counter the machinations of the French and maintain the Venetians' commitment to the Holy League. If his poetry is any guide, he led a solitary and lonely existence in the Signoria, where contact between the Venetian nobility and foreigners, particularly ambassadors was disapproved of, before being prohibited altogether.

The addressee of the letters, Francisco de los Cobos, had been born in Ubeda in Andalusia. He was a protégé of Diego's father. Having been brought up in the household of the secretary for civilian affairs in Granada, Hernando de Zafra, he succeeded him after his death in 1508 (Spivakovsky, *Son of the Alhambra*, p. 46). In 1515 he served alongside Diego's brother Antonio as Procurador for Granada. Later in life Diego described himself and his brothers as 'hechuras' of los Cobos, his creatures (*Algunas cartas*, pp. 33, 62 and 83). Antonio's appointment as first Viceroy of the Indies owed much to los Cobos's influence, as did the nomination of another brother, Bernardino, President of the Council of the Indies in 1545.[19] The content of the letters was frequently scurrilous. Diego informed los Cobos that during the stay of the special Imperial envoy Alfonso d'Avalos, Marquis of Vasto:

> Su Exçelençia vio a los III del presente dos bailerinas y ençendióse de manera que la misma noche fue nouio, en las quales bodas V. Sa. fue harto desseado, y lo es aquí donde no se trata otra cosa sino suspirar por el con cada cosa que nos contente . . . este diablo de marqués, que le uienen las veneçianetas mascaradas de tres en tres a uisitar. (*Algunas cartas*, p. 21. Mendoza to los Cobos, 4 December 1539)

Los Cobos and Mendoza had shared similar sexual adventures in Genoa in 1536. The crude tone and salacious subject matter of the letters from Mendoza about his own relationship were not unprecedented, although references to sex were couched as here in coded references to weddings and

---

[18] On his library, see Anthony Hobson, *Renaissance Book Collecting: Jean Grolier and Diego Hurtado de Mendoza, Their Books and Bindings* (Cambridge: CUP, 1999), pp. 70–92. He also owned copies of Machiavelli and the *Decameron*.

[19] On los Cobos, see Howard Keniston, *Francisco de los Cobos: Secretary of the Emperor Charles V* (Pittsburg: University of Pittsburg Press, 1960). The secretariat he ran is analysed in José Antonio Escudero, *Los Secretarios de Estado y del Despacho (1472–1724): El desarrollo histórico de la Institución*, vol. 1 of 4 (Madrid: Instituto de Estudios Administrativos, 2nd edn 1976).

bridegrooms. Mendoza referred to a visit he paid to a certain Cornelia, then serving in the household of the Countess of Novelara, with whom los Cobos had had an affair in 1530.[20] He relayed to his friend her complaints about his treatment of her and when she lifted up a 'velo' to reveal a portrait of the *Comendador Mayor*, commented 'Paréceme que sabe esta levantar la ropa a este señor'.[21] In June, he requested some 'dechados' (embroidery patterns or samples) and 'bolsas' (purses), before finally revealing why in August:

> sabrá V. S. que yo hize el amore aquí tres meses con una de las bellas [*cortesa / puta / veneçi / marra*]nas de Italia, y venidos a conclusión, en el mismo punto me dixo que estuviese quedo, que ella era judía y ninguna cosa podía hazer por mí si no me tornava judío; yo, como tenía lo uno y lo otro tan poco camino que andar, díxele que passasse adelante, que en aquello poco avía que hazer. V. S. me conseje si me devo circunçidar, y si le parece así y se allega por acá, apareje su preputio, que sigún es hermosa la judía, me parece harto buen mercado.[22]

The manuscript is, unfortunately, illegible at the critical juncture; however, the reading 'cortesanas' or 'veneçianas' rather than 'putanas' seems more likely in the light of subsequent comments about her good head and their not having celebrated the 'wedding' yet, as well as the playful Italianate 'amore'. The temporal construction of the sentence is also suggestive, in that the revelation that she is Jewish and cannot take their relationship any further unless Diego converts, follows on from the description of their three-month courtship. This might imply that he was initially unaware of her origins. However, it may simply be that the rhetoric is calculated to give that impression. Humour in the letters plays on the tension between sexual attraction and adherence to a religious identity. The short path from Christian to Jew, however, is qualified by its enclosure within a clause related to Diego's desire for consummation and it being exclusively related to 'yo'. That the loss of a foreskin is a reasonably good trade for the enjoyment of the Jewess's beauty or his willingness to share his mistress with los Cobos again undercuts any seriousness in the exchange. Eleven days after his first reference to her, Hurtado de Mendoza informed his friend: 'Tengo vna huerta y vna casa fuera de Veneçia, donde si yo fuesse malhechor se podrían hazer ynsultos; pero si quissiesse la judía, presto me passaría a biuir en la sinoga. Muy illustre Señor, en mi uida vi más hermosa judía ni más auisada, y es muger que tiene coca.'[23] The fact that his summer residence on Murano could be the stage for an assault and that his infatuation had now extended to her intelligence and

---

[20] On this affair, see Keniston, pp. 123–42.

[21] *Algunas cartas*, p. 29. Original AGS Estado, leg. 869, fols 105–60.

[22] *Vida y obras*, III, pp. 284–5. Original AGS Estado, leg. 1316, fol. 49. Mendoza to Cobos, 5 August 1540.

[23] *Vida y obras*, III, p. 288. Mendoza to Cobos, 16 August 1540, Murano.

discretion imply that she had accompanied him there. The island was the backdrop for the only interfaith wedding between a Christian and Jewess to appear in Venetian Inquisition records.[24] Mendoza referred to her residence several times in his letters as the 'sinagogue'.

The ambassador acknowledged receipt of the samples or patterns and purses (requested only seven or eight weeks previously) from los Cobos's wife in his next letter, less than two weeks later, although it appears not all of them were destined for the Jewess. Mendoza had alluded to the possibility of marriage in previous letters, despite being touted by friends as a potential future pope (his sexual activities do not seem to have been any obstacle to this).

> Por las bolsas, que eran muy lindas, beso las manos a V. S.; no quiero guantes, que acá son todas asnas; la judía lleuó la azul y no fue mal empleada [. . .] no dexaremos de mirar la judía y yo barba con barba algunas laborcitas; la para quien los quería está aora la más hermosa biuda del mundo y tiene ocho mil ducados de renta: oxalá le pareciese tan hermoso yo como le pareceran los dechados.[25]

The rich and beautiful widow referred to here is probably not to be identified with 'la judía', although an ambiguity remains. Within a few days the Jewess's resistance appeared to be crumbling: 'Los tratos de la judía tornan a bullir, y creo que sin dexar mi lei haremos paz.'[26] Despite the possibility of them 'making peace' without Diego having to renounce his faith, there are still references after this to circumcision and, furthermore, the purses also seem all to have found their way into her possession. The harping on circumcision may have its origins in a practice that was probably still common although clandestine amongst the sizeable *converso* population of Granada during his childhood. However, it is impossible that its theological resonances, in the context of the Reformation, could have escaped someone, who in addition to being ambassador to England in the crucial period after 1536, had renounced the friar's habit, and was also soon to be named imperial envoy to the Council of Trent. The Pauline passages on those of the circumcision related precisely to the interiority of a believer's piety, as opposed to the empty fulfilment of 'ley'. A similar subtext must underlie the words placed in the mouth of the rebel leader Aben Xahuar (Fernando de Valor) when addressing the Morisco gathering in his *Guerra de Granada*: 'como si trajésemos la ley en el vestido y no en el corazón' (p. 117). In November he informed the *Comendador*:

24 Pier Cesare Ioly Zorattini, 'Jews, Crypto-Jews and the Inquisition', in Robert Davis and Benjamin Ravid (eds), *The Jews of Early Modern Venice* (Baltimore: Johns Hopkins UP, 2001), pp. 97–116 (p. 100).

25 *Vida y obras*, III, p. 288. Mendoza to Cobos, 28 August, Venice.

26 *Vida y obras*, III, p. 289. Mendoza to Cobos, 1 September, Venice.

Las bolsas están en la sinoga. Si pensasse que V. S. auía de uenir por acá,
dilataría el día de mi circunçisión para hazerle fiesta. No quiero guantes,
que las de aquy son más asnas y más blancas que doña Constança,
perdónela Dios y perdóneme Dios; mas enbíeme lienço crudo, que esta
judía, antes que uenga la boda, me a començado a dañar el estómago. . . .
Mi retrato es acabado, uime; eme pareçydo de tanto más ruin jesto después
que salí de allá que antes, que aun osé yr a bisperas oy a la judería; mire
Ura. Sa. que tal estaré para contra christianos.[27]

Vázquez and Selden Rose have suggested that Costanza referred to Costanza
Farnese, daughter of Pope Paul III, married first to Bosio III Sforza and then
Stephano Colonna, but it seems more likely to refer to the Constanza,
Condessa di Novelara, whose lady-in-waiting was los Cobos's lover Cornelia
(*Algunas Cartas*, p. 56). Despite his letter in early September, the wedding
had still not taken place and Diego's stomach, seat of his sexual desire and
libido, was beginning to suffer. The translation of 'lienzo crudo' as
'unbleached linen' may disguise a punning, sly and half-serious reference to
the use of erotic painting. If it is a reference to a canvas, then it resonates
with the later allusion to Titian, well-known for his explicit mythological
paintings, and his portrait of the ambassador being finished.[28] The reference
to Diego visiting the Jewess after vespers means that she must have been a
Spanish-speaking Sephardic Jew. The Sephardim were permitted to live
outside the Ghetto Nuovo, which was locked from sunset to sunrise, in the
Ghetto Vecchio, which was open to the rest of Christian Venice. Although
open, relations between Christians and Jews were certainly frowned on. Only
insecurity and wounded vanity, not assuaged by Titian's flattery, drove him to
'dare' to go there after dark. He had commented previously of his portrait
that 'no tengo tan ruin gesto en pintura como byuo en carnes'.[29] The Senate
had forbidden sexual relations between Christians and Jews of the city as
early as 1424, and by 1443 both Jewish men and women were obliged to
wear a recognizable sign, normally a yellow or red headcovering, to avoid
Christians having intercourse with them by mistake, unidentified at night.[30]
The indistinguishability of Jews from Christians continued to destabilize
notions of fixed religious identity, an instability symbolized by the figure of
the *converso*.

His lover was almost certainly the daughter of refugees, who had fled
from Spain in 1492. The Venetian Senate had noted the presence of 'marrano
heretics' in 1497 and ordered them to depart. The term *marrano*, used by

[27] *Vida y obras*, III, pp. 291 and 293: also *Algunas cartas*, p. 58. Mendoza to Cobos,
24 November 1540, Venice.

[28] The painting is in the Pitti Gallery in Florence.

[29] *Algunas cartas*, p. 53. Mendoza to Cobos, 2 October 1540, Venice.

[30] Benjamin Ravid, 'The Venetian Government and the Jews', in *The Jews of Early
Modern Venice*, pp. 3–29 (pp. 6–7).

Diego about himself, referred generally to *conversos* who secretly adhered to or continued to practise their faith following an ambivalent conversion. Her family had probably migrated to Venice later, from Italy via Portugal, where many New Christians and Jews had resettled after 1492, until the introduction of the Inquisition there in 1536 and a second mass exodus. In 1538 Ferrara had offered commercial privileges to all those who spoke Spanish or Portuguese, a phrase clearly designed to include Iberian Jews and *conversos*. The invitation signified the 'beginning of a new phase in which rival urban centres in Italy not only were contending to attract rich and capable Jewish merchants of Iberian descent but were also willing to tolerate the presence of New Christians, who would either return to Judaism or retain their ambiguous religious identity'.[31] Many Jews had fled from Rome, just like their Spanish compatriots in 1529 when Lutheran troops sacked the city, and resettled in Venice. Following the end, despite all of Mendoza's efforts, of Venice's conflict with the Ottomans, there was also a mass influx of Jews from the Eastern Mediterranean to reclaim their part in the trade with the Ottoman Empire. This rapidly led to overcrowding in the Jewish quarters of Venice. There is a reference to the smell this gave rise to when Diego wrote: 'Ayer fuy a uer la judería y vi mi judía que le hiede la casa como una galera, y por esto me voy desauiniendo.'[32] Spivakovsky claimed that this was one of the factors that led Mendoza to bring the Jewess to live in the vicinity of the embassy in the parish of San Barnaba on the Grand Canal, having assumed that she did not simply join Mendoza under the same roof in the ambassador's residence.[33] In an effort literally to contain the influx, the Senate decided that summer to join the Ghettos Nuovo and Vecchio together and gate them off from the rest of the city.

On the surface the letters appear to be the confidences of close friends, whose intimacy is signalled by their opaque, suggestive and idiolectical language. However, their context militates against this understanding of them, since they were simultaneously dispatches from an official Imperial ambassador to Charles V's principal minister. We know that los Cobos's wife María de Mendoza read some of the correspondence, not least because she discovered about her husband's affair with Cornelia from a reference in one of her cousin's letters (Keniston, p. 141). More importantly from marginalia on manuscript copies of Diego's letters, it appears that some of the replies were drafted from annotations made on them by amanuenses of los Cobos, and later transcribed by him or other secretaries.

---

[31] Benjamin Arbel, 'Jews in International Trade: The Emergence of the Levantines and Ponentines', in *The Jews of Early Modern Venice*, pp. 73–96 (pp. 80–1).

[32] *Vida y obras*, III, p. 297. Mendoza to Cobos, 29 January 1541, Venice.

[33] Erika Spivakovsky, 'A Jewess of Venice', *The Chicago Jewish Forum*, 19 (1960–1), 129–37 (p. 132).

Pues v. m. no quiere guantes no se le embiarán; el lienço crudo embiaré con éste sy le pudiere hauer, y creo que la señora judía deue ser causa que lo ayáis menester, y sy assy es, todo deue ser bien empleado. Dios sabe lo que yo querría hallarme presente a vuestra circuncisión, que podría ser que vsassemos della al fuero de Génoua, que creo no se haurá oluidado; aunque no sé sy en este caso querríades vsar de la precedencia, pero no nos desabeníamos. Para la señora Judía os embío otra bolsa. V. m. se la dará; también embío el lienço crudo . . .[34]

Far from being private letters, intimate jokes between two friends, the third person annotation on the letter was certainly dictated by los Cobos. The impliation is that the entire secretariat enjoyed laughing along at Mendoza's scurrilous accounts of his interfaith affair and that los Cobos's jokey replies were written up by him later, while one of his amanuenses noted down an initial dictated response. It alerts us to the constructed, self-consciously witty nature of these interpolations in the serious business of state.

Recybí el lienço crudo, y si uuiesse de rreparar lo que podría gastar doña Talitla, que auía de dezir la signora Ambaxatora, no bastaría una aljama de tela; mas, biue Dios, que la guardo para que V. S. guste uirgo judío, si acá viniere; y podrá ser que hallemos algún jentil, porque no se nos escape ley, sigún aquí son buenas christianas, y el pobre Embaxador, cirçunçidado *capite*, seguirá la instrutión de Génova . . .
. . . si sale la judiíca uergonçosica a la matina, porque también tiene S. E. sus dos leyes como nos, y jentil no le falta, que lo es más que quantas yo e uisto en España y fuera de ella . . .[35]

The 'lienço crudo', from this and los Cobos's previous letter, whatever its other connotations, was clearly linen sent in order to set up Mendoza's mistress as 'lady ambassador', that is to provide her with a trousseau for her 'married' life. It is the first time that Diego referred to her as anything other than 'la judía', here naming her for the first time Talitla. This might be her real name – Talithla is a Sephardic name, found in the Talmud, originally from Aramaic. Diego playfully spiced up the letter by throwing in the arabic word 'aljama', joking that a mosque or synagogue full of cloth would not be sufficient for his mistress. He again plays here on the way that sexuality can

---

[34] *Vida y obras*, III, p. 298. Original AGS Estado, leg. 55, fols 22–7. Cobos to Mendoza, 1 February 1541, Madrid. The marginal note reads: 'que pues no quiere guantes que le embiara lienço sy pudiere, y que cree que la Sra Judía deue ser la causa que haya menester el lienço crudo, que si assy es, todo deue ser bien empleado y que Dios sabe lo que se querría hallar presente a su circuncisión y que podía ser que usasen della al fuero de Genova, que cree que no se le haurá oluidado, aunque no sabe sy en este caso querría el cesar de la precedençia', *Algunas cartas*, p. 56, n. 4.

[35] *Vida y obras*, III, p. 300. Original AGS Estado, leg. 1317, fol. 38. Mendoza to Cobos, 12 March 1541, Venice.

cut across and subvert religious categories and identities, offering los Cobos the chance to enjoy being a 'uirgo judío'. To avoid renouncing their 'ley', the ambassador suggests they seek out gentiles charitable enough ('buenas cristianas') to take pity on the summarily circumcized diplomat and his companion. Los Cobos alluded to employing the Genoese 'fuero' or law at Diego's circumcision, at the risk of their falling out, and again here, there is another reference to following the precedent or 'instrucción' set in Genoa. The density and opacity of the allusions make it impossible to make definitive sense of this passage. However, it seems to refer to a shared sexual escapade involving prostitutes. These exchanges are typified by the sharing of intimacies of and about women between male friends. Mendoza ends the letter cryptically suggesting that the Jewess adheres to two laws, as they do, and is the most 'gentil', kindest or irreligious, woman he has ever met.

Despite the lack of seriousness and marked mysogyny in these letters, there is no doubt that they also reveal a level of playful interest in and tolerance of religious otherness. The possibilities of tolerance were demonstrated within Diego's household itself, with his embrace of heterogeneous religious practices and celebration of both Jewish and Christian festivals: 'Yo estoy bueno y tengo dos pascuas, una tras otra; que mi judía la hace en Viernes Santo y yo en domingo.'[36] The letters reveal that toleration of interfaith relationships in the first half of the sixteenth century was more than possible among the upper echelons of Spain's ruling élite. They show regime insiders openly alluding to and joking about their Jewish lineage, poking fun at the artificiality of religious differences in the face of shared culture and confronting directly the threatening ambiguity and inapprehensibility of the New Christian's fidelity and belief. The underlying ecumenicism and openness of the attitudes revealed here contain lessons for any age threatened by growing sectarianism and fundamentalism. In May, Mendoza seriously injured one of his testicles on a chair. Writing to los Cobos, he insisted:

> Verdad es, illustrísimo señor, que yo e perdido un coxón de un golpe que me dy en una silla, y sin remedio. V. S. se duela con la judía, que ya la traía tan duenda que no fuera mucho tornar a resucitar los güessos de mis agüelos . . . ¿Qué quiere V. S. que escriua de mis buenas andanças? Que la judía está con una calentura que basta a quemarla a ella y todo mi linaje. Guárdeme V. S. los guantes y pésame, que éstas son más asnas que la buena memoria de doña Costança . . .[37]

Américo Castro interpreted the phrase about her reviving the bones of his grandparents as a coded allusion to Mendoza's *converso* lineage. Her

---

36 *Vida y obras*, I, p. 136. Mendoza to Cobos, 8 April 1541, Venice.

37 *Vida y obras*, III, pp. 302 and 303. AGS Estado, leg. 1317, fol. 152. Mendoza to Cobos, 19 May 1541, Venice.

domestication and docility could end in an interfaith marriage, repeating those of his ancestors. Perhaps their bones would be brought back to life in order to be burnt in an *auto de fe* post-mortem. The sexual frustration of his lover, her fever, threatens to burn her and the entire Mendoza line up. He was not completely unaware of the threat from his liaison posed by the fires of the Inquisition. The dense semantics combine imagery of disease, lineage, fire and death. These topoi resonate with the persecution of *marranos*. It may be more than a mere allusion to his New Christian background, but rather an admission of his ambivalent religion and possession of two laws.

When he described himself as *arcimarrano*, are we to take him at his word? The correspondence falls silent about the Jewess after this letter for over nine months, until finally in response to an enquiry by los Cobos, Mendoza informed him: 'Yo no tengo que dezir sino que es una muy ruin uida, dolor de riñones y miedo y sospechas y dar audiençia antes que amanezca a espiones; y con esto se oluidan judías y lo demás.'[38] Spivakovsky has interpreted this last reference in his correspondence to mean that the affair had been ended following the injunction that all Jews return to live in the Ghetto, when the two, Nuovo and Vecchio, were joined together and gated to enclose all of Venice's Jews. However, the first Inquisitorial hearing in Venice involving a Jew did not take place until 1548. It is entirely possible that the relationship continued although it is not referred to again. On the other hand the palpable sense of threat from her in his previous letter might imply that it had become too dangerous for them to continue the affair.

While these letters can be seen as symbolic of liberal attitudes towards *conversos*, heterogeneous religious practices and other faiths, we need to be careful not to wrench them from their context and interpret them anachronistically. Diego Hurtado de Mendoza's attitudes, even in their apparent tolerance, could not escape the orbit of an all-encompassing, monolithic Catholicism or the obedience of a loyal monarchist. While he might ask whether the *moriscos* wore their faith on their sleeves and empathetically lament the passing of a distinctive Arabic culture and ethnicity from Andalusia, he also recognized that the *morisco* problem needed, in line with Pius IV's instructions, to be resolved. The *moriscos* of Granada were 'moros entre cristianos . . . y cristianos entre moros' (*Guerra de Granada*, p. 116). Their ambiguous identity fell between the categories of Moor and Christian. Yet in the notorious speech put into the mouth of Aben Xahuar, after complaining about the financial damage implicit in forcing them to dress in a Christian style (clothing was often the most expensive item owned by someone in the early modern period and a direct reflection of their status), he identifies them with Spain: 'Quítannos el servicio de los esclavos negros; los blancos no nos eran permitidos por ser de nuestra nación' (*Guerra de*

---

[38] *Algunas cartas*, p. 85. Mendoza to Cobos, 29 January 1542.

Granada, p. 117). They are trapped in an intercultural no-man's land, irreducibly different and excluded, despite being of the same nation or race.

The *Guerra de Granada* is typified by this paradoxical attitude, oscillating between sympathy for the servitude of the *moriscos* and criticism of their brutal suppression, and conventional affirmations of Christian superiority, faith and constancy. The unveiling of daughters and wives is symbolically linked in the speech with opening the doors of their houses: '¿Hemos de ser sujetos de ladrones, de malhechores, de atrevidos y desvergonzados adúlteros . . .?' (*Guerra de Granada*, p. 118). Grudging admiration for the chastity of Muslim women had surfaced similarly in the anonymous *Viaje de Turquía*.[39] The whole speech, however, was modelled on Sallust's rendering of Catiline's speech in the *Bellum Catilinae*, a copy of which was owned by Mendoza.[40] While we might admire the rhetoric of Xahuar's plea, ultimately the classical echoes render it a type for treason and conspiracy. Similarly, later in the same book in what could be a quotation from the trial of Jucé Franco, Mendoza recorded how, 'otro crucificaron, azotándole, e hiriéndole en el costado primero que muriese. Sufrióle el mozo, y mostró contentarse de la muerte conforme a la de nuestro Redentor' (*Guerra de Granada*, p. 141). The stock rhetorical resources of medieval anti-Semitism overshadow this history's subversive elements, which ultimately tells a story of Christian triumphalism. Despite numerous threats, inducements and blackmail, 'Fue gran testimonio de nuestra fe . . . [*que*] ninguno hubo . . . que quisiese renegar' (*Guerra de Granada*, p. 141). While tolerance, heterogeneous religious practices, interfaith desire and even marriage were possible in the Spain of the first half of the sixteenth century, by the 1570s they had given way to conventional affirmations of a single religious identity and the demonization of the renegade. Death had become preferable to the recognition of another law.

[39] See Part 2 of *Viaje de Turquía*, ed. Fernando García Salinero (Madrid: Cátedra, 1986), esp. chs 15 and 19.

[40] See Charles Davis's article on 'Tacitean Elements in Diego Hurtado de Mendoza's *Guerra de Granada*', *Dispositio*, 10 (1996), 85–96 (p. 93).

Representing their Sex:
Actresses in Seventeenth-Century Spain

MELVEENA MCKENDRICK

It was probably the Italian players of the *commedia dell'arte* who, in the late 1580s, introduced into the Spanish theatre the idea of using professional actresses. While it is difficult to believe that actors' or actor-managers' wives before then were never recruited to perform, even if actresses were not hired specially, it remains the case that in 1587 an Italian company called *Los Confidentes* had to seek permission from the Council of Castile for its women to act. The licence, when granted, stipulated not only that actresses had to be married and were not to dress as men (a ruling promptly and there-after consistently ignored) but that boys were no longer to play female roles. Actresses were obviously considered to be morally more acceptable than cross-dressed boys, and from then on they became an established feature of the Spanish stage.[1] In England and France, by contrast, it was not until the second half of the seventeenth century that women were licensed to act in public, and even in Italy, where women did appear on stage in the second half of the sixteenth century, boys continued to play female roles into the 1630s.[2]

In the context of the official silencing in the early modern period of women's voices, in the public record as well as in the domestic sphere, this wholesale emergence of female actors on to the Spanish stage at the end of the sixteenth century was a development more remarkable than it is easy now to conceive. That the new practice was permitted only because it was consid-ered by the authorities to be the lesser of two evils does not change the fact that the very sex that was supposed to lead a confined, passive and generally silent life within the domestic space was now treading the boards of the playhouses and speaking out often at great length and with considerable eloquence. It is the prominence of these female voices in the *comedia* that is so striking. Women had been given both a voice and visibility, a public

---

[1] There was a brief hiccup in 1596 when the Council of Castile changed its mind, but to little lasting effect.

[2] See Melveena McKendrick, *Theatre in Spain 1490–1700* (Cambridge: CUP, 1989), pp. 46–50.

platform no less from which to represent the condition and experience of being female. Their behaviour on stage might belong to the world of imagination and popular entertainment, but from within that protected fictional space the words they spoke revealed what it was like to be a woman, and specifically what it was like to be a woman in a man's world. That the actresses who embodied the *comedia*'s female characters were neither peasant women abused by noblemen, nor gentlewomen with violent husbands, nor the marriageable daughters of the urban gentry, but came for the most part from relatively humble if often respectable backgrounds, made no odds. Not all of them had questionable reputations, as the moral opposition to the theatre held, but as a result of their profession and their peripatetic lives they knew more about the world than most of their sex and were amply equipped to act as forceful spokeswomen for a wide range of female causes. So who and what were these women? This chapter returns to the early eighteenth-century compilation *Genealogía, origen y noticias de los comediantes de España* to discover what it can tell us about the actresses and their socio-economic and cultural context.[3]

The fact that performance on a public stage offered women a legitimate arena for creative self-expression, where they could speak and move freely in a way disallowed in normal life, was in itself morally and socially problematic. That they made the most of the opportunity is clear from many a contemporary commentator: Juan de Zabaleta in his *El día de fiesta por la tarde* (Madrid, 1660) describing, slightly satirically, how seriously actors took their roles in their efforts to impress their audiences, recalls:

> . . . yo vi a una comedianta de las de mucho nombre (poco ha que murió) que representando un paso de rabia, hallándose [. . .] acaso con el lienzo en la mano, le hizo mil pedazos por refinar el afecto que fingía; pues bien valía el lienzo dos veces más del partido que ella ganaba. Y aun hizo más que esto, que porque pareció bien entonces, rompió un lienzo cada día, todo el tiempo que duró la comedia.[4]

For many moralists and commentators actresses were loose women whose antics and words on stage set a bad example to other women. A perusal of Cotarelo y Mori's *Controversias* gives the impression that disapproval of the actors' world generally was strongest in the earliest years of the *comedia* in the late sixteenth and early seventeenth century before it achieved a degree

---

3   N.D. Shergold and J.E. Varey (eds), *Fuentes para la historia del teatro en España*, II (London: Tamesis, 1985). The second part of *Genealogía* catalogues actresses, providing 954 entries spanning the years 1631 to 1703. Since there is an alphabetical index of names at the back of the volume, I have not given page or entry numbers. Neither have I cluttered my text with the dates given for actresses in the *Genealogía* since they vary in nature and density and seem to trace no meaningful patterns over time.

4   Ed. Cristóbal Cuevas García (Madrid: Clásicos Castalia, 1983), pp. 312–13.

of respectability and acting companies became better regulated. The diatribe attributed to Lupercio Leonardo de Argensola (1598) is a case in point.[5] Argensola had good reasons of his own for targeting Lope's *comedia nueva*, which was so effectively elbowing out the classicizing drama favoured by Argensola himself and his fellow tragedians, and the litany of cautionary tales he uses as ammunition, while separately not implausible, begins to acquire the strong flavour of myth. The burden is that actresses wreak havoc in the lives of noblemen, sometimes with the complicity of their husbands:

> Un titulado deste reino se enredó de tal manera en los amores de una mugercilla representante que no solamente le daba su hacienda, pero públicamente con notable escándalo de la República le tenía puesta casa y vajilla de plata, le bordaban vestidos y la servían y respetaban sus criados como si fuera muger legítima, y aun la que lo era pasaba a esta causa muchas descomodidades. Y llegó a tanta miseria este caballero que sufría otros rivales infames y del mismo oficio o vicio que trataban con la mugercilla, solamente por tenerla contenta.

And again:

> Otro titulado también estuvo escandalosísimamente metido con otra destas mugeres, tolerando el marido y haciendo ostentación de la riqueza que deste trato le procedía, andando con cadenas y botones de oro, y mostrando cantidad de escudos ganados por su muger.
>
> (Cotarelo y Mori, p. 66)

Myth or not, there is no doubt that the conventional view of actors and actresses throughout the seventeenth century, as it was of course down to the early twentieth century, was that they led rather disorderly lives. Whether this was a general perception rather than the view merely of churchmen, moralists, reformers, and self-righteous burghers it is difficult to tell. Certainly the authorities felt the need to make periodic and fruitless efforts to reinforce the decency regulations that covered performances in the *corrales* – actresses had to be married and wear female clothing at least from the waist down, no men were allowed in the women's dressing room, and so on. No doubt the proximity of actors and actresses in rehearsal alluded to by P. Pedro Fomperosa y Quintana in his tirade of 1683 against the theatre and the acting fraternity (Cotarelo y Mori, p. 267),[6] and the attractions of good-looking and accessible women for gentlemen who could afford to indulge themselves by courting them, did lead to some less than respectable behaviour. However,

---

[5]   E. Cotarelo y Mori, *Bibliografía de las controversias sobre la licitud del teatro en España* (Madrid: Tipografía de la Revista de Archivos, Bibliotecas y Museos, 1904), pp. 65–8.

[6]   See p. 89.

this was by no means specific to theatrical life within the socio-economic context to which actors belonged - two of Cervantes's sisters and Lope de Vega's daughter are cases in point.[7] The range of personal behaviour must have been as wide as the range of ability, professionalism and success, and by and large players with licensed companies escaped the opprobrium poured on the motley collection of unaccredited actors, tumblers, dancers, and musicians who travelled the countryside.

This is a general area where much can be gleaned from the *Genealogía*. In a few cases the record is very specific. Doña [*sic*] Isabel de Mendoza started out as a courtesan in Naples where she was discovered by the *autor de comedias* José Verdugo, and Isabel de la Cruz was a courtesan in Valencia who for a while took to the stage. We learn that María de Heredia spent a spell in prison before she became an *autora*, though unfortunately no more information is given. Elsewhere the catalogue merely raises invisible questions. For example, Josefa Laura left her tailor husband in Córdoba and went off with a company of players to Cádiz. She somehow earned enough to support a younger sister and her husband in spite of not having much talent as an actress. Andrea de Salazar was able to leave a large enough sum of money to endow a chaplaincy in the Chapel of the Cofradía de la Novena (see p. 76); there is no mention of marriage and her sister was her heir. Such cases might have had perfectly respectable explanations, and certainly it is clear from the *Genealogía* that actresses could be virtuous or at least end up leading virtuous lives. María de Riquelme 'fue muger de mucha virtud, por lo que mereció mucho aplauso. Está su cuerpo entero hauiendo muerto el año 1656'. She was remembered later as a superlative actress so beautiful that she was pursued by many admirers, to all of whom she gave short shrift. Damiana Pérez is recorded as 'muy celebrada por su representación y hermosura y mucho más por su honestidad y virtud'. Catalina de Peña was renowned for her virtue, and her confessor confirmed that she only ever let her eyes rest on her fellow actors on stage and never on the audience. Ángela de León, a celebrated musican and the actress daughter of parents who were also theatre musicians, retired with her mother to Alcalá when her father died and devoted herself to charitable works. The famous soprano Juana Roldán remained unmarried, and when she retired led a very pious life. Clara Camacho underwent a Damascene conversion in her later years after performing in an *auto sacramental* (alas, unidentified) and turned to an exemplary life of good works. Damiana López, daughter of Damiana Pérez above, who lived and supported a sister and a freed female slave in Barcelona, was so charitable that a legacy from a prosperous relative stipulated that

---

[7] Cervantes's sisters Andrea and Magdalena both conducted tangled sexual and financial liaisons with philanderers of social standing, while Lope's favourite daughter, Antonia Clara, ran off at the age of seventeen with a nobleman who abandoned her several months later.

she be paid the money in instalments so that she could not give it all away and leave herself destitute. When she died in 1690 the Augustinian and Franciscan orders competed for the privilege of burying her body: the Franciscans won on the grounds that, although she was a member of the Cofradía de la Novena and the actors' chapel was in the Augustinian chapel of Santa Mónica, her membership there was a low-ranking one and the Augustinians therefore had no priority. As for the celebrated La Baltasara, Francisca Baltasara, she ended up even more celebrated for her piety and virtue because, after retiring to the hermitage of San José near Cartagena, various miraculous happenings were said to have marked her passing, included the ringing of the hermitage bells (presumably unaided). Vélez de Guevara, Antonio Coello and Rojas Zorrilla, the catalogue reminds us, wrote a play about her life, conversion and death, *La Baltasara*. The use of the word 'conuersión' here in the *Genealogía* is interesting in its suggestion of a transition from something negative to something very positive. The implication is that the theatre was not the sort of breeding ground that produced saints, but the *Genealogía* itself, as we have just seen, reveals that she was not alone in her embracing of piety. Some actresses even forsook the stage for an enclosed religious life. Isabel Hernández, married to an actor, became a nun (presumably but not necessarily after his death), as did María Agueda when she entered a convent of Discalced Franciscans after listening to a sermon by a Franciscan missionary in Murcia. Josefa Lobaco likewise became a Franciscan nun and died with the reputation of a saint. Mariana Romero, a very successful leading lady, attempted the transition but failed. She retired to a nunnery of Discalced Trinitarians and took the veil, but found the life too harsh for her health, returned home and married the *autor* Manuel Ángel. She did not return to the theatre.

We cannot know the circumstances or motives behind these stories of retirement to a life of pious charity and prayer, though it is to be hoped that they were not all as bleak as those that inspired the unfortunate Teresa Escudo. She was married to an *autor* who treated her so badly that she tried to hang herself from the bedpost – a truly despairing act in seventeenth-century Catholic Spain. Her husband came upon her accidentally and with his dagger cut her down still alive. She left the stage (no further mention is made of her abusive husband) for charitable works and an exemplary life. It is obvious from the inventory that at least after retirement many former actresses did the same.

It is necessary to remember, when thinking about these issues of lifestyle and reputation, that women players lived and worked within the organizing framework of the theatrical world itself. From 1631 when it was first established, the keystone in that world became the actors' guild, the Cofradía de la Novena. Based on the actors' parish church of San Sebastián in the Calle de León in the quarter of Madrid where actors usually lived or lodged, the guild, to which most actors thereafter aspired to belong, shaped their social activities and gave them some degree of status and respectability within a culture strongly shaped by religious devotion and observation.[8]

Whole families were employed by the companies and whole families became members of the Cofradía. Isabel Peregrín, Antonio de Segura, María de Segura, and Lorenzo de Castro el Gallego – mother, father, daughter, and son-in-law respectively - are recorded as acting in the three different companies of Andrés de la Vega, Cristóbal de Avendaño and Salvador de Lara, and all four seem to have become members of the Cofradía in the 1630s. There were entire acting dynasties as well. María Pérez, Francisco de Arteaga and all seven of their children – six daughters and a son – were actors in the company of Manuel Vallejo and were together received into the Cofradía on 26 April 1631. One of the daughters, Francisca, is recorded as marrying another actor, Jusepe Rojo, and subsequently their son and daughter, Jusepe Bernardo and María, followed their parents into the profession. María eventually married an actor and sometime actor-manager, Juan Correa, whose brother Francisco was also an actor married to an actress, María Álvarez *la Perendenga*. The *Genealogía* is threaded throughout with these tentacling family interconnections, many of them (inevitably, given the high incidence of death in or after childbirth at the time) the result of successive marriages. Admission to the Cofradía appears not to have been automatic and some of the players listed seem to have made more than one bid to join, but what the criteria were is not clear. What is clear is that all those connected with the theatre, together with their families, were eligible.

Not all actresses were born into the theatre by any means. The catalogue unfortunately seldom provides information about the provenance of actresses without a theatrical background, but there is some. Although Juana Gutiérrez married an *autor*, thereby initiating an acting dynasty – one of their sons, Francisco, became famous for his *gracioso* roles – she was the daughter of a 'labrador honrado'. María Francisca was the daughter of a mulatto servant of the Duke of Nájera and a washerwoman. Antonia Manuela Sevillano was the illegitimate daughter of a gentleman. Francisca de Córdoba was the daughter of a gardener who worked in the gardens of the Retiro palace. Fabiana Laura was the daughter of gentlefolk – her mother, Doña Salvadora Hurtado, the daughter of a respectable apothecary; her father, Don Matías Andreas de Eslava, a doctor of medicine in Granada. She was raised in the house of an aunt who held 'muchos entretenimientos decentes en su casa y llamaba a ella y a los representantes y representantas' to sing and perform. Fabiana, we are told, would join in. This no doubt explains why she married an actor while very young. Divorced soon after, she became an actress and married an *autor*. Lucrecia López, otherwise known as Lucrecia Chesa, was taken as a little girl from her native Milan to Spain by Fabiana Laura and raised by her.

---

[8]   N.D. Shergold, *A History of the Spanish Stage from Medieval Times to the End of the Seventeenth Century* (Oxford: Clarendon Press, 1967), p. 523.

Such cases must represent the tip of a large iceberg, not least because over
the years there must have been innumerable occasions when families seeking
their fortune in the capital ended up putting a daughter on the stage. Once
there, however, these escapees from everyday life tended to marry into the
theatre and become fully part of the acting world.

The structure provided by the theatre companies, in association from 1631
with their guild, offered the women who worked within them a career path of
sorts, the only one open to them apart from convent life. They offered continuity, some stability, and a certain standing, certainly among the ranks of
working people. At the same time, on the evidence of the *Genealogía*, players
led what was, by the standards of the age, a peripatetic existence. Theatre
companies took their productions on tour after performing in the capital, and
many players during their lives worked for a succession of acting troupes
based in different regional cities and travelled with them round Spain and
Portugal. Not surprisingly given the Spanish presence there, some even
found their way to Italy. Many women at the time, and not merely widows,
tried their hand at running companies of players and seemingly with some
success, although most of the long-serving actor-managers appear to have
been men. Jusepa de Rivas, who played third ladies in her husband's
company and sixth ladies in another, set up her own, and at one stage her
cash flow was sufficiently healthy for her to be able to pay off one of her
employee's debts before the troupe left the town where they had been
performing. Jusepa, however, is a good example of how fluid and in a sense
makeshift the theatrical life was, because while working as an actress she
also worked as the maid of another *autor* and she continued in service after
she retired from the stage. This does not mean that actresses were without
social aspirations. Feliciana de la Rosa successfully nominated her husband,
Carlos Vallejo, for the post of Mayordomo in the elections to the chapter of
the actors' guild in 1693. The renowned actress Antonia Infanta, who was
married to an *autor*, opted for a different form of social one-upmanship by
living up to her histrionic reputation and affecting sheets of black taffeta.
There are many examples in the *Genealogía* of actresses consolidating their
standing within the Cofradía by means of charitable gifts. Of course their
degree of professional success depended on their acting ability, and the range
must have been very great. Whereas bit players moved around more
frequently, leading actors and actresses often stayed with companies for
many consecutive years, and this, together with the hierarchical structure of
companies and the frequency of theatrical dynasties, provided a degree of
continuity and stability absent from the lives of many working people at the
time. The stage itself offered the prospect of fame and attention to those
actresses who were young, comely and successful and, if they were so
inclined, the opportunity to better themselves materially through liaison with
wealthy patrons. Given that the aristocratic rich and even the King
frequented the playhouses and that the theatre companies performed in the

royal palaces and the houses of the great, there was plenty of opportunity for beauty and wealth to come together.

The information the *Genealogía* provides about connections generally between actresses and men of significant social status not only has curiosity value but is revealing in terms of what it says about the permeability of the two social worlds at a certain restricted level. In most of the reported cases a sexual relationship is self-evident, albeit not in every case consensual. In others the circumstances are more opaque. One or two cases, interestingly, involve marriage, although given the varied family backgrounds from which actresses came this is perhaps not entirely surprising. It is another indication, however, that being an actress did not in itself entail social death.

There are several notable liaisons involving the birth of a child. María de la O had a child by the Prince of Parma. He sent the boy to Italy and gave her and her father (an *autor*) enough to live on for the rest of their lives. Her sister Feliciana, by contrast, married an ensign in the service of the prince when María withdrew from the theatre. Both of them are recorded as acting later on in their father's company. Even more notable is the case of the celebrated Inés de Calderón, La Calderona, who became the mistress of Philip IV and the mother of Don Juan de Austria. She continued to perform in Valencia while pregnant but as soon as she gave birth the King put her in a convent where she rose to become Abbess - a singular success story by the standards of the day. Her sister María, on the other hand, a celebrated actress in her own right, died in poverty, 'miserablemente', in spite of her connections. Ignacia Antonia de Morales was taken out of the theatre by the Count of Alba de Liste, who subsequently retired her to Zamora where she became a nun. There is mention of a daughter, who ended up in the same convent as her mother, but none predictably of marriage. One imagines that it was the pregnancy that precipitated the move to Zamora and the convent in the first place. The convent's traditionally ambiguous role as both convenient place of banishment and refuge assumes a more poignant significance in the story of Jusepa López. Nicknamed 'la Hermosa' and from an acting family, her liaison with the Duke of Medinaceli produced a son who was much later on to die in prison in Pamplona. Jusepa subsequently miscarried a child when, journeying through Mombeltrán, she stopped to pray in the chapel of a convent. She died there five days later. Doña [*sic*] Ana de Escamilla seems to have handled her affair more skilfully. The daughter of a theatre musician, she acted in a company intriguingly called *Las muchachas*. She caught the eye of the Marquis of Liche who took her out of the theatre for a while, presumably as his mistress. She then married a theatre money collector and, after his death, a *gracioso*, *autor* and 'grandísimo embustero'. Josefa Nieto, also married to a money collector, managed to navigate more dangerous waters. The Duke of Linares 'la retiró de la comedia' after arranging for her husband to be violently, and as it turned out fatally, removed from the scene. The Duke had two sons by her who lived with their mother in some style and for whom he appears to have secured membership in a military order so that they could maintain 'su casa, familia y coche'. The Spanish Dukes seem to have been particularly susceptible to actresses. The Duke of Osuna fell for Josefa de Robles, a great beauty from an acting family who started playing virgin roles in acting companies in Madrid while still very young. The Duke took her, her sister and her mother out of the theatre and set them up in Madrid at his expense. Acting was a livelihood, and a better one had come along.

Manuela de Escamilla, the daughter of an *autor* from Córdoba, for her part ended up in a liaison at the less illustrious end of the upper classes. She began acting at the precocious age of seven, playing third ladies outside Madrid. She then went to Madrid with her father Antonio de Escamilla, apparently to play young male comic roles, 'haziendo los Juan Ranillas'.[9] At the age of thirteen she married a Miguel Dieste (employment unknown) but her husband died eighteen months later leaving her with a son who later himself became an actor. She had an illegitimate son by the actor and play-wright Alonso de Olmedo, then at some time she secretly married the well-known court poet and wit Francisco Antonio de Monteser by whom she had a daughter. Little good came from this liaison since Monteser met a violent death at court and Manuela died aged seventy-two living off charity in Valencia.

A noteworthy story is that of Francisca Manuela who was certainly no better than she ought to have been. A Madrid courtesan at the end of the seventeenth century, she joined three theatre companies without lasting a year in any of them. There followed an affair with a wealthy gentleman who was page to the King, whom, after he had been away for a while, she tried to deceive (and presumably trick into marriage) by buying the new-born baby of a shoemaker's wife and passing it off as her own. The deceit was discovered when the mother demanded her son back. The shoemaker's wife was publicly shamed, the accomplice midwife received one hundred lashes and Francisca was sent to *La Galera*, a prison for female offenders. By 1712, the year in which the *Genealogía* began to be compiled, she had retired from the stage and was selling chocolate in the Calle de San Juan in Madrid.

The Marquis of Liche crops up again as the patron of three musical sisters, though it is unlikely that that was the limit of his interest in them, given his affair with Ana de Escamilla. He took Ana de Andrade and her sisters, Feliciana and Micaela, from Toledo to Madrid to perform at court and they subsequently worked as musicians in the company of Diego Osorio. Nick-named las Tinientas, or las Toledanas, Ana and Feliciana subsequently took up acting as well. Ana married Félix Pascual, a musician and long-time

---

[9]   It is not entirely clear in the text whether this refers to Manuela or her father, but women did occasionally play male comic roles, and the use of the diminutive suggests that the phrase applies to her.

autor. Feliciana married twice, first the son of a famous theatrical dynasty, Juan Francisco López – probably himself an actor – and later a prompter. Micaela, however, who seems to have been the most gifted musician of the three and to have remained with her instrument, fared considerably better. She married Diego Osorio de Velasco, an actor but also a scion of the house of the Condestable de Castilla, who, after he inherited an entail from his brother, was compelled by the Count to retire from the theatre. He became Governor of Salas de los Infantes, presumably with his musician wife at his side. It is a striking example of the extent to which theatrical activities were embedded in the life of the nation, and the degree of interaction that was at least conceivable if not usual.

There are other, more anonymous, incidences of relations between actresses and men of rank. María Laura, a fostered girl from Granada, abandoned both her husband and her foster mother's legacy to go off to Madrid with a gentleman and others during the plague of 1679. Here she remained hidden for a while – not solely because of the plague perhaps – before taking to the stage to earn her living. The unfortunate Isabel de Andriago, married to an *autor*, was given no choice in the turn her life took. She was violently abducted when leaving Seville for Córdoba by Don Francisco Tello, a gentleman of Seville, who held her captive for some time. She ended her days, not surprisingly, in a convent. As one reads through the *Genealogía*, the plays and novels of the day seem to become increasingly less fictional. There are a few more orderly cross-class relations as well. Luisa de la Cruz, an excellent musician, married Juan Antonio Sandoval, *Procurador de Obras y Bosques*. She was ordered out of retirement by none other than Philip IV to take part in the spectacular production in 1653 of Calderón's *Andrómeda y Perseo* at the Palace of the Retiro. Josefa Ruano was from an acting family but left the stage to marry a gentleman from Tarancón. Josefa Pavía, for her part, married a captain, Juan de Saberiche, a captain being one of the lowest versions of a gentleman.

I think it is safe to assume that, like Josefa Ruano, other actresses who married well would have retired from the stage. Acting was a way of life and not compatible with the duties of a gentleman's wife. In any case, not all actresses (or actors for that matter) by any means remained in the theatre throughout their working lives, as their modern counterparts tend to do. The *Genealogía* shows considerable mobility, with actresses, particularly the minor ones, moving in and out of the profession as opportunity arose or necessity drove. Alfonsa de la Haro y Rojas, who was married to a wardrobe master, was obliged to retire from the stage when she lost her voice. Francisca Agueda, too, had to retire through ill-health, and this must have been a fairly common occurrence although the *Genealogía* rarely mentions illness. Less common, fortunately, but not unknown were serious, even fatal, accidents involving stage machinery: Josefa de Medina fell from a piece of stage machinery while performing in Seville and was killed. Francisca

Fernández, one of three acting sisters, simply realized that acting was not for her and retired with her sister Sebastiana to set up a grocery business. Josefa Guzmán, when she gave up the stage, went on to own and run a tobacco shop in Cádiz. Many not surprisingly retired as they got older and parts dried up, because then, as now to some extent, the careers of women players were far shorter than those of men. The cast lists of nearly all Spanish plays of the time contain roles for mature men and most figure at least one *barba*, the term for the elderly man of authority. Many male actors of the appropriate age specialized in playing *barba* parts, and every theatre company employed at least one of them. One has to search the *comedia* very hard indeed, on the other hand, to find roles suitable for older women. María de Quiñones, the *Genealogía* tells us, retired at seventy and died at ninety, but in all probability she pulled her weight in her later years by doing off-stage jobs. The scarcity of roles for older women meant that actor-managers' wives, who naturally expected leading roles and were financially valuable to the company, sometimes went on playing romantic heroines rather longer than they ought to have done, risking the ridicule of theatregoers. The most notorious example predates the *Genealogía*'s chronological span. When Tirso de Molina's *Don Gil de las calzas verdes* was first performed in July 1615 in Toledo by the company of Pedro Valdés with the part of Doña Juana being played by Valdés's wife, the celebrated Jerónima de Burgos, she was by this time so corpulent that her interpretation of the role of the work's beautiful, dashing heroine was greeted with derision by the audience and the performance was a complete failure. Subsequently, and presumably with more appropriate performers, the play became one of the most successful in the Spanish classical canon.

Older women were written out of plays for one obvious reason: like cinema now, the *comedia* was a commercial venture subject to the laws of supply and demand. This did not prevent great plays being written, but it did determine what sort of plays they were and what elements they contained to attract audiences and sustain their interest. The presence on stage of women playing female roles was one of the *comedia*'s great box-office draws, as the theatre's detractors realized only too well. P. Pedro de Guzmán was clearly speaking from personal experience when, in his treatise *Bienes del trabajo honesto y daños de la ociosidad* (1614), he inveighed against the impact on the audience of women performers on stage:

> Las palabras lascivas echan centellas o ellas lo son; la voz, la música, los afectos, los afeites, la hermosura, el buen cuerpo, la gracia, el talle, el donaire, el cabello, el rizo, el copete, el vestido, el meneo, que aunque parece hecho al descuido, lleva estudiada su malicia y deshonestidad. Todo eso, entrando por los ojos y por los oídos, es fuego, es ponzoña, es secreto veneno, es sutil solimán, que tira al corazón del que lo mira descuidado de sí y de que otros lo noten, porque todos miran un objeto mismo, y le ayudan y le apadrinan. (Cotarelo y Mori, pp. 349–50)

As this over-heated rant reveals, the actresses that drew audiences (women as well as men, if modern response surveys are anything to go by) were the still young, graceful and attractive.

There is, however, a less obvious but crucial reason for the scarcity of roles for older women in the *comedia*. Why are mothers almost as rare as hens' teeth, and why do most fathers appear to be widowers? There is a thin sprinkling of queen mothers, but the complete family grouping that appears in Guillén de Castro's wonderful comedy *La fuerza de la costumbre*, with its strong sense of family bonds based on a palpably loving relationship between father and mother, is almost unique in a hugely prolific theatre. Even female servants are normatively young rather than old. The answer seems to me to lie in the *comedia*'s essentially formulaic identity and its ideological shaping. It inherited, largely from Latin comedy and the *commedia dell'arte*, a recipe based on young love, rivalry, and generational conflict, and these topoi, albeit in different manifestations and combinations and with added complications such as class and politics, remain the basic ingredients of a very large proportion of Golden-Age plays, whether comic or tragic. Rarely does a play not have a love interest, whatever its other preoccupations, and rarely does that love interest not involve a conflict of some sort with authority. Authority at the time, of course, was gendered as male. The preferred *comedia* pattern, therefore, required young women and men (lovers, rivals) to provide the romantic interest, habitually echoed in the often parodic antics between young male and female servants, and additional men to act as authority figures of different sorts: fathers and brothers, feudal lords and, at the higher socio-political level, princes and kings. There are historical plays with royal women but these for the most part are young, as is the rare female authority figure from slightly lower down the social scale, such as the Countess Diana in Lope de Vega's *El perro del hortelano*, where the inversion of authority in the love affair between mistress and servant provides the dynamic for the entire play. In other words, the sort of plays that the acting companies normally commissioned in response to what they perceived to be audience demand simply did not need older women. They were surplus to requirement, and the composition of the licensed acting companies at the time reflects this. The composition of the companies in turn determined the range of roles the dramatists incorporated into the plays: plays were written for specific companies, all with the same configuration. It was a self-reinforcing situation.

Within these limits there was some variety of opportunity for actresses, but hierarchical type-casting was the norm, with actors and actresses hired annually to perform specific kinds of roles. Essentially, aside from employment as singers, musicians and dancers for the plays and the between-act entertainments, the roles available for women in the licensed theatre companies were categorized as first to sixth lady, although the *Genealogía* reports a few versatile actresses as having played male roles as well. In the mid-seventeenth century Josefa Ramón played male *gracioso* parts in *sainetes* by Luis Quiñones de Benavente in addition to third ladies, and was also a theatre musician. María de Navas, whose remarkable story is told below, played female roles 'y asimismo hizo galanes vistiéndose de hombre en la compañia de que hera autora'. Since many female roles required actresses to wear masculine costume in order to pass as men, it would have caused little stir to see women dressed for the part in male roles, but to judge from the *Genealogía* the practice was not widespread and is likely to have been a response to the resources available to the company. Some actresses were good enough to specialize as first or second ladies, but the *Genealogía* shows that over time many were hired to play different categories of parts in different companies. An example late on in the seventeenth century is Ana de Figueroa, who played fifth ladies in 1681 in the company of Agustín Manuel and in 1685 in that of Félix Pascual. In 1686 she was taken on to play fourth ladies in the company of Juan Ruiz and again in 1689 in that of Estéban Vallespir (see p. 85). In 1702 and 1703 she rose to play third ladies in the companies of Joseph de Mendiola (in Portugal) and Manuel Rojo, but by 1707, twenty-six years after her stint with Agustín Manuel's troupe and therefore considerably older, she was reduced to playing sixth ladies in Toledo with Pedro de Alcántara's company. This sort of visible career trajectory is not uncommon, but many of the entries in the catalogue give the impression in any case that for a lot of women acting was merely a job undertaken when the need arose. We have seen that some died in straitened circumstances or even dire poverty: Leonor Ortiz and her husband, Francisco de Casanova, who both acted in her father's company (Juan Francisco Ortiz) and together became members of the Cofradía de la Novena in 1664, ended up so poor that they were reduced to begging for alms from door to door in Madrid. Others moved to other trades or retired to convents. Many lived in reasonably comfortable circumstances with their families, and that some prospered is clear from the alms they gave, and the gifts and bequests they made to the chapel of the Cofradía de la Novena, to hospitals and other charitable causes. Some, we know, found wealthy, even noble patrons, and the most beautiful had followings of admirers; some actresses, like their male counterparts, were bigamists, and some had children out of wedlock, often by their rich protectors.

For the sake of public order and decency, not only were actresses at this time required by the authorities to be married but actors were required to be accompanied by their wives – which largely explains the growth of acting dynasties, of course. Most of the women listed in the *Genealogía* were wives and/or daughters of actors and actor-managers – 'hijas de la comedia' as the saying went – and it was common for actresses whose actor husbands died to marry other actors. The normality of theatrical marriages is indicated by the fact that the *Genealogía* makes a point of signalling marriages 'fuera de la comedia' as if worthy of special mention: Teresa Liñán 'fue casada fuera de la comedia', and of Catalina de Chaves we are told: 'Casó en Valladolid con uno de fuera de la comedia.' However, not all actresses by any means married within the profession in the narrow sense. A considerable number are recorded as being married to musicians, wardrobe masters, money collectors, prompters, and 'criados de la comedia' (presumably general helpers) and, beyond the theatre itself, to scribes, tradesmen, and draughtsmen. Even husbands involved in the theatre did not always stay there. In the middle of the seventeenth century, Manuela Caballero married a prompter in her father's company, but he was a barber by trade and later on became a scribe in Córdoba. Antonia Valdira, renowned for having four breasts, also married a barber before she was exiled from Valencia on the order of the Governor: no reason is given and she returned to Valencia in due course and found work in the company of Bernardo de Vega. This sort of detail confirms that for many men and women the theatre represented gainful employment rather than a calling or a way of life, and jobbing *comediantes* at the time do seem to have been able to turn their hand to a remarkable variety of different trades. Marrying outside the theatre, of course, was no guarantee of a stable, tranquil life. Margarita de Peñarrosa who as a girl, we are told, played angels and other 'papelitos' very prettily, was taken off the stage and married 'fuera de la comedia' by her father, who presumably thought the match an advantageous one. Her husband soon went off to the Indies and was never seen again, a not unusual occurrence at the time.

Some of the information given about actresses' husbands in the *Genealogía* offers vivid snapshots of the lives these women led. Jerónima del Río, from Mallorca, married a fellow Mallorcan, Estéban Vallespir, who was in turn a master cloak-maker in Mallorca, a cold-drinks seller in Valencia, and a pastry cook in the household of a Count in Madrid. He later turned his hand to running a theatre company, which took him at different times to Zaragoza, Cuenca, Valencia, Murcia, Portugal, Zamora, Calatayud, Granada, and Madrid. In Granada in 1690 one of the actresses in his company, Francisca Correa, had him imprisoned for debt and took over his company in lieu of payment. Fifteen years later he was back in Mallorca working as a harbour master's constable. Remarkably, Jerónima, presumably on account of her great beauty, managed to play fifth and sixth ladies roles without ever uttering a word: her Castilian, it seems, was virtually non-existent. Luisa de Robles performed in *particulares* (private performances) for the King but no other details are given of her career. She married a Frenchman who was shipwrecked and presumed dead. She then married an *autor*, Alonso de Olmedo Tufiño (the father of the Alonso de Olmedo who fathered Manuela de Escamilla's son). Some years later when the Frenchman, who had been captured by pirates, reappeared, Olmedo not only handed over his wife to her rightful husband but gave them half of what he owned and undertook to settle all the debts incurred during his marriage with Luisa. The Frenchman took advantage of this generosity but thereafter neither man cohabited with Luisa and the three became close friends and enjoyed excellent relations (though exactly what that means is unclear). María de Cisneros, for her part, married a barber-surgeon turned prompter, José Jimeno, who unbeknown to her was really a friar with an illegitimate wife he had attempted to poison. When he tried to persuade María to leave the stage and go off with him to a job as a military surgeon, she refused and he tried to kill her by purging and then abandoning her. Discovering his real identity, she married Manuel de Mosquera, a painter, actor and *autor*. It later transpired that Jimeno had a third wife as well: apparently María was much amused one day when a woman called to see her saying that the wife of José Jimeno had come to see the wife of José Jimeno. Disappearing husbands seem to have been a fairly common occurrence. Inés Gallo was abandoned by hers, Pedro Carrasco, an actor with a fine tenor voice, in 1670 when he disappeared to the West Indies in the middle of performing in the Corpus Christi *autos sacramentales* in Madrid. Nothing daunted, Inés stayed on in the theatre and raised her stock by becoming an *autora*, but alas in 1678 she and her entire company drowned on the sandbank in the Huelva estuary.

Husbands in one way or another are at the centre of the most sensational entries in the *Genealogía*. Eufrasia María de Reina, married to a master saddler in Seville, went off to Portugal with a company of players and from there wrote to a student admirer, who had seen her in a play and sent her a note, asking him to kill her husband. The latter was warned by friends, went to ground, and the news was spread that he had died. She then married twice, first an *autor* and then in Madrid an actor called Damián de Castro. Imagine her consternation, then, when one day she received a note from her first husband after he saw her performing in a play. She reported his reappearance to the Inquisition and separated from Damián de Castro although, hardly surprisingly, she did not return to her first husband either. She ran her own company instead, and subsequently retired to Seville where she kept busy helping in a hospital and leading an exemplary life. Eufrasia was not the only actress intent on ridding herself of her husband. Bárbara Coronel, who became one of the *comedia*'s best-known actresses and *autoras*, not least because she almost always wore masculine dress, particularly when on horse-back or when travelling, had earlier achieved notoriety by killing her husband with the aid of the young prompter who was her lover. She was saved from execution when the King intervened on her behalf at the request of her uncle, the famous *gracioso* Cosme Pérez, known as Juan Rana. Presumably miti-gating circumstances were cited.

María de Navas, for her part, was the victim rather than the perpetrator of a crime, although there is no doubt that she was a formidably strong-minded woman. Like María de Cisneros, she had the misfortune unwittingly to marry a friar. The account of her fortunes is very confusing, but it seems that after the marriage was annulled she married a prompter and returned to the stage At some point they separated and she retired for a while to a convent. She then made a very successful comeback, playing both female and male roles and setting up her own company. In 1687 she successfully stood for election as the *Mayordoma* of the actors' guild, with her brother Juan actually performing her duties as her proxy. She left Madrid during the War of the Spanish Succession in the early 1700s along with other supporters of the Hapsburg claim, but when she arrived in Zaragoza and the Bourbon King's army marched in she realized she had backed the wrong side and asked for a pardon for her disloyalty. She was allowed to continue with her career but exiled from Madrid. She did return in due course and after failing in an attempt to become a nun she took to the Madrid stage again 'sin la menor repugnanzia suia'.

Such women as these last three sit at the extreme end of the cavalcade of female players – versatile, resourceful and aware – who occupy the pages of the *Genealogía*, working hard to make a living, travelling round the country with their companies, calling on their wits and strength of character to survive and thrive as best they might in a society dominated by men where social disgrace and poverty were never far away. They range from the chaste and respectable to the unruly and the criminal, but, braving the weight of traditional expectation and current prejudice, they all made choices against the grain, lived in the public eye and withstood the public gaze, and this in itself at the time made them a very special band of women. Little wonder the regulations required them to be subject to a husband's control, but little wonder too that they often contrived to elude it.

So usual was it for actresses to be married that when this is not the case the fact is spelt out. In the case of Ana de Cañas, the *Genealogía* specifies: 'Fue música, hizo terzeras y quartas damas en varias compañías, no fue casada.' Most who were unmarried worked alongside relatives, but it is clear that some succeeded in acting without family protection. How the latter managed to get round the regulations is not clear, but their peripatetic lives must have helped. The catalogue notes that María Jacinta la Bolichera, so called after the part of third lady she played 'con tanto primor' in *El garrote más bien dado* (Calderón's *El alcalde de Zalamea*),[10] lived apart from her husband a great deal of the time. In 1663, 1664, 1667, 1668, and 1669 she is recorded in the account books of the Cofradía de la Novena as being the *autora* of her own company. She was obviously, therefore, a woman of energy and independence, and she, like Ana de Cañas and other such women, no doubt found ways of getting round the regulations governing the theatre companies' activities when it suited them. Most of these rules were in any case more honoured in the breach than the observance.

The *Genealogía*, it will be clear, affords us fascinating insights not only

---

[10] This refers to Rebolledo's camp follower, La Chispa, who in Act I (line 630) wishes she could be *la Bolichera*, that is run the *juego del boliche* the soldiers will be playing, presumably in the hope of tips.

into the acting world and the careers of the women who were part of it, but
into the social texture of the period. It does not by any means tell us all we
would like to know - whereas dates of death are commonly given, dates of
birth virtually never are so we have no idea how long these women lived.[11]
On one really crucial issue it is totally silent. The first question that struck
me after reading Part II of the *Genealogía* through from beginning to end
was, could these women read? The *comedia* flourished in a society in which
women by and large were officially consigned to ignorance, invisibility and
silence, and by all indications with the Counter-Reformation this situation
progressively deteriorated. As the beneficent shadow of Erasmus faded from
the Spanish consciousness, the early flowering of concern for female education faded with it. The Index of 1559 banned all vernacular translations of
the Bible and all devotional works in the vernacular,[12] which necessarily
militated against an erudite female readership in a society where few women
had access to Latin. It meant that, where a large and important proportion of
publications in the Peninsula was concerned, even literate women were
reduced to the status of incompetent reader along with the uneducated and
children.[13] This was in sharp contrast to the learning of Latin available to
boys (but not girls) in all market towns in the Latin grammar schools, of
which there were 4,000 in Spain by 1600, although the number declined
dramatically in the course of the following century.[14] After the significant
progress in literacy and education in Europe in the sixteenth century, seventeenth-century Europe generally was educationally much less favoured and
saw a marked decline in literacy as a whole. In Spain the level of education is
judged to have been adversely affected by political and economic decline.[15]

Sara T. Nalle's figures, however, suggest that, in spite of this, the level of
literacy in Castile was actually higher than has hitherto been thought,
although she acknowledges that literacy is an extremely difficult thing to
establish.[16] Signatures, book ownership (the literate did not necessarily own
books), wills, even Inquisitorial records (those investigated were sinisterly
required to state whether they could read and what books they owned) – all
are problematic indicators, not least because most of those investigated by

11 While the compiler of the *Genealogía* had access to the records of the Cofradía de
la Novena that recorded deaths, the parish records that might have yielded birth dates were
beyond reach.

12 Henry Kamen, *The Spanish Inquisition: A Historical Revision* (London: Phoenix,
1998), p. 109.

13 For Santa Teresa's regrets about this, see Richard Pym, 'Negotiated Voices: the
Vida of Santa Teresa de Jesús', *Bulletin of Hispanic Studies*, 77 (2000), 232–3.

14 Richard L. Kagan, *Students and Society in Early Modern Spain* (Baltimore: Johns
Hopkins UP, 1974), p. 42.

15 Carlo M. Cippolla, *Literacy and Development in the West* (Harmondsworth:
Pelican, 1960), p. 53.

16 In 'Literacy and Culture in Early Modern Castile', *Past and Present*, 125 (1989),
65–96.

the Inquisition came from the lower social orders: farmers, artisans, peasants, shepherds, and so on. The problem where women are concerned is even greater because they figure much less in those aspects of life recorded in official documents. Nalle's research in Inquisition archives shows that in Madrid in the middle of the sixteenth century 69 per cent of *madrileños* could sign their names and that 62 per cent of male defendants appearing before the Inquisition in the district of Toledo in the first half of the seventeenth century attested that they could read. Judged by signature, the most literate Castilian women came from Madrid, where in 1650 25 per cent of female testators could sign their wills (although this does not mean that they could write anything else or read, of course). In Toledo, on the other hand, only 7 per cent of women deponents could sign their wills. The figures she records for Cuenca in the period 1591–1637, a good spread for our purposes, show a male literacy rate of 52 per cent and a female literacy rate of 33 per cent (Nalle, p. 69), but clearly this must reflect very variable degrees of literacy. Anecdotal and literary evidence during the first half of the seventeenth century suggests that many urban women, particularly perhaps younger women, from the noble, professional and merchant classes could read, not least because devotional reading in the vernacular by now played a significant part in religious life. We can assume that some gentlewomen in the country and some women from the artisan and tradesman class could also do so. It is interesting, after all, that no maid in the Golden-Age theatre seems ever unable to read the notes she carries between her mistress and her admirer - illiteracy hardly figures on the stage except in a rural setting. It is also relevant that the assumption of all commentators at the time was that the principal consumers of fiction were women.

The case of actresses, I think, has to be recognized as a special one. Women from families of some substance did not have to work and reading for them was an option, albeit one with considerable advantages in terms of leisure and devotional activity. Housewives and women constrained to make an economic contribution to the household, by the very nature of the possibilities available, did not need to read at all. Apart from female heads of religious houses and royal women called upon to carry out political duties, actresses were the only women whose daily work more or less required them to be able to read. They worked with texts, they memorized dialogue and speeches, often extremely long and intricate ones, and I think we can assume that those who played all but very small parts must have been able to read, even if, as was the case with most, they came from a relatively humble background. The evidence given by P. Pedro Fomperosa y Quintana (see p. 74) bears this out. Targeting rehearsals as being a cause of promiscuous behaviour between the sexes, he complains:

> A las mujeres muchas veces se los leen los hombres, unas por no saber leer, otras por abreviar en este ejercicio con lo que han de tomar por memoria.

Ensayan luego todos juntos, siéntanse promíscuamente, míranse y háblanse cara a cara sin reparo, ni nota, ni miedo. A estos ensayos, como son de cada día, es preciso estar las mujeres como de casa y medio desnudas.

(Cotarelo y Mori, p. 267)

Some actresses could not read but others, the indication is, could, although like most actors they found it useful to have help in learning their lines. In view of the pressure Spanish actors generally worked under at the time, this is entirely to be expected. The need to perform a constant stream of new material and the insistent demands made on their time for performances in playhouse, palace, street, and private house made for hectic, and necessarily disciplined working lives, as Agustín de Rojas famously recorded in *El viaje entretenido* (1603):[17]

Pero estos representantes,
antes que Dios amanece,
escribiendo y estudiando
desde las cinco a las nueve,
y de las nueve a las doce
se están ensayando siempre;
Comen, vánse a la comedia
Y salen de allí a las siete;
y cuando han de descansar,
los llaman el presidente,
los oidores, los alcaldes,
los fiscales, los regentes,
y a todos van a servir,
a cualquier hora que quieren.

Josef Oehrlein calculates that the actors had about two weeks to rehearse a new play and rightly observes that while they might have got away with a less then perfectly finished product in the playhouses, for the court and for the Corpus Christi festivities polished performances would have been expected.[18] Companies could not possibly have met such deadlines if actresses playing substantial parts had had to be fed all their lines in order to memorize them – it would have been impossibly labour-intensive and time-consuming. And since a very large proportion of them came from theatre families, they were presumably taught to read as children, as part of their preparation for the stage.

The fact that a large proportion of actresses must have been able to read

17 Libro 2 (Madrid: Aguilar, 1945), p. 313.
18 'El actor en el Siglo de Oro: imagen de la profesión y reputación social', in *Actor y técnica de representación del teatro clásico español*, ed. José María Borque (London: Tamesis, 1989), pp. 17–33 (p. 23).

obviously does not necessarily mean that they were great readers – they would scarcely have had time – but it does mean that they were exposed in the course of their daily lives to writing of considerable sophistication. The stage exposed women spectators to a world of ideas, dilemmas and possibilities that they would certainly not have encountered elsewhere in their lives, but the exposure of the women who created and inhabited that world on stage was necessarily closer and more intense. They had to think and discuss what these ideas, dilemmas and possibilities meant in order to decide how to perform them, they lived the situations, the crises and emotions for the duration of the play, they spoke the powerful verse of great poet playwrights. No doubt the less talented did what they were told, no doubt many were wooden and unconvincing, but if the general level had not been reasonably high the theatre would not have been the success it was – certainly visitors to Spain were very admiring of Spanish actresses. They could not have been unaware that in many of the parts they played, all written for them, they were effectively challenging society's prescriptions for, and assumptions about, women and the way a woman's life was to be lived, that they were articulating in public what women often felt and thought in private. This automatically set them apart from most women, and made them likely to be more sensitive than the average woman at any social level to the predicaments and causes of the female characters they depicted. If they took being able to read for granted, then it is fair to assume that other forms of untraditional female behaviour would have seemed more comprehensible and acceptable to them, particularly given the prominent, very public nature of their work, which in itself was significantly transgressive in the context of contemporary gender expectations at the time. The *Genealogía*'s entries vary significantly in the amount of information they give us about the 954 women it records and quite a few are exiguous, but there is more than enough, both quantitatively and qualitatively, to suggest that their lives as well as their work must have made them receptive to the parts they played and to what these parts signified. Their possible impact on their audiences, women and men, is a matter too complex to go into here, and is not easy to gauge. There can be no doubt, however, that they were a cause of extreme anxiety to the theatre's learned and ecclesiastical detractors, who strongly believed that women on stage, voicing the thoughts and feelings of their sex, were dangerous and subversive creatures, and they were no fools.

Public Morality and the Closure of the Theatres in the Mid-Seventeenth Century: Philip IV, the Council of Castile and the Arrival of Mariana of Austria*

ALISTAIR MALCOLM

On 15 November 1649, Mariana of Austria made her formal entry into Madrid as the new Queen consort of Philip IV of Spain (r. 1621–65). The welcome awaiting her was especially euphoric because her engagement had been announced as long ago as January 1647, almost three years earlier. While moving female Habsburgs around Europe had always been a major logistical enterprise, on this occasion international circumstances had contributed to make the journey particularly hazardous. A Swedish invasion of Bohemia, the outbreak of revolts in southern Italy and the Ottoman siege of Crete had forced the governments in Madrid and Vienna on three separate occasions to revise their complicated travel arrangements. So, it was no wonder that her new subjects were pleased to see her, and their celebrations marked a double triumph because the Queen's arrival also served to restore a sense of festivity to the Spanish court that had been missing for nearly ten years. During the 1640s there had been several deaths in the royal family, along with military defeats, political upheavals, and the enforcement of a variety of unpopular moral reforms that included the closure of the theatres. In fact, the prohibition of *comedias* had still not been officially lifted at the time of Mariana's arrival, but their staging was regarded as intrinsic to the occasion. The reappearance of *comedias* would constitute one facet of a new informality that began to characterize the reign of Philip IV at this time, and

* In the preparation of this chapter I have benefited from the assistance of Teresa Chaves, who kindly provided me with printouts from her new book, *El espectáculo teatral en la corte de Felipe IV* (Madrid: Ayuntamiento, 2004). I would like to express my gratitude to her, as well as to Olivier Caparossi, Trevor Dadson, Bernardo García, Terence O'Reilly and Jules Whicker for their patience with my queries, and to Anthony Lappin, who read an early draft. Much of the research was undertaken thanks to a grant of money from the University of Limerick staff development Seed Fund, which allowed me to spend a month in Madrid during the summer of 2004.

which would be reflected in the way his government came to be conducted and how his court would be presented during the second half of the reign.

This chapter will consider the theatre closure that took place between 1646 and 1651 within the broader context of the movement for the reform of customs and behaviour that briefly flourished during the seven or eight years before Mariana's arrival. Matters such as the closure of the theatres, restrictions on court fashions and the punishment of political corruption were central to the Spanish government's duty to nurture and promote the Catholic credentials of the monarchy, and it is therefore important to see them as a group, rather than as isolated issues. Moral reform was a subject that concerned everyone. For several decades already, court preachers and writers from the religious orders had been expressing their disquiet that the nobility had allowed its rectitude to be undermined. It was also believed that the lower orders – lacking the example of their betters – were wasting their time in taverns, gaming houses and the theatres. Ultimately, however, responsibility for public morality lay with the King, because the particular manner in which he governed (or failed to govern) his dominions was understood to have a direct effect on the overall fate of his monarchy.[1] For this reason, it will be useful to commence with some indication of the expectations that were placed on the ruler during the seventeenth century.

Good kingship in early modern Spain was personal kingship, in the sense that all important decisions had to be made by the monarch on the basis of advice offered to him by his formally appointed councillors and magistrates.[2] For most of the seventeenth century the general practice of Spanish government could not have been more alien to the process of state consolidation that is often seen as typical of the period and which we understand today by the term 'absolutism'. In the Spanish kingdoms, royal authority was usually believed to have devolved upon the ruler from his subjects, in return for

---

[1] The principal exponent of this idea during the 1640s was the Jesuit writer, Juan Eusebio Nieremberg. See Ronald Cueto, *Quimeras y sueños. Los profetas y la Monarquía Católica de Felipe IV* (Valladolid: Secretariado de Publicaciones, Universidad de Valladolid, 1994), pp. 74–5; and Antonio Álvarez-Ossorio Alvariño, 'Virtud coronada: Carlos II y la piedad de la Casa de Austria', in P. Fernández Albaladejo, J. Martínez Millán and V. Pinto Crespo (eds), *Política, religión e inquisición en la España moderna. Homenaje a Joaquín Pérez Villanueva* (Madrid: Ediciones de la Universidad Autónoma de Madrid, 1996), pp. 29–57 (pp. 35–6). The relationship between the good fortune of the state and the morality of its ruler had previously been outlined by Giovanni Botero, *Della ragion di stato libri dieci* (Venice: I Gioliti, 1589), pp. 89–93.

[2] Fray Juan de Santa María, *República y policia christiana para reyes y principes y para los que en el govierno tienen sus vezes*, 3rd edn (Barcelona: Geronymo Margarit, 1617), fols 5 and 29; Andrés Mendo, *Principe perfecto y ministros aiustados documentos politicos y morales en emblemas*, 3rd edn (Lyon: Horacio Boissat and George Remeus, 1662), pp. 25–8, 57–60 and 64 (fourth pagination); Antonio Feros, 'El viejo monarca y los nuevos favoritos: los discursos sobre la privanza en el reinado de Felipe II', *Studia Histórica (Historia Moderna)*, 17 (1997), 11–36 (pp. 16–20).

whose loyalty and obedience the King had to provide security from aggressors and proper administration of justice. If the terms of the contract were violated by either party, then force could be legitimately used to restore the balance.[3] It is true that within court circles there developed an equally legitimate culture of power that portrayed royal authority as being derived from God. This conception was manifested in the *autos sacramentales* that were performed around about the time of the royal marriage. Calderón's *Triunfar muriendo*, which was probably staged in the summer of 1650, contained an elaborate web of metaphors in which the characters representing Philip and Mariana were seen as figures of Christ and the Virgin Mary, and where the wedding itself was portrayed as analogous to Christ's marriage to the Church.[4] Yet this very theocentric approach was perfectly compatible with contractual theories, because the original bestowal of authority on the ruler by his subjects could easily be said to have taken place under the auspices of divine providence.[5] Nobody tried to argue that Spanish kings had a divine right to infringe the law in pursuit of their objectives. On the contrary, their authority was expressed and legitimated by example. As God's representative on earth, the King had to imitate Christ through his individual exercise of virtue, and, if he failed to do so, then the divine favour that for hundreds of years had allowed the Habsburg monarchy to flourish would be withdrawn (Álvarez-Ossorio, pp. 31–6 and 41).

In the seventeenth century, it was generally agreed that the model of good kingship had been provided by Philip II, who was associated in the popular mentality with a particular form of austere and intensive personal government. Philip II was understood to have spent long hours at his desk attending to the minutes of his councils, thus keeping permanently in touch with the operations of his global monarchy and making all the important decisions himself. It was this mode of procedure that his successors chose to adopt, even though their apparent attention to state papers often concealed a failure to distinguish between adherence to bureaucratic forms and real executive intervention. From the 1620s, a faction of noblemen had acquired an ascendancy over the government and sought to disguise and enhance their

---

[3] Francisco Ugarte de Hermosa y Salcedo, *Origen de los dos goviernos divino i humano i forma de su exercicio en lo tenporal* (Madrid: G. Morras, 1655), pp. 17–26, 151–8 and 217–18; Guenter Lewy, *Consitutionalism and Statecraft during the Golden Age of Spain: A Study of the Political Philosophy of Juan de Mariana, S.J.* (Geneva: Droz, 1960), ch. 3; Robert Bireley, *The Counter-Reformation Prince: Anti-Machiavellianism or Catholic Statecraft in Early Modern Europe* (Chapel Hill: The University of North Carolina Press, 1990), pp. 35–7.

[4] Pedro Calderón de la Barca, *La segunda esposa y triunfar muriendo*, ed. Víctor García Ruiz (Kassel: Reichenberger, 1992), ll. 514–61, 652–712 and 1369–1400. See also the editor's comments at pp. 31–2 (n. 1), 57–61 and 176–7 (note to ll. 1679–83).

[5] Diego de Saavedra Fajardo, *Empresas políticas*, 2nd edn (Milan, 1642), ed. Francisco Javier Díez de Revenga (Barcelona: Planeta, 1988), *empresas* 18–19.

usurpation by developing a conception of royal power that was much more authoritarian than anything previously encountered.[6] Under such a scheme the young Philip IV was kept in isolation from most of his subjects, but was accorded a very public role within the ceremony of the court, which meant that he could be seen but not approached. There also took place a short-lived attempt to implement policies that could be understood as absolutist, inasmuch as they attempted to enhance the King's power at the expense of the traditional rights and privileges of the élites. The individual at the centre of these initiatives was Philip's chief minister (or *valido*), the Count-Duke of Olivares, whose twenty-two-year ministry amounted to a systematic violation of everything that was considered to be right and proper in contemporary notions of kingship. So, when the Spanish imperial system was rocked by a series of revolts that broke out in Portugal and Catalonia in 1640, it was easy to conclude that they were the result of divine anger at the King's dereliction of duty.

This crisis, which was followed by the forced retirement of Olivares in January 1643, led to the introduction of a whole body of legislation intended to win God back on to the side of the Monarchy. Measures were promulgated to tighten up discipline within the universities and the ranks of the clergy; attempts were made to prevent men and women from mingling freely at religious occasions; legislation was introduced to control the way in which people dressed; and investigations were opened into the allegedly fraudulent activities of Olivares's unworthy henchmen, whose survival in office was widely considered to be incompatible with the restoration of good government.[7] This was the context of the calls to reform and ultimately prohibit the performance of *comedias* that took place in the 1640s. The promoters of these initiatives together formed an influential political grouping, which came to the fore during the 1640s. For want of a better term, the rather anglicized expression of 'Godly faction' may be used to describe them because they had certain similarities with the English Puritan movement, at least in their moral aspirations and providential view of history. But the French term of *dévots* might be equally appropriate on account of the resemblance between these devout Spaniards and their co-religionists at the French court during the 1610s and 1620s.[8] And, like the Puritans and the *dévots*, the Spanish Godly were a very loose-knit grouping of different people with different priorities. They included grandees like the Duke of Montalto;

6   J.H. Elliott, *The Count-Duke of Olivares: The Statesman in an Age of Decline* (New Haven: Yale UP, 1986), pp. 181–2 and 454–5.

7   BNM MS 13163, fols 70r and 77r.

8   Joseph Bergin, *The Rise of Richelieu*, 2nd edn (Manchester: Manchester UP, 1997), pp. 113–14; Kevin Sharpe, *The Personal Rule of Charles I* (New Haven: Yale UP, 1992), pp. 647–8; J.C.J. Metford discusses parallel trends of hostility towards the theatre in England, Spain and France, 'The Enemies of the Theatre in the Golden Age', *Bulletin of Hispanic Studies*, 28 (1951), 76–92 (pp. 76–7, 81 and 88–9).

leading courtiers, such as the Marquis of Aitona; prelates, such as the Patriarch of the Indies, Don Alonso Pérez de Guzmán el Bueno; and a variety of religious mystics of whom the Franciscan nun, Sor María de Ágreda, was the most celebrated example. Only a small number of die-hards wanted to see moral reform introduced across the board. Some were carefully selective in the measures that they chose to espouse, while others were just inconsistent. A case in point was Philip's first Queen consort, Isabel of Bourbon, who may be credited with providing some form of leadership to the group because many Godly people were connected to her, either because they were members of her household, or because they acted as her religious advisers, or because they were promoted to high office thanks to her influence. Yet the Queen's uneasiness about her husband's dependence on *validos* and her correspondence with renowned holy people do not seem to have prevented her from being an enthusiastic follower of the theatre.[9] Likewise the Cardinal Archbishop of Toledo's authorship of a paper criticizing the performance of *comedias* in 1648 sits ill with the protection that he subsequently gave to the dramatist Agustín de Moreto.[10] Another example of the Godly was Don Diego de Arce y Reinoso, whose appointment as Inquisitor General in 1643 seems to have been instigated at the Queen's behest.[11] Yet he would have little truck with Isabel's religious mystics, and he would later acquire a reputation as a stern and disinterested minister who operated above and beyond any factional alignment.[12] Most obscure of all was Don Antonio de Contreras, a man of deep spiritual convictions that were manifest in his support for numerous religious institutions and charitable causes, and in his clear belief that the theatre was an immoral form of entertainment. Yet Contreras also owed his career to the Count-Duke of Olivares, and was a close friend of Don Lorenzo Ramírez de Prado, the principal instigator for the reopening of the *corrales* in the late 1640s.[13]

[9] *Comedias* were still being performed in Isabel's own apartments as late as January and February 1643: N.D. Shergold and J.E. Varey, *Fuentes para la historia del teatro en España I: Representaciones palaciegas: 1603–1699* [henceforth *Fuentes I*] (London: Tamesis, 1982), pp. 51–2. See also, Alistair Malcolm, 'Spanish Queens and Aristocratic Women at the Court of Madrid, 1598–1665', in Christine Meek and Catherine Lawless (eds), *Studies on Medieval and Early Modern Women 4: Victims or Viragos?* (Dublin: Four Courts, 2005), pp. 160–80 (pp. 172–3).

[10] BL MS Add. 24947, fols 61r–3r; E.M. Wilson and D.M. Moir, *Historia de la literatura española. Siglo de oro: teatro, 1492–1700*, trans. Carlos Pujol (Barcelona: Ariel, 1985), p. 215.

[11] Carlos Puyol Buil, *Inquisición y política en el reinado de Felipe IV. Los procesos de Jerónimo de Villanueva y las monjas de San Plácido, 1628–1660* (Madrid: CSIC, 1993), pp. 340–1.

[12] Puyol Buil, pp. 493–5; Cueto, pp. 144–5 and 149–50. See also Gregorio Marañón, *El conde-duque de Olivares. La pasión de mandar*, 26th edn (Madrid: Espasa Calpe, 1998), pp. 601–2.

[13] Don Lorenzo Ramírez de Prado appointed Contreras an executor of his testament and bequeathed him a painting of the Arrest of Christ that he attributed to El Greco

If the virtuous credentials of these grave and worthy ministers were never in question, for many others, the notion of public morality was just that: how morality was publicly perceived. This emphasis on appearances was in line with the way in which the actions of king and nobility in the seventeenth century were often presented in a manner that was very different from how they were in reality. Ceremony and court protocol, personal demeanour, the manipulation of language, or blatant deception, were all devices that could be used to create impressions and reputations that had immediate and specific purposes for those concerned, with the longer-term side-effect of confusing historians. Nowhere was this more the case than with Philip IV, whose general assumptions and priorities have often been misconstrued because of the conflicting evidence to be found in the state papers, in court gossip, and in the King's celebrated correspondence with Sor María de Ágreda. An examination of Philip's personal involvement in the inception and termination of the programme for moral reform will provide a clearer and more accurate picture of his motives and preoccupations, at least for the middle years of his life.

In the immediate aftermath of the retirement of Olivares, Philip IV made a genuine effort to conform to the accepted requirements of good government by ruling without a formally acknowledged *valido*.[14] Yet, at first, he cut a sorry figure in the absence of his once all-powerful chief minister. Research by Ronald Cueto has shown how, in Zaragoza during the summer of 1643, some of the King's more unorthodox religious advisers came very near to persuading him to dismiss the ministers who had been most closely associated with Olivares and had remained in positions of authority after his removal from the scene (Cueto, pp. 86–7, 131–5 and 141–2). A few weeks later, Philip began to write letters to Sor María de Ágreda, in which, on the one hand, he shows himself to have been completely dependent on the nun's prayers and intercessions for his monarchy, and, on the other, to have had an embarrassing propensity for self-castigation on account of what he professed to regard as his personal responsibility for the disasters that afflicted his

---

(AHPM, protocolo 6280, fol. 413v). In the 1620s, Don Lorenzo had been assisted in his attempts to enter the order of Santiago by Don Pedro de Amezqueta, who was the uncle of Don Antonio de Contreras's wife; see Joaquín de Entrambasaguas, *Una familia de ingenios. Los Ramírez de Prado* (Madrid: CSIC, 1943), p. 57; AHPM, protocolo 9823, fols 1121v and 1124r. Contreras's connections to Olivares have been emphasized by Elliott, *Olivares*, pp. 297, 423, 516 and 560. However, at the end of his life, Don Antonio was outspoken in his hostility to the practice of government by *valido*, Francisco Tomás y Valiente, *Los validos en la monarquía española del siglo XVII*, 2nd edn (Madrid: Siglo Veintiuno, 1990), pp. 21 and 122.

14 R.A. Stradling, *Philip IV and the Government of Spain, 1621–1665* (Cambridge: CUP, 1988), pp. 209–22.

monarchy. In his first letter to the nun, written on 4 October 1643, he protested:

> [. . .] que en todo y por todo deseo cumplir con su santa ley [*de Dios*] y con la obligación en que me ha puesto de Rey, y espero de su misericordia se ha de doler de nosotros y ayudarnos a salir bien de estas aflicciones. El mayor favor que podré recibir de su bendita mano es que el castigo que da a estos reinos, me lo dé a mí, pues soy yo quien lo merezco y ellos no, que siempre han sido y serán verdaderos y firmes católicos.[15]

The King's self-condemnation would be reiterated countless times over the forthcoming years.[16] Yet – as Sor María herself came to realize – there was something rather disingenuous about such highly overwrought expressions of contrition; for they in fact constituted a form of play-acting that was confined to personal letters never intended to be seen by anyone other than their recipient.[17] Philip, like most of his Spanish contemporaries, did believe fervently in the power of intercession that could be exerted by holy people, and it was precisely for this reason that he saw the need to combine his public *persona* as the worthy heir of Philip II with the more intimate *persona* of a contrite sinner. By appearing to take the reins of government into his own hands, he would earn himself the respect of his subjects; by making out that he was aware of his own moral responsibility for the disasters afflicting his monarchy, he would obtain the spiritual benefits of a holy woman's intercessions with the Godhead. Neither role legitimately reflected his real practice of government which, just a few years after the withdrawal of Olivares in 1643, reverted to form with his recognition of a new *valido* in the person of Don Luis Méndez de Haro.

Yet, even though Philip's resort to *validos* amounted to a failure of executive resolve, it was not necessarily a sign of royal weakness, for he always had a very clear awareness of his obligations as a monarch. He was also forceful in his selection of and support for those ministers with whom he found it congenial to work, and could be equally ruthless in the removal of others less favoured. He would therefore not be nearly so submissive with people who attempted to back up Sor María's very deferential and carefully worded advice with importunate recommendations of their own. The evolution of Philip IV's concerns and priorities, from a deep personal insecurity in the immediate aftermath of his dismissal of Olivares towards a more guard-

---

[15] Sor María de Ágreda, *Cartas de Sor María de Jesús de Ágreda y de Felipe IV* [henceforth *CSMA*], ed. Carlos Seco Serrano, 2 vols, Biblioteca de Autores Españoles, 108–9 (Madrid: Ediciones Atlas, 1958), I, p. 5.

[16] For similar expressions, see *CSMA*, I, pp. 19–20, 45, 52, 84, 89, 95–6, 102–3, 158, 188, 194; II, pp. 73, 76, 83–4, 97–8, 101–4.

[17] See below, p. 106 (n. 37).

edly pragmatic, even cynical, attitude towards the Godly faction lies at the heart of our understanding of how the Spanish governing establishment came to adopt a more informal disposition after 1649.

Behind much of the programme of state-directed moral reform in the 1640s was the President of the Council of Castile, Don Juan Chumacero. Chumacero's outlook was not coloured by any of the ambiguities and reservations held by other Godly noblemen; rather, he was an out-and-out zealot. Back in the 1620s he had been responsible for leading the investigations into the alleged malpractices of Philip III's favourite, the Duke of Uceda. Then, in the early 1630s, Chumacero had been packed off to Rome as a means of silencing his criticism of the expense that was then being lavished on the construction and decoration of the Buen Retiro palace.[18] Absent from Spain for ten years, his appointment as President of the Council of Castile in March 1643 suddenly gave him a mandate to impose the viewpoints that had previously kept him at a safe distance from Madrid, and his opinions had not softened for all the time he had been abroad. Once back at the centre of government, he made common cause with like-minded figures, such as Sor María de Ágreda and the notorious Franciscan prophet, Fray Francisco Monterón, whose prayers and intercessions he regarded as necessary for the safety of the monarchy (Cueto, pp. 129–31). Philip – at least during the summer and autumn of 1643 – gave his full approval to the President's efforts, and requested that these holy people commend him to God so that he might better fulfil the Lord's wishes.[19]

It seemed, therefore, as though the King was in a state of dependency that was ripe to be exploited. It was Chumacero who was responsible for obtaining the removal of Olivares from the *madrileño* village of Loeches – where he had been residing since his departure from the royal palace – to the much more safely inaccessible Castilian town of Toro. He was also instrumental in securing the dismissal of the rest of the Count-Duke's immediate family from the royal households during the autumn of 1643.[20] The next year, the President continued the attempts to purge the government of former supporters of Olivares, but his efforts were undermined by the increasing self-possession of the King, as well as by the sudden deaths of Isabel of Bourbon and the royal confessor Fray Juan de Santo Tomás.[21] Not to be

---

[18] Tomás y Valiente, *Los validos*, pp. 158–9; Jonathan Brown and John H. Elliott, *A Palace for a King: The Buen Retiro and the Court of Philip IV*, 2nd edn (New Haven: Yale UP, 2003), pp. 223 and 243.

[19] BNM MS 13163, fols 158r–9r.

[20] Alistair Malcolm, 'Don Luis de Haro and the Political Elite of the Spanish Monarchy in the Mid-Seventeenth Century' (unpublished doctoral thesis, University of Oxford, 1999), p. 71; Chumacero to Philip IV, 4 August 1643, BNM MS 13163, fols 124r–v.

[21] Antonio Carnero to Olivares, 10 February 1644, AHN Estado, lib. 869, fols

outdone, Chumacero spent the next three years plaguing the King with papers that urged him to strike at the root causes of public sin. These were attributed explicitly to perceived shortcomings in public morality that were most clearly evident in the adoption of French fashions in dress and attendance at *comedias*,[22] and, more implicitly, in the continued presence of certain undesirable members of the King's retinue.[23] In a veiled allusion to the Olivares years, the President concluded that 'todo lo veo como de antes, y peor', unless the King should decide to take matters in hand, and reform his household.[24] His coded implications were not lost on Philip, who responded sharply and in a way that suggests a much stronger character than that of the guilt-ridden penitent pouring out his anxieties in his letters to Sor María de Ágreda:

> No dudo q' los pecados son la causa de los trabajos q' padecemos, y assí sienpre os he encargado (siendo vos a quien os toca) el q' se remedian, pues ni yo lo puedo sanar todo, ni remediarlo por mi persona. Yo e descargado mi conciencia con la vra, y si juzgara q' avía escándalo entre los q' entran en mi presencia, lo remediara luego al punto, pues desseo no offender a nada a nro Señor.[25]

Philip's implication was clear: he saw it as Chumacero's responsibility – just as much as it was his own – to deal with matters of public morality; he did not believe that there was any need to purge his household of malefactors, and he was now getting tired of people trying to tell him otherwise.

118v–19r. Olivares wrote bitterly of Chumacero in a letter of 17 October 1644: 'no he tenido cartas del Señor Presidente, ni parece justo apresurarse a escribir a quien vale tan poco, y a quien en todo se ha tratado de despreciar y menospreciar tanto', AHN Estado, lib. 869, fol. 289.

22 BL MS Add. 24947, fol. 53v.

23 Chumacero seems to have been particularly troubled by the low necklines of women's dresses and the way in which young male courtiers had begun to grow their hair long. In a document of 5 February 1646, purporting to be by the *Sala de gobierno* but probably written by Chumacero (see below, pp. 103–4 (n.33)), it is stated that the changes in fashion had begun to appear twelve years before (i.e. in 1634), BL MS Add. 24947, fol. 55v. Velázquez's portraits of a *Lady with a Fan* (Wallace Collection, London) and a *Woman doing Needlework* (National Gallery of Art, Washington) are both datable to this period. See also, Zahira Veliz, 'Signs of Identity in *Lady with a Fan* by Diego Velázquez: Costume and Likeness Reconsidered', *Art Bulletin*, 86 (March 2004), 75–95 (pp. 80–2).

24 BL MS Add. 24947, fol. 49r.

25 BL MS Add. 24947, fol. 50v. This was a response to a *consulta* of 18 April 1645. On an earlier occasion, the King had already defended the rectitude of his entourage: 'agradézcoos lo q' me representáis y no dudo q' si todos nos enmendáramos tubiéramos mejores sucessos. Encárgoos q' de vra parte hagáis lo posible [. . .], y yo de la mía, haré lo mismo, si bien entre los q' entran en mi presencia ay poco q' enmendar', reply to a *consulta* of 20 December 1644 (fol. 46v).

The King's responses to Chumacero are evidence for a gradual strengthening of his resolve. Without abandoning his own providential view of how the world operated, he was now moving away from the recommendations of his Godly advisers towards a more pragmatic outlook. It is within this context of the Godly ministers' gradual loss of control over Philip's religious susceptibilities that the debate over the morality of the theatre may be approached.[26] The supervision of the public theatres was an especially important aspect of the work of the Council of Castile, because they provided the revenue needed to run the municipal hospitals, and because they were considered by some ministers to be a means of social control. If properly regulated, the performance of *comedias* could be a harmless outlet for potentially fractious subjects, but there was also a concern that *comedias* might have a detrimental effect on the moral welfare of those who beheld them (Vitse, pp. 44–6). The renowned cleric, Don Luis Crespí, after half an hour spent thumbing through a volume of plays by Antonio de Solís, could not but express his consternation at the number of dramatic situations he encountered in which men flirted with women who were not their wives; actresses appeared on stage dressed as men; and lascivious dances were included for no other apparent reason than the titillation of the theatregoers (Cotarelo y Mori, p. 195; Wilson, p. 162). A few decades earlier, the distinguished Jesuit theologian, Pedro de Rivadeneira had been of like mind; he regarded Golden-Age theatre as equal in its degeneracy to that of Ancient Rome, where both were responsible for the decline of the civilizations from which they had been born and which they sought to represent (Vitse, pp. 49–52). To their objections were added those of Don Baltasar de Sandoval, the Cardinal Archbishop of Toledo, who acclaimed the Spartans for eradicating the problem of adultery simply by not allowing women to go to the theatre.[27] For these people, and many others of similar views, *comedias* encouraged illicit

---

[26] The standard works on this subject are those of Emilio Cotarelo y Mori, *Bibliografía de las controversias sobre la licitud del teatro en España* (Madrid: Tipografía de la Revista de Archivos, Bibliotecas y Museos, 1904) and Marc Vitse, *Elements pour une théorie du théâtre espagnol du XVIIe siècle* (Toulouse: Université de Toulouse-Le Mirail, 1988). The dramatist Francisco Bances Candamo also provided an account of the controversy in his *Theatro de los theatros de los passados y presentes siglos*, ed. Duncan W. Moir (London: Tamesis, 1970). The different sides of the polemic are most concisely summarized by Metford, 'The Enemies of the Theatre', and by E.M. Wilson, 'Nuevos documentos sobre las controversias teatrales: 1650–1681', in Jaime Sánchez Romeralo and Norbert Poulussen (eds), *Actas del Segundo Congreso Internacional de Hispanistas celebrado en Nijmegen del 20 al 25 de agosto de 1965* (Nijmegen: Instituto Español de la Universidad de Nimega, 1967), pp. 155–70. When writing this chapter I was unaware of the existence of Thomas Austin O'Connor's recent contribution: *Love in the 'Corral': Conjugal Spirituality and Anti-Theatrical Polemic in Early Modern Spain* (New York: Peter Lang, 2000).

[27] BL MS Add. 24947, fol. 62v.

sexual relations and contributed to a national lethargy to which all social ills could be ascribed.

Since the end of the sixteenth century, the theatres had been closed on a number of short-lived occasions, usually as a mark of respect following deaths in the royal family. But these brief remissions were often accompanied by demands for a definitive and permanent prohibition of *comedias*, or (failing that) for more effective policing of the *corrales* by the forces of law and order. At the beginning of the seventeenth century, a series of ordinances were issued that created a model for posterity. It became the duty of the Council of Castile to monitor the content of the plays; to fix the time of day at which they were to be performed; to establish methods of admission and impose rules of segregation of men from women in the audience. The Council also attempted to limit the number of theatre companies operating in any one city, and to prohibit the inclusion of dances and scenes in which actresses appeared on stage in male costume. In order to make sure that these regulations were properly enforced, a legal official, drawn from the *Sala de alcaldes de casa y corte*, was under orders to oversee ticket sales as well as to attend first-night performances in a chair that was positioned prominently to one side of the stage.[28] The overall supervision of the theatres, together with the closely related business of the municipal hospitals, was ultimately the responsibility of more senior magistrates within the Council of Castile itself, who enjoyed the title of *Protectores de los hospitales y corrales*. It was for the *Protectores* to keep an eye on the membership of the theatre companies, as well as to read and license all material before it appeared on stage.[29] They were also allotted a window, or balcony, in each of the two public theatres in Madrid in order to make sure that what had been censored stayed censored once the plays were performed. The President of the Council of Castile was also accorded a balcony, although it is unlikely that Don Juan Chumacero, given his strong views on the subject, would have taken advantage of this privilege (Shergold, pp. 388, 391–2 and 398).

Further research will be necessary before we can know precisely who held the office of *Protector*, and how effectively, or rigorously, each of these officials individually sought to control the theatres. During the 1620s and 1630s, it seems likely that the ordinances would have been fulfilled with some degree of zeal simply on account of the fact that one of the *Protectores* was Don Antonio de Contreras, whose concern about the morality of the theatre

---

[28] John J. Allen, *The Reconstruction of a Spanish Golden-Age Playhouse: El Corral del Príncipe, 1583–1744* (Gainesville: University Presses of Florida, 1983), pp. 43–5. The *Sala de alcaldes* was a lesser tribunal that was subordinate to the Council of Castile and responsible for maintaining law and order in Madrid, Janine Fayard, *Los miembros del Consejo de Castilla, 1621–1746*, trans. Rufina Rodríguez Sanz (Madrid: Siglo Veintiuno, 1982), pp. 23–4.

[29] N.D. Shergold, *A History of the Spanish Stage from Medieval Times to the end of the Seventeenth Century* (Oxford: Clarendon Press, 1967), pp. 386–7, 390–1 and 516–19.

is well documented. Yet there also appears to have been a growing concern that the Council of Castile as a whole was failing to enforce properly its own rules (Cotarelo y Mori, pp. 179 and 194–5; Vitse, pp. 57–8 and 81–2). During the early 1640s, therefore, Contreras saw it as necessary to reissue all the old regulations, together with a variety of new measures designed to counter the dissenting voices. His new reforms insisted that the subject matter of the plays should henceforward be strictly limited to historical events and the lives of saints, and that the use of rich brocades in costumes be forbidden. Henceforward, all actresses would have to be married, and only one new play was to be staged each week. In addition, dances had to be subjected to the approval of the *Protector* before they could take place in the playhouses, whilst all performances of plays, rather than just the opening nights, would have to be attended by an *alcalde de casa y corte*. Finally, the agents of the Council were to carry out regular searches of the actors' houses in order to expel the scoundrels and vagrants suspected of living there (Cotarelo y Mori, pp. 164–5 and 632–3; Shergold, pp. 519–20).[30]

The situation of the theatres, even before the total closures of the 1640s, had therefore become very bleak. The death of the King's first wife, Isabel of Bourbon, in October 1644, obliged the suspension of performances as a temporary mark of respect, which was lifted in April 1645. But, in February 1646, the theatres were again closed by an open-ended ban that would last officially for exactly five years. Varey and Shergold, in their study of this second prohibition, noted how it was particularly significant, on account of its length and the fact that it was not motivated by a royal death ('Datos', p. 290). Yet it is also of interest because hitherto unstudied documents demonstrate that the original decision to close the theatres in 1646 was only provisionally granted, and very much against the better judgement of the King.

The sequence of events that led to this decision began on 26 January 1646, when Don Juan Chumacero addressed a paper to Philip recommending that he establish a committee of theologians whose duty would be to come up with measures that would cut to the root of public sin. Philip's response was to dismiss the idea as unnecessary, on the grounds that it was the Council's job to make sure that social conformity was properly enforced.[31] In doing so, he unwittingly reconfirmed the Council's prerogatives and provided it with a fresh mandate to take action. Ten days later, on 5 February, the senior tribunal of the Council, known as the *Sala de gobierno*, duly came back with a paper advising that the women of the court should appear decently dressed;

---

30 See also J.E. Varey and N.D. Shergold, 'Datos históricos sobre los primeros teatros de Madrid: prohibiciones de autos y comedias y sus consecuencias (1644–1651)' [henceforth 'Datos'], *Bulletin Hispanique*, 72 (1960), 286–325 (pp. 286–7).
31 BL MS Add. 24947, fols 53r–54v.

that male courtiers cut off their long tresses; and that the theatres should be closed, as the efforts of the *Protector de comedias* had clearly been in vain. In addition to these recommendations, the *Sala* rather incongruously included a much more ambitious and complicated request that the Council of War should cease to have jurisdiction over legal cases involving soldiers.[32] Although the paper of the *Sala de gobierno* was signed by five ministers, its authorship may fairly safely be attributed to Chumacero alone on account of its inclusion of several of the President's trademark phrases.[33]

One might guess that the juxtaposition of a highly polemical issue of jurisdictional competence alongside the relatively simple matters of legislation to prohibit excesses in dress and the theatre was a ruse to secure the acceptance of the lesser measures. If this was the case, the plan worked: Philip's reply convincingly refuted the notion that stage plays could have an effect on the behaviour of those who watched them, since it consisted of a ringing endorsement of his soldiers that can be seen as wholeheartedly taking the side of Don Lope de Figueroa against Pedro Crespo. But, having stood his ground on the issue of the military *fuero*, the King felt it incumbent upon himself to abide by the Council's more incidental advice. He therefore promised that the nobility would be made to dress with greater modesty, and a rather apologetically worded decree to this effect was issued the following month.[34] Philip also agreed to the closure of the theatres, and his remarks on this issue are worth citing at length because they amount to the definitive statement of his personal opinion regarding a form of literary and visual expression that has become very much synonymous with his reign.

> El uso de las comedias es y se ha tenido siempre por indiferente y por eso se han permitido para divertimiento del pueblo y escusar otros inconvenientes mayores que la ociosidad y ruines inclinaciones pueden causar, particularmente en la multitud de la corte, y en otros lugares populosos; y en esta consideración, y por no haver juzgado jamás que la representación de comedias aprobadas por el Cons° – como casi lo son las más que se veen en el Reino – fuese acto prohibido de suyo, las he tolerado, aunque en differentes tiempos los ministros mayores y otras personas zelosas han tratado de proponerme lo contrario; y si bien estoi todavía en el mismo dictamen: viendo por otra parte que la sala de

---

[32] BL MS Add. 24947, fols 55r–58v.

[33] The *Sala*'s assertion that women who dressed in the French fashion were 'descubriendo a todos lo que se solía retirar a los maridos' (fol. 55v) is a repetition of words used by Chumacero in a paper that he had addressed to the King in December 1644 (fol. 45r). Reference to the King as 'lei viva' also occurs in both documents (fols 45v and 55v). Chumacero himself later claimed authorship of the *Sala*'s paper: 'y aviendo remitido VM mi consulta [de 26 de enero de 1646] a la sala de govierno hice otra en su nombre, y de su acuerdo' (fol. 67r).

[34] 'Esta reformación de trajes la he resuelto conformándome con el parecer de los ministros que la han juzgado por necesario', royal decree addressed to the *Bureo*, 12 March 1646, AGP, Sección Administrativa, leg. 983.

govierno y algunos hombres graves a quien he mand° se comunique juzgan
por lo mejor que se escusen las comedias vengo en que se suspendan por
aora durante estas occasiones presentes, aunque reconozco que ha de ser
de gran desconsuelo, que se quite este solo divertimiento que ha quedado
en el pueblo, siendo tan continuos y grandes los trabajos que se han
padecido y padezen; y spero en Dios se ha de servir de mudar los tiempos
de manera que, reformándose las comedias en lo que conviniere, se puedan
volver a permitir sin los inconvenientes que aora se consideran, si el mismo
tiempo lo aconsejare.[35]

Philip's line of reasoning closely followed the arguments of many writers
who defended the legitimacy of the theatre. His use of the term 'indiferente'
echoed the belief that there was nothing intrinsically wrong with *comedias*,
but it was rather the way in which they were performed by the actors or interpreted by the spectators that made them potentially harmful (Cotarelo y
Mori, pp. 174 and 237; Vitse, pp. 42–4, 54–6, 62–5 and 70). The King therefore did see some reform as necessary, but in no way did he want to introduce
a total ban of the performance of plays, since he realized how much his
hard-pressed subjects needed this kind of entertainment to distract them from
the affliction of crippling taxation. Philip therefore made no bones about the
fact that he was agreeing to close the theatres against his own better judgement, and only until such time as an alleviation of the present domestic and
international difficulties should allow him to reverse his decision.

These moderate and sensible views contrasted markedly with those
expressed in the letter that Philip wrote to Sor María de Ágreda a month
later, on 7 March 1646, informing her that he was introducing the moral
reforms that she also had been requesting:

Cuanto puedo hago por evitar ofensas públicas y escandalosas de Nuestro
Señor, pues reconozco verdaderamente que cuánto más le ofendamos más
armas damos a nuestros enemigos; y ahora actualmente, se han dado
órdenes para reformar los trajes en las mujeres, y para que cesen las
comedias, por parecer que destas causas proceden parte de los pecados que
se cometen.[36]

In the letter to Sor María, there was no inkling of the temporary nature of the
measures, nor any sign that they had been introduced only reluctantly and as
a sop to his Godly advisers. Whatever Philip himself may have privately felt,
the important thing was that the nun was given the understanding that everything was being done to placate the Almighty so that her prayers might in
turn secure God's favour for the Spanish monarchy. Yet further tragic events
that took place in the course of 1646 suggest that the forcible imposition of

---

[35] BL MS Add. 24947, fols 55r–v.
[36] *CSMA*, I, p. 52.

virtuous codes of conduct on the King's subjects was failing to have its desired effect. The deaths of Philip's sister, the Empress María in May, followed by that of his only son and heir, Baltasar Carlos, in October, turned on its head the association between public morality and divine favour. Theatre closures, which usually provided a mark of respect in the aftermath of deaths in the royal family, had in this instance taken on the form of an ill omen of bereavements still to come. The death of the Prince of Asturias was what necessitated the King's betrothal to Mariana, and it also seems to have increased his scepticism, not so much towards the intercessory power of Sor María and other figures like her – which he never doubted – but towards the assumption that only by implementing a reign of virtue could the monarchy be saved.[37]

In 1646, the theatre prohibition was maintained to the letter, with even the Corpus Christi *autos* being cancelled. But, by the summer of 1647, the *autos* were being performed again, though they were not yet allowed to be staged for money within the playhouses ('Datos', pp. 290–3). In the palace the austerity measures were beginning to be treated with still greater flexibility, when, in December 1647, the Infanta María Teresa and seventeen of her ladies, all wearing dresses of scarlet lined with ermine and silver mantles, danced before the King in the candle-lit hall of the Alcázar palace.[38] Exactly a year later, on the eve of the Queen's fourteenth birthday, the Infanta and a slightly smaller number of her ladies performed Gabriel Bocángel's *El nuevo Olimpo*, a more ambitious event with elaborate costumes, stage scenery, and music provided by the choirs of the royal chapel. While Bocángel was at pains in the introduction to his printed text of the masque to distinguish it from popular *comedias*,[39] there could be no denying that both spectacles flouted the spirit, if not the letter, of recent government legislation to enforce

[37] Over the course of 1647, Sor María became gradually aware that the King was impervious to the kind of advice that she, and others like her, were trying to offer: 'El rey continúa su corespondiencia, cada día mas agradecido de lo q' le digo y mas fino pero menos ejecutibo', Sor María to Don Francisco de Borja, 13 December 1647, ADR F/156, no. 79. See also her letters of 15 April, 16 August and 26 December 1647, 10 January 1648, ADR F/156, nos. 65, 74, 80 and 81. Philip's celebrated letter to Sor María de Ágreda of 30 January 1647, in which he justified his relationship with Haro, may, when read in the context of the nun's letter of 18 January and its enclosures, be taken as a polite warning that his confidante should desist from trying to influence the composition of his government, *CSMA*, I, pp. 90–3 and 259–65.

[38] Gabriel Bocángel y Unzueta wrote a verse description of the masque entitled *La piedra cándida*, *Obras completas*, ed. Trevor J. Dadson, 2 vols (Madrid and Frankfurt am Main: Iberoamericana and Vervuert, 2000), II, pp. 891–913.

[39] Chaves, *El espectáculo teatral*, pp. 143–8; Bocángel y Unzueta, *Obras completas*, II, p. 936. Juan Francisco Dávila, who also wrote a prose and verse account of *El nuevo Olimpo*, was not quite so careful in his choice of words, twice referring to the event as a 'comedia', *Relación de los festivos aplavsos . . .* (Madrid: Domingo García y Morras, 1649?), fols 2v and 3v.

moral reform. *El nuevo Olimpo* lasted for two hours between 6pm and 8pm, and was performed before a select audience of grandees and presidents of the councils, with the King and the Duchess of Mantua presiding over the occasion.[40] Conspicuous by his absence was Don Juan Chumacero, who had been sent into honourable retirement a few months before.

The reopening of the public theatres was also being brought back on to the agenda by the increasingly desperate straits of the hospitals and by the need to find money to pay for festivities to celebrate Mariana of Austria's long-expected arrival. On 28 October 1648, the Council of Castile nominated a new *Protector de comedias*, Don Lorenzo Ramírez de Prado. This, the second of the two offices (in addition to the one still held by Don Antonio de Contreras), had been allowed to lie vacant for over a year after the death of its previous holder, and the new appointment suggests a further softening of the government's attitude towards the theatre. At the beginning of that month, the Ayuntamiento of Madrid had made an offer to pay for the Queen's formal entrance, but only on the condition that the public theatres be reopened, because there was no other way of finding the money necessary to subsidize the hospitals. This offer (or threat) found its way onto the table of the Council of Castile in November 1648, together with a letter written to Ramírez de Prado by the *corregidor* of Valladolid alleging that the situation in the foundling hospitals within his jurisdiction had become so appalling that mothers were throwing their unwanted children into the rivers. The councillors debated the legitimacy of *comedias*, as they had done so often in the past, and, once again, the majority still opposed the reopening of the theatres. But those in the minority, who included the new President, Don Diego de Riaño y Gamboa, would ultimately carry the day. The opening paragraphs of their report (*consulta*) followed the same arguments as Philip's own statement of nearly three years before, to the effect that there was nothing intrinsically harmful in *comedias*, which were a legitimate and necessary source of distraction for the common people. The councillors then went on to make explicit reference to the temporary nature of the 1646 prohibition, 'como dejando puerta abierta para que los daños o conveniencias de aquella deliberación los mostrase la experiencia', before drawing attention to their belief that the domestic and international situation had in fact become much worse than it had been before the theatres were closed (Cotarelo y Mori, p. 166).

In much the same way as the 1646 recommendations of the *Sala de gobierno* can be attributed to Chumacero, the 1648 *consulta* may well have been the work of the new *Protector*, Don Lorenzo Ramírez de Prado. Don Lorenzo had, for nearly forty years, been a leading figure in the Spanish literary world and a close friend of many of the great writers of the Golden

---

[40] AHN Consejos, lib. 2029, fols 24r–v; Dávila, *Relación*, fol. 2r; Bocángel y Unzueta, *Obras completas*, II, p. 943.

Age (Entrambasaguas, pp. 90–113). He had also managed to work his way up through the state administration occupying posts in the councils of Finance and the Indies, as well as conducting a diplomatic mission to the court of Louis XIII. This very successful political career had been pursued in spite of serious impediments stemming from the disgrace of his father, a senior minister of Philip III, who had died in prison in 1608. The public prosecutor who had directed proceedings against Alonso Ramírez de Prado had been a close relative of Don Juan Chumacero, and both men had subsequently used their influence in order to obstruct Don Lorenzo's career (Entrambasaguas, pp. 26–38 and 55–7). The very fact that the latter had managed to survive and flourish in the face of such personal animosity, and to the extent that, in 1645, he was actually able to secure appointment to the Council of Castile during Chumacero's own presidency, is testament to his very special abilities and the favour that he enjoyed with Philip IV and the new ministers who were beginning to sideline the President of Castile in the struggle for influence. Ramírez de Prado's authorship of the *consulta* of November 1648 seems probable on account of its inclusion of correspondence addressed to him, the emphasis it placed on the *Protector*'s ability to ensure that the theatres were properly policed, and its resort to a highly informed discourse, which is unlikely to have been devised by anyone other than someone, like Don Lorenzo, who had very strong literary inclinations. The *consulta*'s argument demonstrated that *comedias* amounted to an 'espejo de la vida humana', in which the public could be persuaded by 'el bien sentir de las frases, lo articulado de las voces, lo accionado de los representantes y lo entretenido de la graciosidad' into discerning and accepting the deeper moral implications of the plays that were being performed on stage (Cotarelo y Mori, pp. 167–8).

Regardless of the authorship of the 1648 *consulta*, its proposals were implicitly accepted when Ramírez de Prado received a third appointment, on 11 May 1649, as *Superintendente de los festejos* in anticipation of the Queen's arrival. This preferment appears to have been made at the behest of Don Luis de Haro, whose recent emergence into the limelight as the King's new *valido* had partly been facilitated by the requirements of the royal marriage. Haro had played an important role in the preparations for Mariana's arrival, providing Philip with detailed advice on the route to be followed by the Queen, the identity of her retinue and the costings for the journey. It was also Haro who was now responsible for the arrangement of the Queen's formal entry into Madrid, a responsibility that he chose to entrust to a competent member of the Council of Castile with well-established connections in the literary world.[41] The growing influence of both

---

[41] Evidence for Haro's direct involvement in the organization of the Queen's journey can be found in AHN Estado, leg. 2779. The anonymous *Noticia del recibimiento i entrada de la Reyna nvestra Señora doña María-Ana de Avstria en la mvy noble i leal coronada villa*

these men ensured that the movement for Godly reform was fast becoming a dead letter. The nobility had already been allowed to violate the restrictions on dress and personal appearance in August 1647, when the emperor's ratification of the marriage capitulations had arrived in Madrid.[42] It seems also to have been the case that, in addition to the expensive and occasional festivities laid on by the Infanta María Teresa and her ladies, more traditional *comedias* were regularly performed within the palace at least from 1649, and possibly from as early as Carnival 1648 ('Datos', p. 301).[43] Furthermore, some of the councillors of Castile had begun to advise Philip that, as the prohibition was being so flagrantly violated in the provinces, he should allow his subjects their source of pleasure as an act of royal grace, rather than run the risk of being perceived to be incapable of enforcing his own laws (Cotarelo y Mori, pp. 166–7).

It appears, therefore, that a convenient sleight of hand was in operation whereby the moral reforms remained in force, but were blatantly disregarded in a working arrangement that pleased everybody except for those few members of the Godly who were still alive and had not yet been sent into comfortable retirement. Happiest of all was the fourteen-year-old Mariana who appears to have had an insatiable appetite for *comedias*. At practically every point along her journey from her disembarkation at Denia, she was entertained by the private performance of plays, and her journey from Vienna to Madrid itself came to provide the backdrop for a *comedia* by Calderón ('Datos', pp. 301–3). *Guárdate del agua mansa* was probably staged before the Queen in the Alcázar palace in December 1649, for, in the final Act, the characters Doña Eugenia and Doña Clara describe the Queen's

---

de Madrid mentions Haro as being the individual 'a cuya protección i cuidado [las fiestas] se deben' (p. 1). See also, Jenaro Alenda y Mira, *Relaciones de solemnidades y fiestas públicas de España*, 2 vols (Madrid: Sucesores de Rivadeneyra, 1903), I, pp. 313–14. When Ramírez de Prado drew up his testament in 1657, he bequeathed a painting, attributable to Giulio Romano, to Haro's son, the Marquis of Heliche, who, by that time, had become the great impresario of court theatre. Ramírez de Prado also left a depiction of Christ as Man of Sorrows, which he considered to be by El Greco, to the Count of La Puebla de Montalbán, and a head of St John the Baptist, supposedly by Titian, to the Count of Puñonrostro. Both noblemen were important courtiers within Haro's political network (AHPM protocolo 6280, fol. 412v).

42 Antonio de León Pinelo, *Anales de Madrid del año 447 al de 1658*, ed. Pedro Fernández Martín (Madrid: Instituto de Estudios Madrileños, 1971), pp. 334–5.

43 Evidence for the performance of *comedias* in the palace during the early months of 1648 is tenuous, as it comes from a letter from Sor María de Ágreda to Don Francisco de Borja of 6 March 1648: 'no podré encarecer a VSª el sentimiento y amargura q' e tenido de q' el rey admitiesse comedias en palacio. No entiendo a este señor y el día de ceniça me escribió una carta de cartujo q' quería hacer grandes cossas en la cuaresma y ser muy perfeto. Quien le pudiera responder lo que siento, q' aun q' diga mucho, no lo q' el desseo me pide' (ADR, F/156 no. 83) She may have been referring to the masque of 21 December 1647, and was almost certainly relying on reports exaggerated by Haro's enemies.

formal entry on the morning of 15 November.[44] Accompanied by her husband, she rode beneath the traditional *pallium* up the Carrera de San Jerónimo, through the Puerta del Sol and the Calle Mayor to the Alcázar palace. Along the way the spectators were entertained by the performance of plays on temporary outdoor stages, while the royal couple passed beneath triumphal arches that had been devised under Ramírez de Prado's direction.[45] Thereafter, the Queen's private apartments in each of the royal palaces would become a venue for the performance of *comedias* in open violation of the ban that would not be formally rescinded until February 1651 (Cotarelo y Mori, p. 635; *Fuentes I*, p. 236).

In the spring of 1650, the newly married Philip IV wrote a letter to another of his epistolary confidantes. The recipient was Sor Luisa de Jesús, a Carmelite nun in a convent situated to the north of Ciudad Real. Before she had taken the veil, Sor Luisa had been ninth Countess of Paredes, governess of the royal children and a personal friend of the King. Philip's letters to her were therefore quite different in tone from those that he wrote to Sor María de Ágreda, and they convey a more intimate and honest depiction of his state of mind. On this occasion, Philip described the Carnival festivities that had been laid on that year when Ramírez de Prado – again acting under the direction of Don Luis de Haro – had organized the production of an elaborate festival play in honour of the new queen. The author and subject of the play are unknown, but substantial sums of money were spent on its staging, and the royal family were delighted by the buffoonery of the celebrated actor, Juan Rana.[46] Philip wrote this letter just a few weeks after the Inquisition had conducted a ten-day investigation into the mystical claims of Sor María de

[44] Pedro Calderón de la Barca, *Guárdate del agua mansa*, eds Ignacio Arellano and Víctor García Ruiz (Kassel: Reichenberger, 1989), vv. 3015–184. Víctor García Ruiz suggests that the play may have been a reworking of an earlier *comedia*, whose performance had itself been prevented by the closure of the theatres in the mid 1640s (pp. 38–9 and 57–61).

[45] J.E. Varey and A.M. Salazar, 'Calderón and the Royal Entry of 1649', *Hispanic Review*, 34 (1966), 1–26 (pp. 6–12). Reproductions of two of Francisco Rizi's sketches for the triumphal arch representing America, which was constructed outside Haro's residence in the Calle Mayor, have been published by María Teresa Chaves Montoya in 'La conquista del Viejo Mundo "América" recibe a Mariana de Austria (1649)', in Wolfram Krömer (ed.), *1492–1992: Spanien, Österreich und Iberoamerika. Akten des Siebten Spanisch-Österreichischen Symposions 16.–21. März 1992 in Innsbruck* (Innsbruck: University of Innsbruck, Institut für Sprachwissenschaft, 1993), pp. 51–65.

[46] Philip IV to Sor Luisa de Jesús, 7 March 1650, *Felipe IV y Luisa Manrique de Lara, Condesa de Paredes de Nava. Un epistolario inédito*, ed. Joaquín Pérez Villanueva (Salamanca: Ediciones de la Caja de Ahorros y Monte de Piedad de Salamanca, 1986), p. 121. For the cost of the play, and Haro's delegation of its organization to Ramírez de Prado, see *Fuentes I*, pp. 52–6. Again I am grateful to Teresa Chaves for having drawn this source to my attention.

Ágreda.[47] Though cleared of any suspected heresy or fraud, Sor María would have had more immediate concerns on her mind than Philip's apparent relapse into moral iniquity. Yet the letters that she wrote to other members of the nobility would mince few words about her continuing frustration about Philip's imperviousness to her advice, and her distress at the expense lavished on the great machine plays that were staged at the Spanish court during the 1650s.[48]

The purported closure of the theatres between 1646 and 1651 had been just one aspect of a broad dissatisfaction about the way in which the Spanish Monarchy functioned as a Catholic society in a providential world. It was believed that morality had a direct effect on personal and national fortunes, and so it was considered necessary to do everything possible to control how society behaved in order quite literally to oblige God to come to the assistance of the Spanish monarchy. Such an assumption, however, was thrown into question by historical events. During the two-year period between 1646 and 1647, when the reforms were being enforced to the full, there took place a whole string of mishaps, which rather belied the view that God was on the side of the virtuous. In addition to the deaths within the royal family, French armies captured the cities of Dunkirk and Tortosa, Philip's ally the Duke of Modena defected to Louis XIV, and Naples and Sicily were plunged into revolt. By contrast, the reopening of the theatres, and the return of a more carefree atmosphere to the Spanish court coincided with a marked improvement in Spain's international situation as the French state collapsed into the civil anarchy of the Frondes. It was clear that moral austerity and court extravagance were having effects diametrically opposed to those they were supposed to have within the theocentric world-view of the Godly.

Mariana's arrival in the autumn of 1649 coincided with a number of important cultural and political changes, which marked a watershed in the reign of Philip IV. Most immediately, the movement for moral reform was now dead. While decrees seeking to control the behaviour of the King's subjects were issued throughout the seventeenth century, enforcement of such legislation was never as intense as during the 1640s. There was also a clearing of the political air, as factional alignments became much less polarized. With the sidelining of extremists, like Chumacero, a much larger body of people came to the fore that believed in some form of compromise. As a

---

[47] T.D. Kendrick, *Mary of Ágreda: The Life and Legend of a Spanish Nun* (London: Routledge & Kegan Paul, 1967), pp. 76–7.

[48] Writing at the time of the preparations for the performance of Calderón's *La fiera, el rayo y la piedra*, she expressed her sorrow that 'el rey se dibierta aora con comedias de tramoxa. No sé para q' busca otras q' las q' ay en su reino y gobierno. [. . .] Canssadissima me tiene y aflijida', letter to Don Francisco de Borja, 3 May 1652, ADR F/156, no. 152. A year later, and in relation to the performance of *Las fortunas de Andrómeda y Perseo*, she voiced her discontent about the King 'porq' gasta tanto en comedias y se acuerda tan poco de lo q' su corona a menester', same to same, 30 May 1653, ADR F/156, no. 156.

consequence, the character of the Spanish court during the 1650s was by and large apolitical, as was evident in the existence of friendships between ministers of sharply differing opinions, such as Contreras and Ramírez de Prado.[49] This merging of the factions itself mirrored the resolution of long-standing divisions over the way that the King should rule and present himself to his subjects. On the one hand, there had been those who had favoured a sober, restrained, hidden monarchy in which the King was surrounded by a small group of people and dedicated his time to government business and religious devotion – the style that had been adopted by Philip II during the second half of his reign. On the other hand, there were those who saw such an approach as incompatible with the ceremonial requirements of the early modern state. It was the reversion to a more public, or 'baroque' style of kingship after 1649 that allowed Philip to give formal recognition to Don Luis de Haro as his *valido*, a distinction towards which the latter had been discreetly moving over the course of the previous six years.

In the final analysis, all of these developments had been brought about by a ruler who has often been misjudged by historians. Philip IV was no doubt indecisive, prone to crises of conscience, a little too good at self-deception, and rather over-credulous about the ability of religious mystics to help his foreign policy. But these were characteristics that were common to most of his contemporaries. What he certainly was not was the debauched hedonist with a tortured soul, which is the image so often conveyed by writers who have taken his correspondence with Sor María de Ágreda at face value (Marañón 2004, pp. 297–302; Kendrick, pp. 100–3).[50] Rather, the King was a pragmatist who was more perceptive than many of his ministers about what his subjects would and would not be willing to tolerate, and possessed a great deal of natural guile in the lip-service that he came to pay towards the aspirations of the Godly. While Philip has rightly been blamed for failing to fulfil his executive role within his government, he was nonetheless highly successful in defining how the Spanish Monarchy should be presented to the rest of the world in such a way as to suit his own tastes, the requirements of his nobility and the personality of his new teenage consort.

---

[49] Ramírez de Prado also appears to have been close to Juan Eusebio Nieremberg, Entrambasaguas, pp. 102 and 108. For the relative absence of faction at the Spanish Court in the 1650s, as well as further assessment of the personalities of Philip IV and Mariana, see Alistair Malcolm, 'La práctica informal del poder. La política de la Corte y el acceso a la familia real durante la segunda mitad del reinado de Felipe IV', *Reales Sitios*, 38 (2001), 38–48.

[50] See also, José Deleito y Piñuela, *El Rey se divierte* (Madrid: Alianza, 1988).

The Politics of Memory in *El Tuzaní de la Alpujarra*

MARGARET RICH GREER

Yten, es asentado e acordado que sus altesas e sus decendientes para syempre jamás dexarán biuir al dicho Rey Muley Baaudili [. . .] e caualleros e escuderos, y viejos e buenos onbres, e comunidat, chicos e grandes, e estar en su ley; [. . .] e que sean judgados por su ley xaraçina, con consejos de sus alcadís, segunt costunbre de los moros, e les guardarán e mandarán guardar sus buenos vsos é costunbres.[1]
Capitulations, Boabdil and the Catholic Kings, 25 November 1491

The religious and cultural tolerance that the conquering Catholic monarchs promised their Islamic subjects 'forever and ever' in the 1491 Capitulations lasted but a decade, as Cardinal Francisco Jiménez de Cisneros's policy of forced conversions replaced the patient evangelization efforts of Granada's first archbishop, Hernando de Talavera, at the turn of the century. The downward spiral into what Francisco Márquez Villanueva characterizes as religious persecution and cultural genocide stretching over more than a century is a tragedy of Spain's history both too complex and too well known to merit repetition in one more essay.[2] My concern herein is with the question of how the trauma of that historical tragedy was negotiated in the dramatic tragedy Pedro Calderón de la Barca wrote on the 1568–70 rebellion of the *moriscos*, brutally put down by troops commanded by Don Juan de Austria. Events of the twenty-first century have propelled us to a point in time and space that invites us to salvage from the wreckage piled at the feet of Walter Benjamin's angel of history a baroque pearl,[3] Calderón's puzzling drama, *El Tuzaní de la Alpujarra*. This work (its title in the 1682 Vera Tassis edition is

---

[1] Manuel Barrios Aguilera, *Granada morisca, la convivencia negada. Historia y textos* (Granada: Editorial Comares, 2002), p. 39, citing M. Garrido Atienza, *Las capitulaciones para la entrega de Granada* (Granada: Universidad de Granada, 1992), pp. 273–4.

[2] For an up-to-date bibliography of the abundant work on the history of the *moriscos*, see Barrios Aguilera.

[3] Walter Benjamin, *Illuminations. Essays and Reflections*, trans. Harry Zohn, ed. Hannah Arendt (New York: Schocken Books, 1968), pp. 257–8. The 'baroque pearl' is my adaptation of Hannah Arendt's use of the metaphor, pp. 33–51 *passim*, from Shakespeare's *The Tempest*.

Amar después de la muerte) has long intrigued me.[4] Why would Calderón –
famous for his service to the Catholic faith in his *autos sacramentales* long
before he was ordained a priest in 1651 – write a work that from its first lines
conveys much sympathy for a rebellious Granadine *morisco* population, decades
after their final expulsion from Spain between 1609 and 1614?

To understand the politics of cultural memory at work in and around this
baroque pearl, I will explore the intersections of multiple facets: (1)
constructions of space that Calderón deploys successively in the text; (2) the
bodies – individual, fictional, communal or corporate – those spaces
convoke; (3) laws of religion, of state and of class invoked; and (4) the
layered dialogues in time of his work with the events it portrays, the era of its
probable composition, and our contemporary readings of both. I will begin
with time, as the most direct path to answering the 'why' question of
Calderón's composition of this tragedy and my reading of it. Then, turning to
the issue of how he could communicate sympathy for the *morisco* rebels to his
audience, I will focus on spaces and bodies – on the dramatic spaces he
constructs, the fictional bodies he deploys therein, and the manner in which that
intersection interpellates the body of the audience, individually and collectively.
Last, I will consider the subject of law and of naming practice by which
Calderón inscribes characters under those laws in *El Tuzaní* and other dramas
centred on Christian–Muslim relations over the length of his career, to argue for
the legitimacy of reading a dissenting practice in this very Catholic author.

Calderón's dramatization of the history of the Alpujarras rebellion was a
post-figuration of its significance from the world he inhabited, a use of
history common to other dramas of his era, in Spain as in England. Jonathan
Boyarin proposes that memory, too, is a 'creative collaboration between
present consciousness and the experience of expression of the past.'[5] The
past itself, in Benjamin's poetic formulation, turns like a sunflower toward
the power of the rising sun of history (p. 255). Given the long ascendance of
a unified and religiously purified Catholicism as the ideological solar power
of early modern Spain, is it feasible to read a sympathy for *morisco* rebels in a
drama Calderón apparently penned in the 1630s, the same decade in which he
was awarded the habit of the Order of Santiago for his service to the Catholic

---

4   The play was first published in the defective *Quinta parte* of Calderón, which he
disowned as plagued with errors; the second title, taken from the penultimate line of the play,
appeared in the Juan de Vera Tassis edition of 1682, along with other alterations and significant omissions. Vera Tassis was much given to 'correcting' Calderón texts according to his
own criteria. Pedro Calderón de la Barca, *El Tuzaní de la Alpujarra*, ed. Manuel Ruiz Lagos
(Alcalá de Guadaira (Sevilla): Editorial Guadalmena, 1998), pp. 56–70. Quotations from the
play will be from this edition.
5   Jonathan Boyarin, 'Space, Time, and the Politics of Memory,' in *Remapping
Memory: The Politics of TimeSpace*, ed. Jonathan Boyarin (Minneapolis: University of Minnesota Press, 1994), p. 22.

monarchy with his court plays and *autos sacramentales*?[6] Political treatises and emblem books of early modern Spain insisted repeatedly that religious unity was the basis of national unity, an argument still reiterated by Bernardo Blanco-González to defend the expulsion of Jews and Moors in his introduction to Diego Hurtado de Mendoza's *Guerra de Granada* during the last year's of Franco's Spain.[7]

Official documents of the era and most histories have reported that the expulsion of the *moriscos* received substantial popular support in 1609 and only limited criticism during Philip III's reign.[8] Recent investigations indicate, however, that as Márquez Villanueva pointed out, that support was far from unanimous (see the first chapter in this volume) and the expulsion much less than complete.[9] Although technically there were no more Muslims on Spanish soil after 1526, when forced conversion or expulsion had been extended to all Spanish realms, opponents of the *moriscos* argued that true conversion and acculturation were limited, particularly in concentrated *morisco* areas and among the lower classes. Christian repression – religious, cultural, and economic – and *morisco* resistance, banditry and Mediterranean piracy had produced a climate of mutual suspicion and resentment, augmented by Christian fears that the *moriscos* constituted a fifth column within Spain that could or did conspire with Turks and/or French Huguenots to invite an invasion. Whatever the balance of truth at the time, by the decade of the 1630s, a good number of Spaniards saw the expulsion in another light, in view of its economic consequences. In 1633, the royal confessor Antonio de Sotomayor wrote: 'Muy poco tiempo ha que se hizo la expulsión de los moriscos, que causó en estos reinos tales daños que fuera bien tornarlos a recibir, si ellos se allanaran a recibir nuestra Santa Fe.'[10]

A.A. Parker and Anne Cruz have linked Calderón's inspiration to another question of that decade – the status of the Portuguese *conversos* and the

---

6   The date regularly cited for the play is 1633, which, as Parker points out, citing María Grazia Profeti, is based on an erroneous Cotarelo y Mori interpretation of the title *Mas puede amor que la muerte* performed that year. Alexander A. Parker, *The Mind and Art of Calderón: Essays on the Comedia* (Cambridge: CUP, 1988), p. 403. Parker too suggests 1632–3, as the period of the discussion of the status of the Portuguese *conversos* he advances as having inspired Calderón's writing of the play (p. 320). The decade of the 1630s or early 1640s remains the most probable, as the theatres were closed between 1644 and 1649, and Calderón ceased writing for the playhouses in 1651 although he continued to write court plays and *autos*. *La niña de Gómez Arias*, a related *comedia*, is thought to date from around 1637–8.

7   He maintains that, albeit for different reasons, neither Jews nor Moors were entitled to legal existence in Spain: *Guerra de Granada* (Madrid: Castalia, 1970), pp. 54–5.

8   Antonio Domínguez Ortiz and Bernard Vincent, *Historia de los moriscos. Vida y tragedia de una minoría* (Madrid: Alianza, 1984), pp. 24–5.

9   Francisco Márquez Villanueva, *El problema morisco (desde otras laderas)* (Madrid: Ediciones Libertarias, 1991), pp. 4–6.

10   J.H. Elliott, *La España imperial: 1469–1716*, trans. J. Marfany, 5th edn (Barcelona: Vicens Vives, 1986), p. 335.

debate during the decade prior to Portugal's 1640 secession from the Habsburg monarchy between those who recommended giving the *conversos* a general pardon and those who advocated their expulsion. That link should certainly not be ruled out. Although the worsening *morisco* 'problem' had not served to alleviate that of the *conversos* by bringing about an elimination of the blood purity statutes in the sixteenth century as *conversos* had hoped,[11] the economic consequences of the *morisco* expulsion in the seventeenth might dissuade policy makers from another blow to the economy.

A more direct and immediate inspiration, however, could well have been provided by the 1632 transportation of the 'Libros Plúmbeos' and the Torre Turpiana parchment to Madrid and their exhibition over the following decade beside the high altar of the Iglesia de San Jerónimo, as Thomas Case has pointed out.[12] In 1588, during the demolition of the Torre Turpiana, which had been the minaret of the principal mosque in Granada, a worker found amid the rubble a tablet with an image of the Virgin Mary painted on it and a lead box that contained a parchment with a prophetic text written in Arabic, Latin, Greek, and Spanish, a cloth supposedly used by the Virgin to dry Christ's tears, and a bone said to be that of the protomartyr St Stephen. Relics purporting to be the remains of other martyrs and saints, including the bones of Granada's patron saint, San Cecilio, were found between 1595 and 1599 in caves in the hill of Valparaíso on the outskirts of the city, as well as a series of round lead plates, linked together to form something akin to books and inscribed in a 'salomonic' form of Arabic. The books, 'miraculously' discovered in Granada, were supposedly written by San Cecilio and his brother, San Tesifón, apostolic disciples of Arab origin, who served as transmitters of messages from the Virgin or Spain's patron saint, Santiago.

The discoveries in the caves of Valparaíso – renamed the Sacromonte – quickly became the focus of a cult of popular devotion and also the centre of a controversy over their authenticity. Their most tenacious defender was the archbishop of Granada, Pedro de Castro, Vaca y Quiñones, who founded an abbey on the Sacromonte where the *Libros Plúmbeos* were placed at the high altar of the collegial church. Archbishop Castro and his allies resisted for decades the efforts of several popes to have the books transferred to Rome to be judged by papal authorities. A decade after his death in 1623, they were transported to Madrid and given a similarly prominent display, by the San Jerónimo altar, again generating considerable popular interest. There they remained

---

[11] As Márquez Villanueva points out, the *converso* intelligentsia thought that the *moriscos* could be assimilated: 'Dejarán su pertinacia sólo si se les abren las *honras*, al menos en sus escalones ínfimos, y si se reconociera el trabajo como valor social antepuesto a la casta y a las exclusiones apriorísticas. La España que deseara asimilar a sus moriscos tendría así que desmantelar, a la larga, todo el sistema de Inquisición, estatutos y menosprecio de la actividad productiva' (p. 23).

[12] Thomas Case, 'Honor, Justice, and Historical Circumstance in *Amar después de la muerte*,' *Bulletin of the Comediantes*, 36 (1984), 55–69.

another decade, as disputes dragged on over who should examine and judge them, the *Consejo Real*, a special *junta*, the Spanish or the Roman Inquisition. The books were dispatched to Rome in 1642, where another forty years passed before they were finally declared falsifications in 1682. The books, which contain a syncretic blend of Christian and Islamic doctrine, were almost certainly prepared and hidden by *moriscos* attempting thereby to avoid expulsion and assure the survival of their culture. They were probably the work of two assimilated *moriscos*, Miguel de Luna and Alonso del Castillo, who served as translators for the Crown, perhaps with collaboration of figures from the Church in Granada who, like Archbishop Castro, were fervent defenders of the Immaculate Conception of the Virgin, a thesis included in the books' messages. Despite the opposition of several distinguished scholars, the books and relics were accepted as legitimate and highly significant for a good number of Christians. As A. Katie Harris puts it:

> For Granada's Old Christian majority [. . .] the finds became key elements in the process by which Granada, the emblematic city of Spanish Islam, was transformed into a model Christian city. The relics and the writings of their patron saint enabled Granadinos to imagine themselves as the legitimate heirs to an ancient and now restored Christian heritage.[13]

Thus, Madrid by the 1630s afforded the conjunction of space and time for reshaping the collective memory of the *morisco* revolt, with the *Libros Plúmbeos* on display, a new regime in place, a longer view of the consequences of expulsion, and the question of the Portuguese *conversos* in debate. In M.A. de Bunes' words, 'La resolución de 1609 empieza a pesar como una gran losa sobre la conciencia de los españoles e, incluso, se considera injusta e innecesaria la deportación de cerca de 400,000 habitantes de la peninsula.'[14] Three accounts of the Alpujarras uprising had been published, whose titles alone give a first indication of their differing perspectives: *Historia de la rebelión y castigo de los moriscos* (Málaga, 1600) by Luis del Mármol Carvajal; *Guerra de Granada* (Lisbon, 1627) by Diego Hurtado de Mendoza; and Calderón's principal source, the *Guerras civiles de Granada* by Ginés Pérez de Hita (1619?).[15]

Barbara Simerka suggests in *Discourses of Empire* that historical drama emerged at the end of the sixteenth century as a new form, an indeterminate genre that facilitated the expression of conflicting ideologies, a counter-epic discourse and a critique of the military ideology dominant in Spain.[16] Simerka

---

[13] 'The Sacromonte and the Geography of the Sacred in Early Modern Granada', *Al-Qantara. Revista de estudios árabes*, 23:2 (2002), 517–43 (p. 518).

[14] *Los moriscos en el pensamiento histórico* (Madrid: Cátedra, 1983), p. 22.

[15] *Segunda parte de las guerras civiles de Granada*, ed. Joaquín Gil Sanjuan (Granada: Editorial Universidad de Granada, 1998). It may have appeared in 1604, 1610 or 1612, but the surviving editions date from 1619.

[16] *Discourses of Empire: Counter-Epic Literature in Early Modern Spain* (University Park, PA: Pennsylvania State UP, 2003).

draws on Phyllis Rackin's study of Shakespeare's Tudor history plays, in which Rackin points out the parallel between the historiographic debates in the sixteenth and the end of the twentieth centuries. Both eras debated questions of evidence and legitimate witnesses, the possibility of acceding to 'true' history, and the problem of anachronistic readings. A foremost concern in the sixteenth century was that of causality. Was the motor of history divine providence or a more-or-less Machiavellian individualism? What was the impact of will and individual actions? The attitudes of the three principal chroniclers of the Alpujarras rebellion differ on that question, reflecting both their personal experience of the rebellion and their social position.

Mármol, son of a scribe to the *Audiencia* in Granada, a soldier-historian with many years of service in North Africa, including six years of captivity to the Moors, and a military bureaucrat charged with overseeing supplies for the army of Don Juan de Austria, wrote a minutely detailed and well-documented account that exhibits a fully providential conception of history 'donde Dios y el Rey están siempre del mismo lado' (l. 11).[17]

Pérez de Hita, a shoemaker by trade, is more ambivalent on the question of causality; on one hand, he underlines divine - or demoniac - causality. Not even a leaf moves without God's will, he says (*Segunda parte*, p. 2); the 'Moors,' in taking up arms against Philip II's 1567 decrees, were

> incitados de una infernal furia y movimiento, predominando sobre ellos algún furor celeste. Porque se entiende no poder ser menos este movimiento, sino que el sangriento Marte se moviesse a les incitar, haciéndoles tomar armas y tender vanderas contra las christianas legiones, baxando al furioso infierno, y despertar a la cruda guerra que ya olvidada estava y descuydada del bullicio de las armas. (*Segunda parte*, p. 4)

On the other hand, he blames individual words and actions as the efficient cause of the rebels' withdrawal to the Alpujarras, describing a confrontation between Fernando Muley, the Granada *morisco* who would be elected king of the rebels as Abenhumeya and Pedro Maza, *veinticuatro* of Granada, when Fernando removed his sword but not his dagger on entering municipal chambers:

> Esta desazón, y las demás que antes hemos contado, fueron parte para que el reino se levantase. Maldita sea la daga, y malditas las demás ocasiones de que tantos males resultaron, y tanto derramamiento de sangre cristiana en las civiles guerras que se tuvieron, y que así pueden llamarse; pues fueron cristianos contra cristianos, todos dentro de una ciudad y de un reino. (*Segunda parte*, p. 10)

---

[17] *Historia del rebelión y castigo de los moriscos del reino de Granada*, ed. Angel Galán (Málaga: Editorial Arguval, 1991), pp. 8–11.

Hurtado de Mendoza, younger son in the powerful family that had passed the Captaincy General of Granada from father to son since its reconquest, was a humanist by education and a disciple of Tacitus in his chronicle, in which he criticized government by *letrados* full of ambition and lacking military experience, rather than a military aristocracy. He makes occasional passing reference to divine providence, but concentrates on very human errors of judgment. In thus providing two explanations of historical causality, Pérez de Hita and Hurtado de Mendoza adopt the same practice as English historians of the age and various characters in Shakespeare's historical dramas. They displayed the two possibilities before their public, leaving to them the relative value of the two motors of history.

Going one step beyond them, Calderón neither invokes the power of divine providence nor pays much attention to religion in dramatizing the conflict. Rather, he centres on a debatable political decision and a complex of individual actions. He distributes responsibility for the tragedy between *moriscos* and Christians, from the most humble to the highest rank.

Calderón's use of space within this drama plays an important role in transmitting to his Madrid public an almost visceral comprehension of the experience of the *moriscos* who rebelled and the Christian forces challenging their mountain stronghold. Space in drama is by nature always double: the literal space of the stage, occupied by actors, and the virtual space evoked in the imagination of the audience through words, with or without the help of scenery and iconic objects on stage. To appreciate the efficacy with which Calderón manipulates that double space, we should consider the three-stage process by which human beings develop a concept of space. Roger Hart describes what he calls the phenomenological landscape of children and their attitude toward their environment – their spatial behaviour, use of space, and the perception of space they develop by means of negotiations with parents and other authority figures. The first stage is an egocentric space of action; the second, a topographic concept of space – the capacity to draw the route from home to school, for example; and the third, that of the adult, is an abstract concept of space, seen from a Euclidean or metric perspective, as in Mercator-style maps. The more advanced concepts of space do not displace the earlier ones, however. Both the space and time of the child continue active in the adult, as the source of desire, of individuality, of patterns of behaviour, and psychic symptoms.

With the first words of the play, Cadí's question, '¿Están cerradas las puertas?' (l. 1). Calderón opens the drama by evoking the intimate space of a house, the space of our first human identifications – and of our primordial fears, one of which is the fear of seeing that intimate space invaded. The actors' attire, specified in Calderón's first stage direction, has already signalled wordlessly that it is a *morisco* residence: 'Salen todos los *moriscos* que pudieren, vestidos a la morisca, jaquetillas y calzoncillos, y las Moriscas en jubones blancos, con instrumentos.' The invaders they fear are Christian, the

officials charged with punishing violations of Philip II's edict banning the use of
morisco dress and traditional ceremonies – and requiring that *moriscos* keep the
doors of their houses open to prevent secret violations, such as singing and
dancing the *zambra* that follows. Insistent knocking on the door interrupts their
celebration, and while Cadí, whose name means 'judge,' speaks of edicts and
justice, codes and enforcers of the symbolic order, it is the *gracioso* Alcuzcuz
who pronounces that basic fear with all its corporality. Saying 'Pues ya escampa'
(l. 37), he abbreviates an ironic expression that in its unspoken continuation, '¡y
llovían guijarros!', presages trouble, which he suspects will strike the centre of
his physical identity:

> Al abrir del porta, temo
> que ha de darme con la estaca
> cien palos el alguacil
> en barriga, a ser desgracia
> que en barriga de Alcuzcuz
> el leña, y no alcuzcuz haya. (ll. 48–53)

The report of the caller, Don Juan Malec, transports the spectator/reader to a
public space, that of the city council chambers, to witness with the listening
moriscos his story of the reading of the edict, his protest against of the cultural
violence of its application, and the abuse then heaped on him and his people by a
Christian nobleman, Don Juan de Mendoza. The *morisco* nobleman, in contrast
with Alcuzcuz, cannot articulate the physical affront he has suffered at
Mendoza's hands, an offense he says touches them all:

> ¡Mal haya ocasión; mal haya
> sin espadas y con lenguas,
> que son las peores armas,
> pues una herida mejor
> se cura que una palabra!
> Alguna quizá le dije
> que obligase a su arrogancia
> a que (aquí tiemblo al decirlo)
> tomándome (¡pena extraña!)
> el báculo de las mano;
> con esto basta, esto basta;
> que hay cosas que cuestan más
> el decirlas que el pasarlas. (ll. 156–67)

Later in the act, Calderón places us in a virtual space that is both private
and public, as Don Álvaro Tuzaní proposes marriage to Doña Clara Malec,
taking upon himself the obligation of redressing her father's dishonour by
Mendoza. He hides as her father and other *morisco* notables arrive and we
listen with him as they propose marriage between Doña Clara and Mendoza.
Calderón then repeats this divided scene with Isabel, the Tuzaní's sister, in love

with Mendoza, hiding in his house as he duplicates his insults to the *morisco* nobles in rejecting such a mixed marriage that would sully his Christian nobility with Moorish blood. These parallel scenes are more than the standard dilemmas of the *comedia*, in which lovers regularly hide when fathers or brothers arrive inconveniently. Here, they dramatize a hardening of policy and changed attitude toward mixed marriages, which had been considered a key to assimilating *moriscos* in the reign of Charles I. From 1568 on, such marriages were disapproved of in favour of more radical policies aimed at eliminating this minority.

The virtual space with which Calderón opens the second act is a polar opposite of the intimate household space of the first. Now he places us before the mountain stronghold of the *morisco* rebels, the Alpujarra, alongside Christian forces charged with ending their rebellion, here represented by Don Juan de Mendoza and Don Juan de Austria. The latter, now charged by his half-brother the King with putting down the rebellion, angrily challenges the 'rebelada montaña',

> . . . infame ladronera
> que de abortados rayos de tu esfera
> das, preñados de escándalos tus senos,
> aquí la voz y en África los truenos. (ll. 878, 884–6)

Not only is this an external vision of the Alpujarra, but also a reminder to the spectator of the short distance that separates it from the feared assistance of North African Berber soldiers and Turkish troops. Don Juan de Mendoza extends the external panorama of this formidable natural fortress, this

> rústica muralla
> [. . .] bárbara defensa
> [. . .] por su altura difícil
> fragosa por su aspereza,
> por su sitio inexpugnable
> e invencible por sus fuerzas. (ll. 934–43)

drawing a topographic map that paints the region from a bird's-eye view:

> Catorce leguas en torno
> tiene, en catorce leguas
> más de cincuenta que añade
> la distancia de las quiebras,
> porque entre puntas y puntas
> hay valles que la hermosean,
> campos que la fertilizan,
> jardines que la deleitan. (ll. 944–52)

But if the Alpujarra is a formidable fortress, Calderón also makes it a metaphorically unstable space. Various characters call it a labyrinth, as Diane

Sieber notes.[18] In her reading of the play, the labyrinth is symbolically linked to that of Crete in which Theseus slays the Minotaur – not the rebellious *morisco* community, but the fierce Christian soldier Garcés, who kills Clara (Maleca) for her jewels, and is in turn slain by el Tuzaní. As various critics have observed, the sierra is visually compared to the sea three times: first, a lovely sea in the eyes of Don Juan Malec,

> . . . aquesta sierra
> que al sol la cerviz levanta,
> y que poblada de villas,
> es mar de peñas y plantas,
> adonde sus poblaciones,
> ondas navegan de plata,
> por quien nombres las pusieron
> de Galera, Berja y Gabia,   (ll. 180–7)

second, an unstable sea in Mendoza's image of Galera as a galley moving with the wind on a sea of peaks and waves of flowers (ll. 1702–5); and, finally, in Don Juan de Austria's projected desire, a sea-space in which to repeat his naval victory at Lepanto:

> Dadme, cielos
> fortuna, como en el agua,
> en la tierra, porque opuestos
> aquella naval batalla
> y este cerco campal, luego
> pueda decir que en la tierra
> y en el mar tuve en un tiempo
> dos victorias, que, confusas,
> aun no distinga yo mesmo,
> de un cerco y una naval,
> cuál fue la naval o el cerco.   (ll. 1803–13)

Thus, Calderón gives us a space that has been undermined in the imaginary even before the explosives ignite.

For the spectator with an abstract concept of space, Calderón suggests the European extension of Spanish forces, as troops arrive from different parts of the monarchy: from Granada, those of the Marqués de Mondéjar, from Murcia, troops led by the Marqués de los Vélez, from Baeza, with Sancho de Ávila, and from Flanders, those commanded by Don Lope de Figueroa. Thus he paints for the audience an image of the extended power of the Spanish

---

[18] Diane M. Sieber, 'El monstruo en su laberinto: cristianos en las Alpujarras de *Amar después de la muerte*' in *Actas del XIII Congreso de la Asociación Internacional de Hispanistas*, 4 vols (Madrid: Castalia, 2000), I, pp. 740–6.

Habsburg monarchy uniting its forces to turn them against the focal point of internal dissent, what Mendoza labels the 'doméstico enemigo' (l. 927). He brings them all together at one point in time and space and in harmony, a utopian view, given that Calderón knew from reading Pérez de Hita and Hurtado de Mendoza that significant tensions and rivalries between Mondéjar and Vélez and Don Juan de Austria had in reality hindered their unity of action.

In narrating this union of forces, Calderón makes another significant temporal modification of the historical record, putting Don Juan's 1671 victory in Lepanto ahead of the defeat of the *moriscos*. He preserves, however, the sequence between his Alpujarras campaign and that of Flanders of 1576–8, evoked in *El Tuzaní* in an exchange with Don Lope de Figueroa:

> D. Juan   ¿Cómo llegáis?
> D. Lope   Como quien
>   Señor, a serviros llega
>   de Flandes a Andalucía;
>   y no es mala diligencia,
>   pues vos a Flandes no vais,
>   que Flandes a vos se venga
> D. Juan   Cúmplame el Cielo esa dicha (ll. 1212–7)

Rearranging the sequence in this fashion, he makes Don Juan progress from a decisive victory that halted the eastward advance of the Turks, to a pyrrhic victory over the *morisco* rebels, one which he says is 'matar y no vencer,' to failure in his attempts to pacify the rebellion in Flanders. In so doing, Calderón avails himself of the creative and didactic freedom that Alonso López Pinciano and other *preceptistas* of early modern Spain, following Aristotle, credited with making poetry superior to history. In terms of the politics of memory, this is a present–past dialogue in which his drama engages present understanding with events of the past, reordering them to distinguish between a war against an aggressive external enemy and wars against internal subjects of the monarchy who follow another religious law.

Law, *ley*, is the term used repeatedly in the drama to denote religious faith and affiliation; from the opening *zambra*:

> *Cantan:*   Aunque en triste cautiverio
>   de Alá, por justo misterio,
>   llore el africano imperio
>   su mísera suerte esquiva
> Todos (*Cantando*):   ¡Su ley viva!

In effect, however, there are two laws, two fundamental codes and two axes of division that operate in *El Tuzaní*, religious law and that of caste or class, each intersecting at key points with a third law, that of the state.[19] Calderón's drama reveals the intersection of what Anthony Cascardi calls the two historical axiologies of early modern Spain, that which Américo Castro saw as that of the three religions, and the descriptions of social estates of Maravall, Marx, Weber and Foucault.[20] According to Cascardi, they represent the clash of incompatible modes of socio-historical orientation, one based on traditional hierarchies and their caste values, the other on the structure of social classes. Writers of the 'Golden Age', he says, usually transmitted a vision of history oriented toward a past or a future that produced imaginary worlds in which this clash was effaced, thus resisting social transformation – in the happy endings that were the general rule in the *comedia*. But in *El Tuzaní*, they are not erased; they cross, with tragic consequences.

The key third term that provokes the tragedy is a change in state policy. Although official ideology portrayed the primary aim of the state, the Spanish Catholic monarchy, as that of upholding Catholicism, in practice the two laws were imperfectly harmonized. The religious and cultural tolerance guaranteed by the 1491 Capitulations in part reflected a Peninsular history of *convivencia*, but also the more strategic state goal of securing the surrender of the last stronghold of Arabic Spain. The balance soon shifted to give religious law priority with the beginning of forcible conversions in 1501. During Charles I's reign, there was a tacit, if see-sawing, balancing of the two laws, with state law increasingly specifying obligatory conversion and assimilation but with officials in practice often turning a blind eye to non-compliance with the statutes. Philip II's pragmatic specifying the strict enforcement of the statutes radically shifted that balance toward religious law, classifying any cultural deviation from the Christian norm in codes such as dress or language as indicative if not productive of religious impurity. That shift in state policy also impinged on the operation of the less-codified but powerful class law. Upper-class *moriscos* who had converted prior to 1492 and cooperated with Ferdinand and Isabel had long been exempted from the ban on carrying arms and from paying the *farda* tax levied on *morisco* communities, and a number had occupied municipal or other administrative offices (Barrios Aguilera, p. 137), as does Calderón's *veinticuatro*, Juan Malec, a character based on a compound of two historical figures, Francisco Núñez Muley and Jerónimo el Maleh (Calderón, *Tuzaní*, p. 93, n. 55). The 1567 pragmatic and the consequent rebellion did threaten at

---

[19] My classification is a pragmatic description of the laws operant in the drama. Political theorists of the era would classify the three types of law as divine, human, and natural law; see Stephen Rupp, *Allegories of Kingship: Calderón and the Anti-Machiavellian Tradition* (University Park, PA: Pennsylvania State UP, 1996). The institution and conservation of hierarchy, my third 'law', was included by different theorists as a part of divine, natural, or human law; see ch. 3 in José Antonio Maravall, *Teoría del estado en España en el Siglo XVII* (Madrid: Centro de Estudios Constitucionales, 1997).

[20] Anthony J. Cascardi, *Ideologies of History in the Spanish Golden Age* (University Park, PA: Pennsylvania State UP, 1997), pp. 1–3.

least for a time even such assimilated upper-class 'New Christian' *moriscos* in Granada who did not join the rebellion. Like Calderón's Don Juan de Mendoza, many Old Christians considered Moorish ancestry, however exalted, an almost irradicable stain (Domínguez Ortiz and Vincent, pp. 89–90). It is, however, ironic that Calderón should make a Mendoza, of the house of the Marqués de Mondejar (ll. 114–16), the spokesman for this insult, on two counts: (1) though there was regional variation, anti-*morisco* sentiment tended to be most concentrated among the lower classes, resentful of their protection by aristocratic landholders who valued their agricultural skills, diligence, and willingness to work for low wages; and (2) the Mendoza family generally favored the maintenance of the status quo concerning the *moriscos*, and the least punitive quelling of the rebellion.[21]

As Dámaris Otero Torres points out, Calderón dramatizes the contradictions and injustices of a violent policy of ethnic and religious inclusion and exclusion, while implicitly upholding the 'truth' of the law of class.[22] On the one hand, he creates sympathy for the ethnic minority, contrasting the nobility of spirit and action of the descendents of the old aristocratic *morisco* families with the quite negative portrayal of Don Juan de Mendoza. At the same time, he maintains an image of an unassimilated *morisco* lower class in Alcuzcuz, an object of laughter for his audience and also a human subject on which base human interests are projected. Along with corporeal fear and the weakness of the flesh he displays in getting roaring drunk on Garcés's 'veneno' (wine), he exhibits the economic interest of the small merchant who sees in the retreat to the Alpujarra a 'negociazo' for his 'tendecilia,' reciting with delight the array of merchandise that he will carry there on his back, and social ambition, which leads him to anticipate that this little store will move him up the social ladder:

> me he de ver, si llegan
> a colmo mis esperanzas,
> de todos los Alcuzcuces,
> marqués, conde o duque. (ll. 322–5)

Calderón's noble characters confess economic preoccupations as well, channeled in modes coherent with their social status: the Tuzaní laments that his poverty has kept him from proposing to Clara until Malec's dishonour

---

[21] Don Juan claims the superiority of his descent from the 'montañas de Castilla,' the stronghold of Old Christian pride as the cradle of the Reconquest (ll. 810–31). Garcés says that a New Christian like Malec has no right to challenge a 'González de Mendonza' (ll. 569–72); see Ruiz Lagos's notes to these lines.

[22] Dámaris Otero Torres, 'Amor y silencio: Ecos del discurso minoritario en *Amar después de la muerte*', in *El escritor y la escena VII: Estudios sobre teatro español y novohispano de los Siglos de Oro. El espectador y el crítico: problemas de recepción*, ed. Ysla Campbell (Ciudad Juárez: Universidad Autonóma de Ciudad Juárez, 2000), pp. 195–203.

gave him the chance to take on that offense as a negative dowry. Don Juan de Mendoza praises the *moriscos'* agricultural skills, for which the great Andalusian landlords had opposed their expulsion. And Don Lope de Figueroa, in possession of la Maleca's pearl necklace, describes the abundance of the sack of Galera, recycling both the myth of the *moriscos'* wealth and suggesting the actual motivation of many of the Christian soldiers enlisting in the Alpujarras campaign. Of course Don Lope makes clear that he did not take her pearls, but bought them from the Christian foot-soldier, Garcés.

Calderón makes the gulf that separates noble from commoner wider than that which divides Christians from *moriscos*. Once he has changed his dress, the Tuzaní can pass unnoticed among Christian forces,[23] and he reassures a fearful Alcuzcuz, as uncomfortable in Christian dress as in Castilian language, that he too will pass unnoticed, not because of his cultural assimilation but because of his social inconsequence: 'en fin, en un criado/ ninguno reparará' (ll. 2541–2). Such assurance does nothing to relieve Alcuzcuz's fear of meeting Garcés, from whose captivity he has escaped. It is not fortuitous that Calderón criss-crosses the fortunes of Alcuzcuz and Garcés. Although he claims to be ambitious for honour, not for gain, Calderón makes Garcés the incarnation of the most destructive passions of war, greed, lust, and the desire for revenge, as well as racial–religious prejudice. This characterization is in fact relatively accurate in an era in which military service was no longer the distinctive province of aristocrats and their subjects, but depended on an army populated by mercenary soldiers and ill-paid (or unpaid) draftees. The army was left halfway between a professional, disciplined force and one which depended on anticipation of its share of enemy wealth and captives, something which both Pérez de Hita and Hurtado de Mendoza condemn as a factor that enlarged the rebellion, provoking otherwise peaceful *morisco* communities to join it.

While difference of class marks his characters more distinctly and permanently than religious difference, we should not read the evidence of Calderón's sympathy for the *moriscos* in this drama as indicating any acceptance of tolerance for Islam. In his 1629 drama *El príncipe constante*, he makes the fifteenth-century Portuguese prince Fernando a heroic martyr who elects degradation and death in captivity over liberty in exchange for the cession of Christian Ceuta, and whose impassioned oratory rejects the surrender of Catholic churches and souls to the devil. And Dorotea in *La niña de Gómez Arias* (1637–8?), sold to the bandit Cañeri by her faithless Christian lover, rejects conversion with equal determination. Rather, the target of his critique in *El Tuzaní* is, as Antonio Regalado argues, a reason of state that justifies the use of any means to achieve its end, exemplified in this play in the brutal repression

---

[23] Pérez de Hita, Calderón's source, explains that Álvaro was raised among Christians (p. 297), but Calderón, by omitting that explanation, naturalizes the invisibility of religious difference.

carried out by an arrogant Don Juan de Austria and the troops under his command (ll. 837–8). In Alcuzcuz's comically biblical mode, 'En vano llama a la puerta / quien no ha llamado en el alma' (ll. 40–1).

Just how could Christianity effectively 'call in the soul'? Calderón's naming practice in this and related plays on Muslim–Christian relations affords an entry to his stand on religious conversion. His practice functions in accord with Slavoj Zizek's version of Saul Kripke's anti-descriptivism. This holds that the identity of an object does not derive from the meaning of a word designating a cluster of descriptive features and referring to objects in the real world possessing those features, but is rather the discursive construction of the object, 'the retroactive effect of naming itself'.[24] In *El Tuzaní*, Mendoza spells out the obvious significance of name changes marking the *morisco* reversion to open allegiance to Islam: Don Fernando Valor to Abenhumeya, King of the rebels; Doña Isabel Tuzaní to Lidora as his melancholy Queen consort; and Doña Clara Malec to Maleca. Less obvious but equally telling is Calderón's use of Juan for three principal characters; not only the historic Don Juan de Austria, but also Don Juan de Mendoza - who may or may not have an approximate historical referent, but whose confrontation with Don Juan Malec is based on an incident Pérez de Hita attributes to Don Pedro Maza – and most significantly, Malec himself, renamed Juan rather than Jerónimo (*Segunda parte*, pp. 8–12). Juan is, according to Tyler and Elizondo, Calderón's favorite name for noblemen and *caballeros*.[25] In Calderón's practice, I suggest, the name Juan constructs its holder as essentially Christian, just as renaming re-constructs the subject differently, as ordered under a different law.

A detour through two other names he employs, Isabel and Alcuzcuz, illustrates that naming practice. Isabel is a wholly fictional character, who first appears veiled in Mendoza's house, provoking his surprise at her arrival, veil and dress:

> ¡Isabel, señora!
> ¡Tú en mi casa, y tú en este
> traje, fuera de la tuya! (ll. 641–3)

She acknowledges that she comes disguised (l. 664), presumably in *morisco* attire, because Garcés hesitates to admit her. She will be renamed Lidora as Abenhumeya's wife and Queen, but at the play's end, as she reports his death

---

[24] Ernesto Laclau, 'Introduction' to Slavoj Zizek, *The Sublime Object of Ideology* (London: Verso, 1989), pp. xiii and xiv.

[25] Richard W. Tyler and Sergio D. Elizondo, *The Characters, Plots, and Settings of Calderón's Comedias* (Lincoln, NB: Society of Spanish and Spanish-American Studies, 1981), pp. 16–17.

and pleads for her brother's pardon along with the rest of the surrendering rebels, she will tell Don Juan de Austria:

> Doña Isabel Tuzaní
> soy, que aquí tiranizada
> viví ajustada en la voz
> y católica en el alma. (ll. 3199–3202).

In bringing the tragedy to what Ruiz Lagos considers an idealized 'happy ending' with a pardon and social reintegration (34–5) that effaces the forthcoming expulsion,[26] she effects a measure of poetic justice (for the Tuzaní and Alcuzcuz at least) that parallels the ending wrought by Queen Isabel la Católica in the contemporary *La niña de Gómez Arias*, when the Queen dictates the death of Cañeri and of Gómez Arias, once he has married the woman he had dishonoured and sold. The choice of 'Isabel,' a name Calderón rarely uses for noblewomen, subtly links her to the historic Queen Isabel, as a sincere Christian trapped by circumstances into 'adjusting' her name to the dictates of Islamic law.

Calderón gives us two other *graciosos* named Alcuzcuz, one in the *auto sacramental El cubo de la Almudena* of 1651, an *auto* shaped on the metaphor of the Bread of Life in a year characterized by famine and bread riots. The allegory conflates three moments of danger for Madrid and Iglesia (the union of the faithful in her living walls): a siege by Muslim forces against her centre (Toledo), the death of Alfonso VI, and the contemporary siege of hunger.[27] Alcuzcuz is a delightfully comic, cowardly foot-soldier for Spanish Islam, dispatched as a '*maxador*' (ambassador) to demand Iglesia's surrender, then caught in a dangerous battle, drunk on Christian 'poison' wine, and hopelessly tangled in the ladder he brings to breach her walls. Here, it is Alcuzcuz who 'calls at the door' of Iglesia, and it opens to him, saying:

> Pues de la paz la seña he visto,
> abriré, porque las puertas
> de la Iglesia no han sabido
> cerrarse jamás a quien
> con la seña de paz vino.[28]

---

[26] It is not a happy ending for Doña Isabel Tuzaní herself, however, as it provides no hint of marriage to the man she loves, Don Juan de Mendoza.

[27] See Margaret R. Greer, 'Constituting Community: A New Historical Perspective on the *Autos* of Calderón', in *New Historicism and the Comedia: Poetics, Politics and Praxis*, ed. José A. Madrigal (Boulder, CO: Society of Spanish and Spanish-American Studies, 1997). Spanish version in *Nuevo Historicismo*, eds Antonio Penedo and Gonzalo Pontón (Madrid: Arco/Libros, 1998).

[28] Pedro Calderón de la Barca, *El cubo de la Almudena*, in *Obras completas*, ed. Ángel Valbuena Prat, III (Madrid: Aguilar, 1952), p. 570.

That 'opening' is dramatized anew in one of his last dramas, *El gran príncipe de Fez, don Baltasar de Loyola*, on the conversion of Prince Muley Mohammed of Fez to Christianity in 1656. A highly symbolic drama, it gives us two scenarios for conversion, an intellectual conversion from within, and conversion inspired by a saintly model of faith. The first is that of Muley Mohammed, a noble military leader and intellectual seeking an answer for a question neither the Koran nor his teacher Cide Hamet can give him. Captured and awaiting ransom in Malta, he finds the answer when a book in the library of Don Baltasar de Mandas (of the order of San Juan) opens miraculously, as it did for St. Augustine. At baptism, he chooses the name Baltasar Loyola, for his wise host and for the Jesuit leader whose missionary efforts he intends to join. The second model converts our third Alcuzcuz, servant of Muley Mohammed. Rather than returning to Fez, he stays with his captured master, intending to be 'ni crestiano por el haz,/ ni moro por el revés, sino así, así, entre dos luces, cresti-moro,' in other words, a classic lower-class *morisco*.[29] But Calderón does not leave him in that condition; instead, as master and servant trek as pilgrims toward Loreto, the newly baptized Baltasar de Loyola performs the same operation verbally on Alcuzcuz, now renamed Juan:

> Esta, *Juan* (¡dichoso tú,
> cuya buena *ley* te alienta,
> [no] sólo a quedar conmigo,
> mas a pasarla de buena
> a mejor, pues de su gracia
> quiso que aun el *nombre* tengas!) (p. 1445) (my italics)

'In the beginning was the Word, and the Word was with God, and the Word was God' (John 1:1). If in Calderón's naming practice, 'Juan' reconstructs a coarsely materialistic Moor like this last Alcuzcuz as Christian,[30] I propose that implicit in the triple Juans of *El Tuzaní* is the message that Juan Malec was also Christian; and that conversion can only be brought about voluntarily, from within, or by the transformative effect of good spiritual models. A very different approach from that adopted by Philip II, Don Juan de Austria, and Don Juan de Mendoza toward the *moriscos* of Granada.

This power of naming and of the word also leads back to the *Libros Plúmbeos* and their possible role in Calderón's decision to write *El Tuzaní*. If these strange books in Arabic might perhaps be legitimate discoveries recovering an early harmony between Arabic and Christianity and pointing to the remains of Christian martyrs in the Sacromonte, then the whole policy of

---

[29] Pedro Calderón de la Barca, *El gran príncipe de Fez, Baltasar de Loyola*, in *Obras completas*, ed. Ángel Valbuena Briones, II (Madrid: Aguilar, 1959), pp. 1441–2.

[30] Not only Alcuzcuz converts, but thanks to one last miracle, Cide Hamet turns from trying to poison Baltasar Loyola for his treachery to Islam to following his law, and an incorrigibly picaresque soldier, Turin, vows to become a good Christian.

cultural genocide of the *moriscos* surely merited being remembered differently. I
suggest that both the fascination and the doubts about the *Libros Plúmbeos*
might offer the key for the curious conclusion of the drama. When Don Juan de
Austria pardons the Tuzaní in response to Isabel's plea, he does so saying that his
'amorosa hazaña' should remain written 'en los bronces del *olvido* y de la *fama*'
(ll. 3250–2, my italics). This is a curious oxymoron, as Otero Torres has noted.
But it is one that might be explained as a subtle reference to the lead plates that
composed those books, supposedly 'forgotten' for centuries, suddenly famous,
but still of uncertain legitimacy in Spanish history in Calderón's era. Like those
books, Calderón leaves the fate of the surviving *morisco* population suspended
in time, awaiting judgments present and yet to come.

'Seguid la guerra y renovad los daños':
Implicit Pacifism in Cervantes's *La Numancia*

JULES WHICKER

Cervantes's play, *La destruición de Numancia* probably dates from 1583 and draws on Ambrosio de Morales's continuation of Florián de Ocampo's *Crónica general de España* (1574–86) and Alonso de Guevara's *Epístolas familiares* (1539) to depict the fall of the last indigenous stronghold in the Celtiberian Wars (154–133 BC).[1] The opening scene of the play centres on the character and tactics of the Roman Consul Scipio Aemilianus Africanus (185–129 BC), who has been sent by the Roman Senate to pacify the fortified hilltop town of Numantia, whose inhabitants have risen in revolt against Roman rule. Scipio's decision to take the city by siege drives the Numantians to the most desperate actions and ultimately they resort to the destruction of their city and to self-annihilation.

Throughout Cervantes's play, the Numantians are repeatedly identified by the Romans, not only as *hispanos* but also as *españoles*, and the allegorical figures of España, El Río Duero, Guerra and Fama also support the idea of an intrinsic connection between the Numantians and the inhabitants of sixteenth-century Iberia.[2] Nevertheless, several studies of the play have justly

---

[1] Ambrosio de Morales (1513–91), *Los cinco libros postreros de la Corónica general de España/ que continuaua Ambrosio de Morales [. . .] prossiguiendo adelante la restauración de España, desde que se començó a ganar de los Moros, hasta el rey don Bermudo el tercero deste nombre . . .* (Alcalá: Juan Iñiguez de Lequerica, 1574). The portion of the *Crónica general de España* (books i–v) written by Morales' predecessor Florián de Ocampo (1495–1558) ends just prior to the Roman conquest of Hispania. Morales added eleven books (VI–XVII), which were published at Alcalá in three volumes in 1574 (books VI–X), 1577 (books XI–XII) and 1586 (books XIII–XVII). The uprising, resistance and fall of Numantia are related in book VIII of the first volume, which begins in 209 BC and covers the entire period of Roman rule. The themes of fame and glory, and his identification with the Numantians as Spaniards, are prominent in Morales's account: 'llega ya aquí la historia de *España* a lo más alto de *gloria y fama*, que en estos tiempos pudo subir: pues se ha de comenzar a escribir la guerra de los Romanos con *nuestros* Numantinos' (fol. 121), as is his attribution to them of particular qualities of courage and physical strength: 'el grande *esfuerzo* y *valentía* de los nuestros' (fol. 122 [my italics]).

[2] In *La Numancia*, itself the Numantians are referred to as 'Hispanos' by Scipio in ll. 126, 164, 323; by El Río Duero in l. 507; and by Guerra in ll. 1981, 1989. However,

observed that the Spaniards of Cervantes's day were more often the besiegers than the besieged and have drawn interesting parallels between the campaign waged against the Numantians by Cervantes's Scipio and those of Don Juan de Austria in the Alpujarras (Hermenegildo), García Hurtado de Mendoza in Chile (King), and the Duke of Alba in the Netherlands, specifically in relation to the sieges of Galera, and Haarlem.[3] In addition, Spaniards figure as besiegers in a number other *comedias*, among them Lope's *El asalto de Mastrique* and Calderón's *El sitio de Bredá*, yet as far as I am aware, only in *La Numancia* are they portrayed as the besieged.[4]

In Lope and Calderón's plays one is made aware of the existence of two distinct approaches to warfare, one of which is characterized by *fuerza* and the other by *prudencia*, though both claim to possess the virtue of *valor*. Clearly informed by Lipsian neo-stoicism on the one hand and by Machiavelli's *Art of War* on the other, both plays indicate that *fuerza* is only effective when governed by *prudencia* and emphasize the importance of rationality, discipline, military engineering, and artillery at least as much as they seek to reaffirm *fuerza* and *valor* as aspects of the Spanish national character.[5] These two concepts of military virtue are present in Cervantes's

Scipio also refers to them as as 'españoles' in ll. 115, 144, 2426, as do Teógenes in l. 547 and Caravino in l. 565. Line references are taken from *Miguel de Cervantes Saavedra: Obras Completas*, ed. Florencio Sevilla Arroyo and Antonio Rey Hazas (Centro de Estudios Cervantinos, 1993–95).

   3   See Alfredo Hermengildo, *La 'Numancia' de Cervantes*, Biblioteca de Crítica Literaria (Madrid: Sociedad General Española de Librería, 1976), and Carroll B. Johnson, 'La Numancia y la estructura de la ambigüedad cervantina', in *Cervantes: su obra y su mundo: Actas del I Congreso Internacional sobre Cervantes, Madrid, 1978*, ed. Manuel Criado del Val (Madrid: Edi-6, 1981), pp. 309–16. Johnson draws further historico-literary parallels: with the *Aeneid* and with the Roman siege of Masada in AD 66, whose inhabitants also committed mass suicide, raising the possibility that Cervantes may also have conceived of his Numantians as Trojans (Turks?) or Jews. See also Willard F. King, 'Cervantes's *Numancia* and Imperial Spain', *Modern Language Notes*, 94:2 (1979), 200–21 (p. 214). King makes a number of persuasive connections between Ercilla's *Araucana* and Cervantes's *Numancia*, especially as regards Canto XV of the *Primera Parte*, which deals with: 'la batalla, en la cual fueron muertos todos los Araucanos, sin querer ninguno dellos rendirse'; see Alonso de Ercilla, *La Araucana* (Salamanca: Domingo de Portonariis, 1569), p. 364. Taken together with the conflict most immediate to the composition of the play, Spain's annexation of Portugal, the set of historical parallels offered by Hermenegildo, Johnson and King comprehensively collapses Imperial Spain's attempts to define itself by its opposites.

   4   Other plays include Juan de la Cuesta's *El saco de Roma*, Lope's *El cerco de Santa Fe, El cerco de Viena por Carlos V* and the anonymously authored *El saco de Amberes*.

   5   See Jules Whicker, ' "La caballería bajo fuego": La representación de la virtud militar española en *El asalto de Mastrique* de Lope y *El sitio de Bredá* de Calderón', in *Calderón 2000: Homenaje a Kurt Reichenberger en su 80 cumpleaños. Actas del Congreso Internacional IV centenario del nacimiento de Calderón*, Universidad de Navarra, septiembre, 2000 (Kassel: Reichenberger, 2002), pp. 411–23.

play too, but as we shall see, Cervantes's treatment of them differs significantly from that of Lope or Calderón.

In *la Numancia*, therefore, Scipio – like Don Juan de Austria, García Hurtado de Mendoza and the Duke of Alba – is the representative of an imperial power, employing sophisticated military doctrines to succeed in his mission to subdue the revolt of a subject people in the interests of a greater imperial project. As such, his values are in line with the political and moral doctrines of Spanish rulers from Ferdinand the Catholic (who so impressed Machiavelli) to Philip IV. Consequently, his fears are also those of Counter-Reformation Spain: effeminacy and moral degeneracy leading to disorder, disobedience, and ruin. For Scipio, only those who live by his scheme of values deserve to call themselves Romans, and those who ignore or reject these values are despised as foreigners (ll. 71–72), barbarians (l. 164), or beasts (l. 1191) to be tamed (*domado*) by enforced confinement (l. 1192). This policy of restraint is also applied to his own soldiers, albeit with considerably less severity, as he berates them for their effeminacy and debauchery, decrees the expulsion of whores from the camp, bans luxuries such as beds, perfumes and feasting, and harangues them about the paramount importance of military discipline as a means to victory. Such ideas were of course repeatedly expressed in relation to Spanish national identity in the Golden Age, and even put in several appearances in the polemic regarding the moral legitimacy of the *comedia*.

Scipio's harangue seeks to restore discipline by reminding his men of their sense of manhood, national identity, and the glory of an empire whose martial character they are supposedly betraying by their pleasures. Although his speech relies heavily on an appeal to honour, and its counterpart shame, it does not do so exclusively, since it concludes with the promise of rewards more material than fame alone:

> os prometo por mi diestra y juro
> que, si igualáis al ánimo las manos
> que las mías se alarguen en pagaros,
> y mi lengua también en alabaros. (ll. 165–8)

Nevertheless, it proves an impressively effective means of galvanizing his troops to action, as his protégé Caius Marius subsequently reports:

> De hoy más, con presta voluntad y leda,
> el más mínimo de estos cuida y piensa
> de ofrecer sin revés a tu servicio
> la hacienda, vida, honra en sacrificio. (ll. 189–92)[6]

---

6   Caius Marius (155?–86 BC) subsequently rose to such prominence as a soldier and politician that his biography was included by Plutarch in his *Lives*.

However, as soon as Scipio begins to outline his battle plans to his brother, Quintus Fabius, it is apparent that the reality of this war will occupy their hands in a much less heroic form of physical activity, as they are set to work digging the ditches and ramparts for the siege:

> Ejercítense agora vuestras manos
> en romper y a cavar la dura tierra,
> y cubrirse de polvo los amigos
> que no lo están de sangre de enemigos. (ll. 325–8)[7]

Yet, for all the similarities between the Rome of Scipio and Counter-Reformation Spain, it is the Numantians and not the Romans who are explicitly identified in the play as 'Spaniards' and as representative of the essential character of the Iberian native.[8] The Numantians display values frequently represented in the *comedia*, and especially in military plays, as traditionally and innately Spanish, namely: physical courage and endurance, a passionate preoccupation with honour, a preference for demonstrating their valour through prowess in open combat, and, particularly in this play, an insistence on the supreme value of liberty. They also favour a form of politics that seeks to achieve unity through consensus in determining policies that are agreed rather than decreed, and here one is reminded of the numerous village councils and elections that appear in the *comedia* in general, and in particular of the unity of the villagers in *Fuenteovejuna*. In contrast to Scipio, who is depicted as solitary and without emotional ties, the Numantians are repeatedly represented in terms of fundamental social relationships: as council members, as comrades-in-arms, as friends, as lovers, and as husbands and wives, sons and daughters. The intimate and universal qualities of these relationships do more than illustrate the inequality of a war between an army and a people; they inevitably foster a degree of empathy with the Numantians on the part of the audience, a feeling that is re-enforced by the allegorical figures of España and El Río Duero. At the same time, the rocky hill on which the Numantians have built their citadel stands in strong contrast to the

---

[7]   The entire Roman force is to be occupied in this task, from its commander down: '[Scipión:] No quede de este oficio reservado/ ninguno que le tenga preeminente./ Trabaje el decurión como el soldado,/ y no se muestre en esto diferente./ Yo mismo tomaré el hierro pesado/ y romperé la tierra fácilmente./ Hacen todos cual yo; veréis que hago/ tal obra, con que a todos satisfago' (ll. 329–36). The attitude of Alejandro Farnese in Lope's *El asalto de Mastrique* closely resembles that of Cervantes's Scipio; see Lope de Vega, *El asalto de Mastrique*, in *Obras de Lope de Vega*, 27, *Crónicas y leyendas dramáticas de España*, ed. Marcelino Menéndez Pelayo, Biblioteca de autores españoles, 225 (Madrid: Atlas, 1969), pp. 1–59 (pp. 32b–33b).

[8]   History supports the identification the play inclines one to make between the soldiers of Roman army and those of Golden-Age Spain, because it records that two-thirds of Scipio's force was made up of auxiliaries form the local tribes.

temporary fortifications of the Romans, and its elevation above their camps in the valley below seems in itself to imply an inherent moral advantage.

Despite all this, the comparisons drawn between Scipio and his Spanish sixteenth-century counterparts in studies by Hermenegildo, Johnson and King are sufficiently forceful that it becomes necessary to entertain the possibility that the Numantians are not merely representative of the common people of Spain, or even of the soldiery of a Spanish army, however much they may resemble the portrayals of these in the *comedia*, but also of the *moriscos* in the Alpujarras (especially at the siege of Galera), or the Arauco (Mapuche) Indians assailed in their unnamed stronghold in Cantos XIV–XV of the *Araucana*, or the Dutch at Haarlem, or perhaps all of these on the basis of a shared identity as victims of Spanish imperial ambitions, and as non-Catholics, whatever their ostensible differences as *conversos*, Muslims, Protestants and pagans.

The result is a kind of double vision, and the implication of this vision is not just that peoples represented by the regime as inimical to Spain's interests and alien to her identity have more in common with the outlook of the Spanish people than her leaders do, but also that the ordinary people of Spain are as much victims of her policies as anyone born in a distant land or into another religion. Thus, while both the Romans and the Numantians are historically distant from Cervantes's audience, they possess an intense immediacy as representatives the doctrines of the élite, on one hand, and the preferences of the people, on the other.

For all that, the play is written as history and as tragedy; the events depicted have happened and are beyond any possible reversal. The old tribal ways of the Numantians have proved obsolete in the face of sophisticated military organization and strategy and the immense resources available to the emergent empire. The *moriscos* in the Alpujarras have already met a similar fate, and the likelihood is that the Arauco Indians will go the same way, though the Dutch, thanks to the modernity of their own approaches to warfare, politics and finance, will go on to exhaust the efforts of the Spanish Crown to subdue them and ultimately to create a brutal empire of their own.

It is odd, then, that Fama should portray Spain as avenging the Numantians by subjugating Rome twice in the sixteenth century (first when Charles V's army besieged and sacked the Eternal City in 1527 and again in 1557, when the Duke of Alba compelled the Pope to accept a peace while refraining from a direct attack upon Rome in order to avoid a repetition of the events of 1527), since the virtues of those directing these actions are identifiably those of Scipio rather than the supposedly more intrinsically Spanish virtues associated with the Numantians. The solution to this apparent paradox would seem to be that, like so many avengers, the Spaniards have, wittingly or unwittingly, assumed the character of their former abuser, an observation that invites one to reassess the validity of Fama's assertion at the close of the play that the Spaniards of the sixteenth century are really the 'herederos' of the Numantians (l. 2427).

This claim, is in any case undermined by the fact that the audience has just witnessed the last of the Numantians, a child named Bariato, throw himself to his death from a tower in defiance of the blandishments of Scipio, who wishes to preserve his life in order that the boy may play a part in his triumph.[9] With Bariato's death the Numantian race has been so emphatically exterminated that it seems impertinent to speak of the relation between the Numantians and modern Spaniards in terms of 'padres' and 'hijos'. There is, in fact, only one sense in which the Spaniards or Cervantes day might regard themselves as the inheritors of the Numantians, and that is – appropriately enough, since it is Fama who proposes the idea – in terms of fame, or to put it another way, the creation of a myth. And, since the allegorical figures of España, El Río Duero and Fama invoke the myth of the enduring presence of Numantian heroism in the Spanish character as something intrinsic to Spain's claim to an Imperial destiny, it will be as well to consider whether it is as open to a sceptical reading as the myth of Imperial Spain itself.

First, however, I should like to return to Scipio. Scholars have understandably differed in their evaluation of the moral character attributed to Scipio by Cervantes. Some have catalogued his virtues, but most have noted his lack of empathy for the Numantians – a lack that one suspects distances him from the majority of the audience – and the arrogance to which the Numantians themselves attribute his refusal to agree to a peaceful settlement in Act I or to decide the outcome of the conflict 'con una breve y singular batalla' in Act III (l. 1160).[10] Several critics regard him as being punished for his coldness and arrogance in Act IV when he pleads in vain with the Numantian child Bariato not to throw himself from the tower. Yet Scipio has been sent to Spain with a mission, and he prosecutes that mission in an unflinchingly systematic manner: haranguing his troops so as to reform his army before marching to Numantia, accepting the embassies of his enemy with the aim of deriving

---

[9]   King argues that the name 'Bariato' is a corruption of Viriato and refers to Viriatus, the Lusitanian leader who led a successful uprising against Roman rule in 147 BC. Though repeatedly victorious in battle, Viriatus ultimately fell victim to a Roman assassination plot in 139 BC: 'Cervantes [. . .] baptized the previously nameless boy with the name of Viriato, doubtless because he was a Lusitanian hero, and, after all, it was the union of Lusitania with the rest of the peninsula which was uppermost in Cervantes's mind when he began the play (The name appears as 'Bariato' in the faulty manuscript on which Schevill and Bonilla based their edition of the play; Sancha corrected [this], sensibly, to Viriato. The Lusitanian's exploits are recounted, in Morales and other historians, immediately prior to the relation of the siege of Numancia. Surely there is no need to look further for the ancestry of the name utilized by Cervantes.)' (King, p. 220, n. 25).

[10]   Earlier in his military career (151 BC) Scipio had in fact faced and defeated a Spaniard in single combat, a deed recorded by Polybius, Pliny, Pluarch, and Appian, among others.

intelligence from them, assessing their weaknesses and their strengths alike, constructing his siege works, and successfully turning their strengths against them.

The Roman model of warfare, which is essentially the one followed by the theorists and practitioners of Golden-Age Spain, is the only one that promises to achieve the strategic objective of imperial control; but this approach to warfare requires reserves on a scale that only an empire can muster. It is, for example, far beyond the scope of the Numantians to mount a counter-siege, and their proud emphasis on freedom and independence has led to an isolation from which they have no allies to call upon for assistance, as the Dutch could call upon the English. However, the application of such tactics requires the establishment of standing armies, and these, as Scipio points out, must be kept continually engaged in military operations if they are not to degenerate into the disorderly rabble that is such anathema to the imperial ideal.[11] Scipio may have his orders from Rome, but he also has an army that is showing advanced signs of enjoying the pleasures of peace and this, in his view, and in this many Golden-Age moralists – though I suspect, not Cervantes – would have agreed with him, can only be rectified by the initiation of a military campaign, regardless of the benefits of making peace with the Numantians.

What this line of thinking leads one to recognize is that the injustices that have led the Numantians to rebel probably took the form of oppressive efforts on the part of previous consuls to derive increased revenues from their Iberian provinces, and that these revenues were in all likelihood required for the maintenance of the very military forces established to ensure their collection. It is within this vicious circle – of revolt provoked by excessive taxation imposed for the purpose of suppressing revolt – that the characters of Cervantes's play, and the *moriscos*, Arauco Indians, Dutch, and Spaniards of his own day find themselves, as with their property and with their lives they fuel a war machine that offers them nothing in return but the promise of fame. One can only wonder how Cervantes's experiences at Lepanto and afterwards shaped his outlook on war, though I would suggest that *la Numancia* gives as true an impression of his disillusionment with heroic discourse as any of his subsequent works.

Despite Scipio's supposed failure – an idea that is undeniably expressed in the play, and universally affirmed by modern critical studies – in strictly military terms his strategy could scarcely have been more successful: by the end of the play he has lost only half a dozen out of his force (estimated by historians to have comprised 50,000–60,000 men), yet the Numantian revolt

---

[11] Compare Scipio's actions with Espínola's assertion in Calderón's *El sitio de Bredá* that: 'si no están entretenidos/ los soldados en algunos/ de los sitios que se ofrecen/ para victorioso asunto/ de nuestras armas, podrán/ amotinarse, y no dudo,/ que la esperanza del saco/ pueda sufrir con más gusto/ el grave peso a las armas' (ll. 203–11).

has been entirely extinguished and its stronghold laid waste. Indeed, there is
no indication either that the example of the Numantians has been anything
other than salutary for the remaining Iberian tribes, and the Duero's account
of Iberian history until the time of Ferdinand and Isabella – itself the era in
which the Roman approach to warfare was resurgent in Europe – is characterized by humiliation and defeat. Roman history also records that Scipio did
not fail to take sufficient captives and booty at Numantia to have his triumph
in Rome, and that he was dubbed 'Numantinus' after his victory at Numantia
just as he was earlier given the name 'Africanus' in celebration of his victory
over the Carthaginians.

It is apparent therefore that in his play Cervantes has chosen to argue that
even the most efficiently conceived and executed military strategy has its
limitations; that however fully the military objectives may be met, the
outcome will always be most truly reckoned in terms of absence and loss, as
it is here, where Scipio's sense of victory evaporates in the face of the
absence of booty, the absence of captives and the consequent absence of
glory. At a personal level, Scipio is undeniably represented by Cervantes as a
consummate practitioner of the art of war as described by theorists from
Vegetius to Machiavelli to Huarte de San Juan and Bernardino de Mendoza.
Yet this comes at a price; it dehumanizes him, causing him to scrutinize
without listening, analyse without thinking, and predict without imagining,
so that even when he witnesses the horrors he has caused at the end of Act IV,
he can think of nothing but his own loss of fame. Thus, the military 'virtues'
that enable him to overcome the Numantians also appear to suppress his own
humanity, and leave general and audience alike wondering about the value of
his victory.

Returning to the Numantians, Scipio is clearly not just their adversary, but
also their obverse. Just as his virtues enable him to win but make him hard to
admire, their virtues bring them fame but cause their downfall. The
Numantians claim to have had just cause for their rebellion in the oppressive
treatment they have received at the hands of previous consuls:

> [. . .] nunca de la ley y fueros
> del senado romano se apartara
> si el insufrible mando y desafueros
> de un cónsul y otro no le fatigara.
> Ellos con duros estatutos fieros
> y con su extraña condición avara
> pusieron tan gran yugo a nuestros cuellos
> que forzados salimos de él y de ellos;   (ll. 242–8)

They offer to accept Scipio as their 'señor y amigo' (l. 264) on the basis of
what they claim to know about his 'virtud y valor' (l. 261) and they flatter
him, speaking of his 'real grandeza' (l. 231) and promising that Numantia
will be his 'vasallo' (l. 288) if he accepts their terms for peace, as if he were a

king in a feudal society rather than the agent of the Roman senate. They evidently cannot see, or do not wish to admit, that he has come to Numantia not to make peace but to make an example of them, to demand or compel their unconditional surrender and to ensure their humiliation as a demonstration of the might of Imperial Rome. The reasons for their revolt are immaterial to him because he is not a judge or a diplomat but an enforcer.

The Numantians are inflexible too, however. Their offer of peace is conditional upon their being permitted to resume their former lives as if their revolt had never happened, and upon their new consul behaving in a way that meets with their approval. When Scipio rejects these unrealistic proposals the Numantians take umbrage, accuse Scipio of arrogance and adopt a posture of defiance that leaves them no room to manoeuvre. At no time do they express regret, admit responsibility, or seek forgiveness for their uprising. No doubt they believe their cause is just, but their pride is undeniable nonetheless, and lends an ironic note to the accusations of arrogance they direct against Scipio.

What both the Romans and the Numantians regard as arrogance in their adversaries derives directly from the subservience of each side to its imperial or national ideal. For the Numantians this ideal seems founded upon the concepts of honour, liberty and valour. These are fine words. What could be better than personal integrity and the respect of others, or the freedom not to pay tribute to anyone and to determine by common consent the character and direction of one's society, or the courage to confront adversity and the readiness to sacrifice one's life for the good of the community? Seen in these terms, it is not hard to understand why the Numantians are so often described as 'heroic', but it worth looking at what these virtues actually lead to in the play, aside from earning the Numantians fame and creating a myth of 'Spanish' virtue.

The least of it is that the Numantians' world-view makes them appear ingenuous in their misunderstanding of Scipio's mission, and archaic in their proposal to resolve their conflict with the Romans by single combat. But these are not the only acts their much-vaunted virtues lead them to: they make a suicidal attack on the Roman camp, they celebrate their own ferocity by killing and eating their Roman prisoners, they kill their own comrades, they seek to persuade their families (who play no part in their councils) that death is preferable to life under any terms but their own, and then they hunt down and murder anyone who remains unconvinced, and all in the name of honour, liberty and valour.[12] It is hard to imagine that such actions are held up by Cervantes as examples to emulate.

---

[12] '*Sale una mujer huyendo, y tras ella un soldado numantino con una daga para matarla.*/ [Mujer:] ¡Eterno padre, Júpiter piadoso,/ favorecedme en tan adversa suerte!/ [Soldado:] ¡Aunque más lleves vuelo presuroso,/ mi dura mano te dará la muerte!' (ll. 1928–31).

The Numantians destroy first their property, then their families, who for all their sentimentality they still treat as their chattels, and then their comrades, and finally themselves, solely to uphold their pride by denying these to the Romans. If Scipio is arrogant, how much arrogance is there in preferring murder and suicide to humility? This seems to me to be the crucial question of the play, since praise of the Numantians' 'heroism' implicitly but necessarily assumes acceptance of the view that 'honour' really is more valuable than life, and at the same time requires one to forget how many Golden-Age texts oblige us to question this claim.

The climactic event of this play as regards the themes of honour and fame is the suicide of Bariato. Fearing death, this young boy had hidden from the Numantian warriors when they began their slaughter of the city's women and children and now finds himself the only survivor of the massacre. As the only Numantian to escape death, and in view of his youth, it is tempting to regard him, when he first appears from the ruins, as a symbol of hope for the future. After all, here is a child whose heirs might indeed create a noble race of Spaniards. At the very least, he is alive, a survivor of a cataclysm in which so may others have suffered and perished. When Scipio is made aware of Bariato's existence, he begins to plead with him not to follow the example of his compatriots. The realization that Scipio values the boy's life because Bariato is essential to the triumph to which he aspires in Rome is shocking enough, yet it is less chilling than to find a modern critic asserting that the continued existence of Bariato necessarily leads the audience to fear that the 'heroic' sacrifice of the Numantians might prove futile, since this implies that one cannot recognize the Numantians' heroism without also desiring the death of this child, and that social conformity and fame may still be regarded as patently sufficient grounds for desiring a child to commit suicide.[13] The point here, surely – and surely it is Cervantes's point too – is that they are not. Scipio's cold cynicism provokes revulsion, it is true, but the mania for honour and fame that insists upon the necessity of Bariato's death is more repugnant still, as is the idea that his plunge from the tower should provoke relief and applause rather than horror and dismay.

---

[13] 'The discovery of Bariato, a mere child who in an earlier scene had fled from the threat of death, is clearly intended to arouse the fear that previous events were not, as promised, the seed of tragicomedy, but the prelude to a greater tragedy – one depicting the utter wasting of the Numantians' heroic sacrifice' (Paul Lewis-Smith, 'Cervantes's *Numancia* as Tragedy and Tragicomedy', *Bulletin of Hispanic Studies*, 64 (1986), 15–26 [pp. 22–3]). Lewi-Smith regards *la Numancia* as a play 'with a moral purpose', as I do, but for him that purpose is 'to reinforce or awaken in Spaniards the spirit of perfect patriotism and to strengthen the nation's self-confidence in time of war'. As a result, whereas he recognizes that 'the Numantians are obliged by honour to suffer and eventually to kill themselves', he appears not to detect the least hint of irony in this, and categorizes this simply as 'a tragedy on the theme of the cruelty of fate' (pp. 20–1).

Only if the Numantians were less concerned with honour could they avoid war and with it their own annihilation, but then there would be no myth of Numantian heroism either. And if Scipio were less intent on enhancing his personal reputation and that of Rome he also might have avoided a war that Cervantes represents as having had an entirely contrary outcome. It is therefore the pursuit of honour, and the fear of its loss, that bring about the atrocities Cervantes depicts in his play, and that in turn perpetuate the nationalistic myth of Numantian heroism as the prototype and model for Spanish military virtue. The figure of Fame invokes this myth to portray Spanish aggression against Rome as justified, and indeed moderate, retribution against the one-time aggressors of Numantia. Yet the parallels between the Numantians and the *moriscos*, the Arauco Indians and the Dutch, each in their own way the antithesis of Rome, remind us that this is a myth that is both misconceived and misapplied in every theatre of conflict. If it is the myths of fame, honour and nation that bring this about, it is in warfare that these myths find their focus.

What this play shows us, therefore, is that in pursuit of imperial ideals, imperial captains such as Scipio invoke the idea that honour, valour and love of freedom are inherent in the common people as a *ruse de guerre*, cynically exploiting this myth as a tool to motivate a soldiery that they then restrain with military discipline. Moreover, it shows us that this myth and the imperial ideal are both profoundly conditioned by the larger notion of honour, and that this notion repeatedly informs actions that are cruel, futile and self-destructive. What is more, despite its frequent association with notions of patriotism, the myth of honour transcends questions of race or nationality. Thus, in Cervantes's view, sixteenth-century Spaniards are 'Romans' insofar as they identify with the imperial ideal and Numantians insofar as they identify with a domestic or national stereotype of honour.

Nevertheless, for all its power, in Cervantes's play the myth of honour is less compelling than the images of physical and emotional suffering that it causes, and this suffering in turn allows us to see how the incorporation of individual virtues into myths of national patriotism and imperial glory, which are themselves but provinces of the global myth of honour, results in the perversion of virtue itself.

Virtue is attributed to, and apparent on, both sides in the conflict portrayed in *La Numancia*, though the Roman approach to virtue is more cerebral and the Numantian approach more visceral. Yet in both cases virtue produces only harm because it is not linked to a respect for the rights of others. It is not that the virtues of the Numantians are unattractive in themselves; indeed the rooted, confident, and markedly consensual character of Numantian society has a nostalgic or utopian quality that is both appealing and preferable to the alien, dictatorial and remorselessly modernizing imperial vision. The problem is that the Numantians' blindness to the destructive nature of the myth of honour is if anything even greater than the Romans', and thus they are similarly, and tragically, unable to reject it.[14]

It is not only the myths of fame and honour, imperial glory and national patriotism that are called into question in this play, however; religion is under scrutiny too. Several critics have observed that the rituals performed by the Numantian priests are reminiscent of the rites of the Catholic Church and that the symbolism of bread and blood in Marandro's final scene has a proto-Christian resonance, and have concluded from this that Numantians prefigure Spaniards in their piety as much as they do in their valour. Yet this reading seems to overlook the fact that the priests of Numantia are explicitly engaged first in a pagan blood sacrifice and then in an act of necromancy, and that if this recalls the rites of the Christian religion then the comparison is not necessarily a flattering one. In the case of Marandro, his self-sacrifice, which is motivated by his love for Lira, and that of his friend Leonicio, which is motivated by his love for Marandro, combined with its imagery of bread and blood, inevitably recalls the self-sacrifice of Christ, but it achieves nothing, merely allowing the two youths to die fighting, the form of death preferred by the men of Numantia, and bringing even greater grief to Lira and death to half a dozen luckless Roman soldiers.[15] As for the bread, stained with her lover's blood, she does not eat it, and it has no evident restorative or redemptive powers, whether of a material or a spiritual kind. If this were not

---

[14] A comparison of *La Numancia* with Calderón's *El sitio de Bredá* is worth making here. In Calderón's play, Justin of Nassau and the beseiged inhabitants of Breda put up a determined resistance against the Spanish forces commanded by Ambrosio Spínola, but ultimately come to realize that further resistance is futile and offer to capitulate. Spínola famously responds by offering them generous terms. Thus the Dutch emerge from the conflict without the wanton loss of life or property seen in Numantia, and yet with their self-respect also largely intact. The Spaniards, for their part, win a reputation for magnanimity that amply compensates them for what they lose in booty, not least because Spínola ensures they are well rewarded for their services. It seems likely, therefore, that if the Numantians had sued for peace once they had satisfactorily demonstrated their capacity for enduring hardship, Scipio would also have been satisfied that he had sufficiently demonstrated his skill and resolve as a commander, and been prepared to come to terms. In fact, he suggests as much when he enters Numantia in the last Act: '[Escipión:] ¿Estaba, por ventura, el pecho mío/ de bárbara arrogancia y muertes lleno,/ y de piedad justísima vacío?/ ¿Es de mi condición, por dicha, ajeno/ usar benignidad con el rendido,/ como conviene al vencedor que es bueno?/ ¡Mal, por cierto, tenían conocido/ el valor en Numancia de mi pecho,/ para vencer y perdonar nacido!' (ll. 2335–43), and he subsequently does what he can to demonstrate these qualities to Bariato, who by his suicide tragically demonstrates that he understands the etiquette of modern war no better than his compatriots.

[15] '[Quinto Fabio: . . .] en un punto seis soldados/ fueron de agudas puntas traspasados./ [. . .] / Queda Fabricio traspasado el pecho;/ abierta la cabeza tiene Eracio;/ Olmida ya perdió el brazo derecho,/ y de vivir le queda poco espacio./ Fuéle ansimismo poco de provecho/ la ligereza al valeroso Estacio,/ pues el correr al numantino fuerte/ fue abreviar el camino de la muerte' (ll. 1754–5, 1764–71).

enough for the audience to perceive a note of scepticism in Cervantes's presentation of religion, it might also be noted that the Numantians have their priests perform their rituals in a desperate search for reassurance, and that at least some of the onlookers at this performance express doubts about the value and authenticity of such proceedings.[16]

Far from offering a solution to their problems or providing a remedy to them, the Numantians' religious practices merely serve to compound their despair and to confirm their sense that disaster is inevitable. The irony here, and there is always irony in this play, is that the only alternative to such fatalism that any of the characters can envisage is to attempt to determine his future through warfare, an attitude which, as we have seen, is largely responsible for creating the situation in which the Numantians find themselves.

It might be argued that the pagan setting of this play ensures that its religious imagery can only foreshadow Christianity, and that, as only Christianity itself can deliver redemption, we should not expect to find it here. That may be so, for the Numantians are clearly ignorant of a crucial quality inherent in the Christian portrayal of Christ, that is, his humility, since for them, and even for those as generous in spirit as Marandro and Leonicio, self-sacrifice means giving up everything *except* their pride. Perhaps this should not surprise us either, for living as they do outside the Christian faith, the only kind of immortality they can aspire to is that offered by fame. Such observations, however, leave unanswered the question of whether the price of such fame is worth paying, even for pagans, and indicate an essential incompatibility between the myth of honour and the much-vaunted Christianity of the Spanish state.

Finally, there seems to be a tendency among critics of the play to regard the allegorical figures in *La Numancia* as infallible, omniscient judges of the action. Yet in view of the play's sceptical presentation of the idea of fame, the figure of Fama must herself fall under suspicion, as must her judgements. Fama is not necessarily more admirable than Guerra, whose companions, we should note, are Hambre and Enfermedad, not glory and honour. This leaves España, El Río Duero and his tributaries. As allegorical figures rather than individuated characters, they represent precisely the kind of myths that prove so damaging to the human characters in the play. Though España may appear to be on the side of the Numantians, she bears the name given to their land by Rome and restored to it by the founders of the expansionist state about which

---

16 '[Marandro:] Leonicio, ¿qué te parece?/ ¿Han remedio nuestros males/ con estas buenas señales/ que aquí el cielo nos ofrece?/ ¡Tendrá fin mi desventura/ cuando se acabe la guerra,/ que será cuando la tierra/ me sirva de sepultura!/ [Leonicio:] Marandro, al que es buen soldado/ agüeros no le dan pena,/ que pone la suerte buena/ en el ánimo esforzado,/ y esas vanas apariencias/ nunca le turban el tino./ Su brazo es su estrella o sino;/ su valor, sus influencias./ Pero si quieres creer/ en este notorio engaño,/ aún quedan, si no me engaño,/ experiencias más que hacer' (ll. 907–26).

the play is so critical. What is more, her costume, with its castles, illustrates the truism that 'España', as often as not, really means Castile. España, no less than Scipio, seeks to stir up the patriotic feelings of her people, and to redirect their sense of past injustices in support of the military aims of the empire. For his part, the Duero appears at first to represent fertility, family and continuity, even an unbroken historical connection between the Numantian past and the Spanish present, yet the lesser rivers so charmingly clustered around him are not in fact his children, but rather his tributaries, and as such they remind us of the extent to which the master narrative of Castilian history depends on tribute from its contiguous regions.[17] In short, all of these allegorical figures belong to the world of pageantry and propaganda and so are expressions of partial rather than universal truths. The action of the play makes, or should make, its audience suspicious of such expository discourse and of the rhetoric of principle and of necessity, just as it should lead it to lend most credence to, and take most deeply to heart, the emotional imprint of the horrors committed in the name of honour that it has been obliged to witness.

In conclusion, then, it seems to me that La Numancia does more than express scepticism about the official values of a Spain that seeks to emulate and surpass the glories of the Roman Empire. Cervantes's criticism is both more engaged and more urgent. Far from promoting a popular view of the Spanish national character as fanatically devoted to ideals of honour, valour and liberty, the play denounces such a view, with esperpentic irony, as a dangerous myth, and it lays the blame for the perpetuation of that myth at the door of a ruling élite for whom it serves as an effective means of political control and exploitation. Consequently, La Numancia portrays the pursuit of fame as hollow and posited on loss, absence and destruction. Nevertheless, the play is not written as a treatise, and for all its bitter irony, it recognizes that the choice between honour and humiliation, resistance and capitulation is by no means an easy one. After all, honour would not be so powerful or so dangerous a myth if it were so easy to dispel.

---

[17] The expansionist tendencies of Habsburg Spain seem implicit in the Duero's description of his relationship with his tributaries: 'Con Orvión, Minuesa y también Tera,/ cuyas aguas las mías acrecientan,/ he llenado mi seno en tal manera/ que usadas márgenes revientan' (ll. 449–52).

Here and There, *acá* and *allá*:
The Origins of Authority in Oviedo's
Historia natural y general de las Indias

B. W. IFE

Any examination of the 'official' ideological landscape of early modern Spain, and of the language in which that ideology was couched, must embrace the principal linguistic challenge encountered by Spaniards on both sides of the Atlantic during the sixteenth century: that of reporting, interpreting and classifying the European encounter with the New World. Few events in history can have put such strain on pre-existing narrative strategies as were placed on the linguistic resources taken by the *conquistadores* to America in and after 1492. Generations of eye-witnesses struggled to bridge the gaps between what they saw, what they understood and what they could communicate. Some, like Columbus, brought their accounts back with them, so at least could vouch for them in person. Others, like Cortés, had to achieve similar feats of communication entirely at a distance, conjuring vivid images of the unimaginable in reports that were not brought back, but sent back in their absence.

The scale of the challenge faced by the Spanish writers about the New World is underlined in Anthony Pagden's study *European Encounters with the New World*, and particularly in his second chapter, 'The Autoptic Imagination'.[1] As Pagden makes clear, the key challenge for the chroniclers of the New World was to establish their narrative authority. The discovery and its associated literature cut across the traditional view that knowledge depended on textual interpretation and exegesis: 'all that could be known had to be made compatible with what had once been said by a recognized canon of sacred and ancient authors' (Pagden, p. 12). But for the most part there was, by definition, no place for the New World in the ancient canon, and the men who went there and wrote back were having to create texts where none

---

[1] *European Encounters with the New World* (New Haven: Yale UP, 1993). See also Pagden's *The Fall of Natural Man. The American Indian and the Origins of Comparative Ethnology* (Cambridge: CUP, 1982) and *Lords of All the World. Ideologies of Empire in Spain, Britain and France c.1500–c.1800* (New Haven: Yale UP, 1995).

existed before (p. 54). For many of these eye-witnesses, the first-person narrative was the cornerstone of their claim to authenticity.

The challenge facing a man like Cortés – a man of action, but one constrained by the general requirement of the Crown that he should account, in writing, for his actions at all times – was not in fact unique to America and the sixteenth century.[2] In his fifth *Carta de relación* of 1526 – a long account of his overland expedition to Honduras to put down a rebellion by Cristóbal de Olid – Cortés draws a clear parallel between similar incidents in his own career and that of Julius Caesar. While crossing the delta of the river Usumacinta, Cortés comes to a particularly wide stretch of water and decides to build a bridge. Of all the ways of crossing a river, a bridge is almost always the most time-consuming and the most resource-intensive. Cortés reviews all the options: turning back, crossing in canoes, wading, finding a better place to cross. But he rejects them all. Instead he builds a bridge a mile long over water that is four fathoms deep plus two fathoms of mud. He uses over a thousand timbers between fifty and sixty feet long, all of them at least the girth of a man, and countless smaller timbers. And he finishes the job in four days. It was, he writes, 'la cosa más estraña que nunca se ha visto'.[3]

Cortés relied on his readers to make the link between this bridge and another they would have known from their schooldays. In Book IV of *De Bello Gallico*, Julius Caesar builds a similar bridge, over the Rhine, in similar circumstances, although he takes ten days to complete it. In both cases, their purpose in building the bridge, rather than taking one of the easier options, is to make a series of statements: to impose their will on their soldiers, to impress the enemy, and to leave a highly visible mark on the political and geographical landscape. And in each case, the bridge is a rhetorical as much as an architectural construct. It stretches across a much greater void than the mile or so of water that has to be crossed on the journey; it is built to stretch across the vast gulf that separates the discoverer from the audience back home.

Like the *Cartas de relación*, the books of the Gallic War were sent back from the western front to the seat of power, in Rome. They were written to be read aloud in the Forum, and they were composed to keep alive the influence and credibility of the absent warrior in the minds of the forgetful and sceptical senators.[4] Cortés's reports were also written to remind the Emperor and his advisers of the extremes of suffering that were being undergone in his

2 B.W. Ife and R.T.C. Goodwin, ' "Many expert narrators": History and fiction in the Spanish chronicles of the New World', in *Remapping the Rise of the European Novel* (Oxford: Voltaire Foundation), forthcoming.

3 Hernán Cortés, *Cartas de relación*, ed. Angel Delgado Gómez (Madrid: Castalia, 1993), p. 557.

4 T.P. Wiseman, 'The publication of *De Bello Gallico*', in *Julius Caesar as Artful Reporter: The war commentaries as political instruments*, eds Kathryn Welch and Anton Powell (London: Duckworth, 1998), pp. 1–9.

name in the New World. It is hard to know how a man like Cortés, who dropped out of university to become an adventurer, learned to write so well. Was he, to put the question in Pagden's terms, glossing a pre-existing, canonical text, or was he composing a text where none existed before and using his first person 'I' witness to authenticate it? In a sense Cortés's writings are a classic example of the autoptic imagination, in which the 'yo' not only guarantees the veracity of the account by his presence, but in this case by his primary role as agent. Not only did he see it, he did it; and the suffering he underwent in the process warrants the veracity of the report, the extent of his service, and his fitness to receive reward.

This cluster of issues – seeing and making sense of something new; communicating the nature and extent of that novelty in language which, by definition, is ill-suited to expressing it; enabling the absent reader to reconstruct the nature and extent of the new experience from his reading about it; persuading the absent reader of the veracity of the account in terms both of its nature and impact; convincing the absent reader of the political, economic and religious significance of the new experience; and obtaining reward both for the service itself and for the effort of communicating it – lies at the heart of one of the most important eye-witness accounts of the New World experience, the *Historia natural y general de las Indias*, compiled by the imperial chronicler Gonzalo Fernández de Oviedo y Valdés. Only Part I of this monumental work appeared in Oviedo's lifetime, published in Seville in 1535; Parts II and III were not published until the 1850s, and the complete work is still in need of a full critical edition.[5]

Unlike the majority of the discoverers and chroniclers of the New World, who might be described as outsiders trying to get in,[6] Oviedo wrote from the centre as well as from the margin. He was an established writer; a former courtier in the household of Prince Juan; secretary to the 'Gran Capitán', Gonzalo Fernández de Córdoba; notary and treasury official to Pedrarias Dávila in Darién; and in 1532 he was appointed constable of the royal fortress at Santo Domingo. He was well-read and well-travelled in Europe, especially in Italy; a humanist by inclination and application; a man of

5   Gonzalo Fernández de Oviedo y Valdés, *Historia general y natural de las Indias, islas y tierra firme del mar Océano*, ed. José Amador de los Ríos (Madrid: Real Academia de la Historia, 1851–5). This edition was republished with a new introduction by Juan Pérez de Tudela y Bueso (*Biblioteca de Autores Españoles*, vols 118–22, Madrid, 1959). An electronic version of Part I (books 1–19), prepared by B.W. Ife and David McGrath, can be consulted at http://ems.kcl.ac.uk/content/etext/e026.html together with a version of Book 1 prepared for use with this paper. The remainder of the electronic text of Oviedo is in preparation.
6   B.W. Ife, 'The literary impact of the New World: Columbus to Carrizales', *Journal of the Institute of Romance Studies*, 3 (1994–95), 65–85.

quality, but one who was ultimately driven to find his fortune in the New World by a life of mild disappointment in the Old.[7]

Oviedo therefore occupied an ambivalent position in social, political and cultural terms. His career left him poised, or torn, between three main points of geographical and cultural reference. Italy to the east was the cradle of renaissance humanism; Spain in the centre was the epicentre of political power; and to the west lay the exotic margins of the Habsburg Empire whose vastness, novelty and incommensurability represented the biggest challenge yet to the authority of classical and biblical knowledge. It is fair to say that Oviedo never really reconciled the pull of these three major influences in his life. In his writing he constantly affects stern criticism of classical precedent but hardly a page is free from dependence on those precedents; and he is frequently in two minds about the real source of his authority as a writer.[8] In the remainder of this chapter, I will look in some detail at how these themes are worked out in the very first chapter of the *Historia*, a prologue to the first part of the work, and illustrate how Oviedo uses the conventions of the prologue to establish a dialogue between several different concepts of authority.

Before embarking on this analysis, however, it is worth noting the preview of these issues in the title of the work as it appeared in 1535. In the long, wordy title, characteristic of the period but no less significant for that reason, Oviedo or his publisher rehearses many of the topics that he will weave together in the first of the twenty books of this, the first part of the *Historia*:

> Primera parte de la historia natural y general de las indias, yslas e tierra firme del mar océano; escripta por el capitán Gonçalo Hernández de Oviedo e Valdés, alcayde de la fortaleza de la ciudad de Sancto Domingo de la ysla Española, y cronista de la sacra, cesárea y cathólicas magestades del emperador don Carlos quinto de tal nombre, rey de España, e de la seveníssima e muy poderosa reyna doña Juana su madre nuestros señores. Por cuyo mandado el auctor escrivió las cosas maravillosas que ay en diversas yslas e partes destas indias e imperio de la corona real de castilla,

---

[7] D.A. Brading, *The First America. The Spanish Monarchy, Creole Patriots and the Liberal State 1492–1867* (Cambridge: CUP, 1991), pp. 31–4. The standard biography of Oviedo is the introduction by Juan Pérez de Tudela to the *BAE* edition of the *Historia general y natural de las Indias* (Madrid, 1959), pp. i–clxxv. See also Alberto M. Salas, *Tres cronistas de Indias* (Mexico: Fondo de Cultura Económica, 1986), pp. 69–173; Antonello Gerbi, *La naturaleza de las Indias Nuevas* (Mexico: Fondo de Cultura Económica, 1978), pp. 149–477.

[8] B.W. Ife, 'Alexander in the New World', *Renaissance and Modern Studies*, 30 (1986), 35–44; Alvaro Félix Bolaños, 'The historian and the Hesperides: Fernández de Oviedo and the limitations of imitation', *Bulletin of Hispanic Studies*, 72 (1995), 273–88; Jesús Carrillo, 'From Mt Ventoux to Mt Masaya: The rise and fall of subjectivity in early modern travel narrative', in Jaś Elsner and Joan-Pau Rubiés (eds), *Voyages and Visions. Towards a Cultural History of Travel* (London: Reaktion, 1999), pp. 57–73.

según lo vido e supo en veynte e dos años e más que ha que vive e reside en aquellas partes. La qual historia comiença en el primero descubrimiento destas indias, y se contiene en veynte libros este primero volumen.

Several aspects of this title are striking, in spite of their conventional nature. Oviedo presents himself initially as a man of action, a captain and governor of the fortress of Santo Domingo, and then as a writer, chronicler of the Emperor and of his mother Doña Juana. The double reference to Carlos and Juana is striking for a text published in 1535 and constitutes an unusual, and rather belated, reminder of Doña Juana's unfitness to rule and the problems that lay behind Charles's succession to the thrones of Castile and Aragon in 1516. Why stir this up again twenty years later? Oviedo may be trying to do two things: first, given a later reference to his appointment by King Ferdinand in Book 1 of the *Historia* (44),[9] he was undoubtedly underlining, none too subtly, that his association with royalty stretched over several generations; second, and consistent with the rather ambivalent attitude towards imperial authority that runs throughout the work, Oviedo may rather subtly have been using Juana, as he consistently uses God, to put the Emperor in his place.

The royal commission ('por cuyo mandado') shifts the perspective in the second part of the title away from the Emperor and his mother, to the marvels of the Indies themselves, 'destas indias' as he twice calls them, emphasizing the transatlantic viewpoint from which the *Historia* is written, before going on to underline the length of service the author has given in the New World and the extent of his first-hand acquaintance with 'aquellas partes'. The sudden shift back to the European viewpoint serves as a queasy reminder that, for his readers, 'these Indies' are 'over there'. The Indies may be the centre of Oviedo's attention, but they are in the peripheral vision of the reader in Seville. It is hard to be certain whether this rapid movement back and forth between demonstratives is attributable to Oviedo or his publisher; but the toing and froing between both sides of the Atlantic will become a major feature of the text of Book 1 and the subtext of the rest of the *Historia*. The title ends with a coded reference to the dual nature of the history, 'natural y general', by explaining that it will begin at the beginning, with the discovery itself. But there are other literary and historiographical conventions to be dealt with first, and it will be several pages before this history can be fully under way.

Book 1 of the *Historia* differs from all the rest in being much shorter, and in not being subdivided into a *proemio* and a series of chapters. In fact, the whole of Book 1 is one continuous text of over 4,000 words; it is billed as a *prohemio* or introduction to the whole work, and is set as a single unbroken

---

[9] References in parentheses are to anteposed sentence numbers added to Oviedo's text (see extracts below).

paragraph in double-column format from the top of folio 2r to the foot of 4v in the edition of 1535. Although Book 1 has many of the characteristics of a prologue, and rehearses many of its conventions, it is extremely difficult to discern a clear sectional structure, and the continuous, unbroken format of the 1535 edition may not simply be the result of poor typographical design and failure to consider the needs of the reader. There is a real sense in which this text asks to be read as a single, complex statement in which several strands of argument are skilfully woven together.

Inasmuch as this 'prologue' reworks conventional material, the sequence of ideas or themes could be broadly divided into twelve main statements, as in the following abbreviated text, though it should be stressed that there is nothing in the original *mise en page* that suggests that this schema is intended in any way:

(1)   This is not a book about Asia

[7]Quiero significar y dar a entender por verdadera cosmographía, que aquí yo no tracto de aquestas Indias que he dicho, sino de las Indias, yslas e tierra firme del mar océano, que agora está actualmente debaxo del imperio de la corona real de Castilla, donde innumerables e muy grandes reynos e provincias se incluyen, de tanta admiración e riquezas como en los libros desta historia general e natural destas vuestras Indias será declarado.

(2)   A plea for the Emperor's attention, and the divinity of knowledge

[8]Por tanto suplico a Vuestra Cesárea Magestad haga dignas mis vigilias de poner la mente en ellas pues naturalmente todo hombre dessea saber, y el entendimiento racional es lo que le haze más excelente que a otro ningún animal; y en esta excelencia es semejante a Dios en aquella parte que El dixo: *Hagamos el honbre a nuestra ymagen e semejança*; desta causa no se contenta nuestra voluntad, ni se satisfaze nuestro ánimo con entender y especular pocas cosas, ni con ver las ordinarias o próximas a la patria, ni dentro della misma; antes por otras muy apartadas provincias peregrinando [. . .] pospuestos muchos y varios peligros no cessan de inquerir en la tierra y en la mar las maravillosas e innumerables obras que el mismo Dios y Señor de todo nos enseña [. . .]

(3)   The abundance of the New World is a tribute to Castile

[10][. . .] sé que ay en este imperio de las Indias, que Vuestra Cesárea Magestad, e su corona real de Castilla posseen, tan grandes reynos e provincias y de tan estrañas gentes e diversidades e costumbres y cerimonias e ydolatrías, apartadas de quanto estava escripto (desde *ab inicio* hasta nuestro tiempo), que es muy corta la vida del hombre para lo poder ver, ni acabar de entender o conjecturar. [11]¿Quál ingenio mortal sabrá comprehender tanta diversidad de lenguas, de hábito, de costumbres

en los hombres destas Indias? [. . .] [18]¿Quántos montes más admirables y espantosos que Ethna o Mongibel, y Vulcano, y Estrongol [. . .]? [19]No fueran celebrados en tanta manera los que he dicho por los poetas e hystoriales antiguos si supieran de Massaya, e Maribio, e Guaxocingo, e los que adelante serán memorados de esta pluma o escriptor vuestro [. . .] [29]¿En quál tierra se oyó ni se sabe que en tan breve tiempo, y en tierras tan apartadas de nuestra Europa, se produziessen tantos ganados e granjerías y en tanta abundancia como en estas Indias veen nuestros ojos traydas acá por tan amplíssimos mares?

(4)   The New World as bountiful mother

[30]Las quales ha rescebido esta tierra no como madrastra, sino como más verdadera madre que la que se las embió: pues en más cantidad y mejor que en España se hazen algunas dellas, assí de los ganados útiles al servicio de los hombres como de pan, y legumbres, e frutas, e açúcar, e cañafistola; cuyo principio de estas cosas en mis días salió de España, y en poco tiempo se han multiplicado en tanta cantidad, que las naos buelven a Europa a la proveer cargadas de açúcar, e cañafistola, e cueros de vacas. [31]E assí lo podrían hazer de otras cosas que acá están olvidadas, y aquestas Indias antes que los españoles las hallassen, produzían e agora produzen. [32]Assí como algodón, orchilla, brasil, e alumbre, e otras mercadurías, que en muchos reynos del mundo las dessean [. . .] [33]Lo qual nuestros mercaderes no quieren por no ocupar sus navíos sino con oro, e plata, e perlas [. . .]

(5)   The difficulties of communicating the abundance of the New World and the wider significance of the commission

[34]Y pues lo que deste grandíssimo y nuevo imperio se podría escrevir es tanto e tan admirable la leción dello, ella misma me desculpe con Vuestra Cesárea Majestad, si tan copiosamente como la materia lo requiere no se dixere. [35]Baste que como hombre que ha los años que he dicho que miro estas cosas, ocuparé lo que me queda de vivir, en dexar por memoria esta dulce, agradable, general e natural hystoria de Indias, en todo aquello que he visto, y en lo que a mi noticia ha venido e viniere, desde su primero descubrimiento, con lo que más pudiere ver e alcançar dello en tanto que la vida no se me acabare. [36]Pues la clemencia de Vuestra Cesárea Magestad como a criado que en estas partes le sirve e persevera con natural inclinación de inquerir (como he inquerido) parte de estas cosas, ha seydo servido de mandarme que las escriva y embíe a su Real Consejo de Indias, para que assí como se fueren aumentando e sabiéndose, assí se vayan poniendo en su gloriosa Crónica de España. [37]En lo qual Vuestra Majestad, demás de servir a Dios Nuestro Señor en que se publique y sepa por el restante del mundo lo que está debaxo de vuestro real ceptro castellano, haze muy señalada merced a todos los reynos de christianos en darles ocasión con este tratado para que den infinitas gracias a Dios por el acrecentamiento de su santa fe cathólica.

(6)   The stylistic shortcomings of the book weighed against its truthfulness

[39]Materia es muy poderoso señor en que mi edad e diligencia por la
grandeza del objecto e sus circunstancias no podrán bastar a su perfecta
difinición por mi insuficiente estilo e brevedad de mis días. [40]Pero será a lo
menos lo que yo escriviere, hystoria verdadera e desviada de todas las
fábulas que en este caso otros escriptores sin verlo, desde España a pie
enxuto, han presumido escrevir con elegantes e no comunes letras latinas e
vulgares, por informaciones de muchos de diferentes juyzios, formando
hystorias más allegadas a buen estilo que a la verdad de la cosa que
cuentan; porque ni el ciego sabe determinar colores, ni el ausente assí
testificar estas materias, como quien las mira. [41]Quiero certificar a Vuestra
Cesárea Magestad que yrán desnudos mis renglones de abundancia de
palabras artificiales para combidar a los lectores; pero serán muy copiosos
de verdad. [42]Y conforme a ésta diré lo que no terná contradición (quanto a
ella) para que vuestra soberana clemencia allá lo mande polir e limar.
[43]Con tanto que del tenor e sentencia de lo que aquí fuere notificado a
vuestra grandeza, no se aparte la intención e obra del que tomare cargo de
emendar la mía, diziéndolo por mejor estilo.

(7)   The arduousness of service in the New World

[44]Siquiera porque no se ofenda mi buen desseo, ni se me niegue el loor del
trabajo que en tanto tiempo y con tantos peligros yo he padescido,
allegando e inquiriendo por todas las vías que pude saber lo cierto destas
materias, después quel año de mill e quinientos y treze de la natividad del
redentor nuestro Jesu Christo, el cathólico rey don Fernando de gloriosa
memoria abuelo de Vuestra Cesárea Magestad me embió por su veedor de
las fund[i]ciones del oro a la Tierra Firme, donde assí me ocupé quando
convino en aquel oficio, como en la conquista e pacificación de algunas
partes de aquella tierra con las armas, sirviendo a Dios y a Vuestras
Majestades (como su capitán e vassallo) en aquellos ásperos principios que
se poblaron algunas cibdades e villas que aora son de cristianos [. . .]
[46]Porque la salvajez de la tierra y los ayres della, y la espessura de los
ervajes e arboledas de los campos, y el peligro de los ríos e grandes
lagartos e tigres, y el esperimentar de las aguas e manjares, fuesse a costa
de nuestras vidas y en utilidad de los mercaderes e pobladores, que con sus
manos lavadas agora gozan de muchos sudores ajenos.

(8)   Comparison of this work with the *Sumario* (1525)

[47]Y porque estando Vuestra Cesárea Magestad en Toledo el año que passó
de la natividad de Christo de mill e quinientos e veynte e cinco años, yo
escreví una relación sumaria de parte de lo que aquí se contiene, e de
aquélla fue su título: Oviedo, *De la natural hystoria de las Indias*; mas
aqueste tratado se llamará *General e natural hystoria de las Indias*; porque
todo lo que en aquel sumario se contiene se hallará en éste y en las otras
dos partes, segunda y tercera dél, mejor e más copiosamente dicho, assí

porque aquello se escrivió en España, quedando mis memoriales e libros en esta cibdad de Santo Domingo de la ysla Española (donde tengo mi casa) como porque yo he visto mucho más de lo que hasta entonces sabía destas materias en diez años que han passado desde que aquello se escrivió [. . .] [48]Y demás desto es de notar que todo lo que aquel reportorio, o sumario contiene, avrá en este tratado e sus partes acrescentado, e otras cosas grandes e muy nuevas, de que allí no podía yo hazer memoria por no averlas visto, ni sabido.

(9)   The book as testimony to the power of Castile

[49][. . .] justo es que tales hystorias sean manifiestas en todas las repúblicas del mundo; para que en todo él se sepa la amplitud, e grandeza de estos estados, que guardava Dios a vuestra real corona de Castilla en ventura y méritos de Vuestra Cesárea Magestad [. . .] debaxo de cuyo favor y amparo ofrezco la presente obra e humilmente suplico en pago del tiempo que en esto he trabajado, e de la antigüedad que en vuestra real casa de Castilla me dan quarenta e más años (que ha que soy del número de los criados de ella) sea servido de aceptar mis libros. [50]Porque aunque éstos que aquí yo escrivo no son de mucha industria o artificio, [. . .] no han sido poco laboriosos [. . .]. [51]Pero es a lo menos muy aplazible leción, oyr y entender tantos secretos de natura.

(10)   The presence of native words in the text

[52]Si algunos vocablos estraños e bárbaros aquí se hallaren, la causa es la novedad de que se trata, y no se pongan a la cuenta de mi romance que en Madrid nascí, y en la casa real me crié, y con gente noble he conversado, e algo he leydo, para que se sospeche que avré entendido mi lengua castellana. [53]La qual de las vulgares se tiene por la mejor de todas; y lo que oviere en este volumen que con ella no consuene, serán nombres o palabras por mi voluntad puestas para dar a entender las cosas que por ellas quieren los indios significar.

(11)   Oviedo's approach as compared with that of Pliny

[54]En todo recompense Vuestra Majestad con mi desseo las faltas de la pluma, pues dixo Plinio de la suya en el prohemio de la *Natural hystoria*, que es cosa difícil hazer las cosas viejas nuevas; e a las nuevas dar auctoridad. [55]Y a las que salen de lo acostumbrado, dar resplandor; e a las obscuras, luz; y a las enojosas, gracia; e a las dudosas, fe. [57][. . .] conténtese el lector con que lo que yo he visto y experimentado con muchos peligros, lo goza él y sabe sin ninguno; y que lo puede leer sin que padezca tanta hambre y sed, e calor, e frío, con otros innumerables trabajos, desde su patria sin aventurarse a las tormentas de la mar, ni a las desventuras que por acá se padescen en la tierra. [74][. . .] e pues los lectores me han de escuchar desde tan lexos, no me juzguen sin ver esta tierra donde estoy, y de quien tracto; y que les baste que desde ella escrivo en tiempo de innumerables testigos de vista, y que se dirigen mis libros a

Vuestra Cesárea Majestad cuyo es aqueste imperio. [75]Y que se escriven por su mandado, y que me da de comer por su cronista destas materias, y que no he de ser de tan poco entendimiento que ante tan altíssima y Cesárea Majestad ose dezir el contrario de la verdad [. . .].

(12) Remuneration and praise of the Emperor

[78]Espero en Dios que guardará la mía de tal peligro, e que como fiel escriptor seré dél remunerado, por la amplíssima liberalidad de su clemencia e real mano de Vuestra Cesárea Majestad cuya gloriosa persona largos tiempos nuestro Señor favorezca y dexe gozar de la total monarchía, como vuestro excelso coraçón lo dessea, e vuestros leales y verdaderos súbditos desseamos, e toda la universal república cristiana ha menester, *amén*. [79]Pues entre todos los príncipes que en el mundo se llaman fieles e cristianos, sólo Vuestra Cesárea Majestad al presente sostiene la cathólica religión, e yglesia de Dios [. . .[86]]

Oviedo uses the bare bones of this extremely skeletal and inconsistently real-ized schema as a framework on which to hang the central questions of the conventional prologue: what is the nature of the author's authority? What is his right to speak? What are the precedents for what he says and how does he relate to them? How can he guarantee the veracity of what he says? What kind of recompense can he expect? The answers to all of these questions are problematic and ambiguous, and their ambiguity is underlined by a dual geographical perspective: the values that he discusses in the prologue are strongly associated with one side of the Atlantic or the other. Some belong 'here', *acá*; whereas they do things differently 'there', *allá*. As the prologue unfolds, it becomes clear that a conventional typology couched in the language of an 'official' ideology gradually becomes undermined by an alternative value system in which all of the polarities are reversed. A conven-tional view of Europe as the fount of authority, power and civility is gradu-ally eroded and replaced by a different, and stronger, set of values located 'here', *acá*.

The fundamental question addressed in any sixteenth-century prologue is the author's right to speak. As Oviedo signals in the title of the *Historia*, he grounds a large part of his authority as a writer in the mandate he has from the Emperor, both by virtue of his position as imperial chronicler, and by implication, because he has been specifically instructed to produce the work that the reader has in his hands (36). And with that mandate comes every-thing that the Emperor stands for: the centrality of political power in Europe and the defence of the faith. These are values that have their origin 'over there', and with them go traditional values of scholarship and eloquence. Europe is the seat of biblical, philosophical and literary precedent, of civility and rhetorical polish (42, 85).

In the context of these Old World values, *acá*, by contrast, is the 'distant' site of subservience, savagery and apostasy. What the absent author – absent, that is, from the seat of power in the Old World – loses in authority by virtue of his absence he has to make up for in authority borrowed from the Emperor. And from a literary standpoint, set alongside the ancient world of the classics, the New World is precisely that, recently discovered, short-lived, without history or literature (19). Oviedo underlines the geographical opposition between *acá* and *allá* with another contrasting pair, *aquí* and *allí*, which he reserves wholly for drawing literary distinctions: 'here', *aquí*, in this book, 'este volumen', 'esta primera parte', rather than 'there', *allí*, where they write with style and finesse.[10]

In broad terms, one could attribute these political, religious, historical and literary value systems to east and west of the Atlantic in tabular form:

acá – the New World as a source of negative values	The Atlantic Ocean	*allá* – the Old World as a source of positive values
subservience		authority
marginality		centrality
dependence		power
obscurity		recognition and reward
apostasy		defence of the faith
novelty		literary precedence
plainness		rhetorical polish
savagery		civility

But there is another source for the writer's authority that reinvents and even subverts the traditional contrast between civilization and barbarism, and that resides within the author himself. Oviedo's years of service throughout the New World are not just a token of his loyalty; they are the source of his right to speak and a guarantee of his veracity (36, 47). He has been there/lived here and seen for himself, unlike the many more polished authors who have sat at home and written their histories without getting their feet wet; they may reside at the centre of power, but their work is characterized by absence, absence from the reality they purport to describe and account for (40). Loyal service, effort, and suffering have their compensations: first-hand experience makes the writer better able to comply with the Emperor's request (46). Deficiencies of style will be compensated for by greater credibility. And what might be seen as shortcomings in the nature of the land itself also have their compensations: the New World may not have the longevity and

---

10 Oviedo respects the difference between *acá/allá* and *aquí/allí* with remarkable consistency: aquí yo no tracto de aquestas Indias (7); del tenor e sentencia de lo que aquí fuere notificado (43); yo escreví una relación sumaria de parte de lo que aquí se contiene (47); otras cosas grandes e muy nuevas, de que allí no podía yo hazer memoria por no averlas visto, ni sabido (48); éstos que aquí yo escrivo no son de mucha industria o artificio (50); Si algunos vocablos estraños e bárbaros aquí se hallaren (52).

maturity of Europe but its abundance is greater, and its variety is a greater
cause of wonder and a greater stimulus to the glory of God (30–2).

At the heart of this last observation lie two paradoxes: the first is that
caused by the apparent mis-match between the natural abundance of the
newly discovered lands, and the brevity to which the writer would normally
aspire (34). Oviedo is insistent, perhaps disingenuously so, that his
encroaching old age and the little time he has left to live will prove a real
challenge to his doing justice to the reality of his topic (35). Nevertheless, he
will do his best to tell the story in as plain a language as he can, in the hope
that the Emperor's chroniclers 'over there' will polish it at a later stage (42).
And if the account contains some native words, that is not because he cannot
write Spanish: he was born in Madrid and educated at court, and though he
may be geographically distant, he is linguistically and culturally a man of the
centre (52).

The second paradox has to do with the correlation that Oviedo sets up
between the ever-increasing extent of the new lands, the consequent growth
in the political power of the Habsburg Empire, the ever greater commitment
of the Emperor to defending the faith, and the greater and greater evidence
all this gives of the glory of God (37). But whereas the growth in the
Emperor's power is linear, the growth in divine power is exponential. Several
times, Oviedo appears to use this as a way of reminding the Emperor of his
mortality *sub specie aeternitatis*: the greater the Emperor appears to become,
the less significant he appears to grow in comparison with his creator. This
inverse correlation is particularly important in the extremely convoluted
sentence in which Oviedo finally gets around to addressing the question of
his remuneration (78). A loyal servant of the Crown such as Oviedo does not
expect to benefit from his writing; all he asks is that his efforts be dignified
by the Emperor's attention and that such important matters as the extent of
the lands that God had reserved for the Crown of Castile should become
known throughout the world; and that his truthfulness and faithfulness
('como fiel escriptor' – the double meaning of 'fiel' is vital) may be rewarded
by God in the form of the Emperor's ample generosity: please God, make the
Emperor pay me!

In the light of this oppositional subtext, we might revise the previous
table, which attributed positive values to the eastern side of the Atlantic
(*allá*), with a complementary schema. Now the negative values associated
with the New World (*acá*) are transformed into the real sources of his
authority as a writer.

acá – the New World as a source of negative values	The Atlantic Ocean	*allá* – the Old World as a source of positive values
subservience marginality dependence obscurity apostasy novelty plainness savagery		authority centrality power recognition and reward defence of the faith literary precedence rhetorical polish civility
negative becomes positive		positive becomes negative
service loyalty effort experience truthfulness presence abundance admiration		overweening power advantage exploitation book learning ornament absence lesser abundance decadence

Of necessity, this discussion has drawn out the two schemas in a more reductive manner than is consistent with the text itself, where the two discourses, at once opposing and complementary, are woven together with some considerable skill. A close reading of what at first sight appears to be a rather conventional text reveals a high degree of ambiguity in Oviedo's view of the role he is playing, the political and religious system in which he is functioning, and, ultimately, the various discourses of power and authority within which he is required to work. With great skill, Oviedo turns the source of his authority against itself: the Emperor's mandate may appear to condemn the author to the margins of power, but Oviedo's loyal service and long experience in the New World become the source of a new kind of historiographical authority, and he puts his fidelity as a narrator at the service of the God to whose greatness the marvellous abundance of the newly discovered lands bears witness.

WORKS CITED

Manuscript sources

ADR F/156, nos 65, 74, 79–81, 83, 152 and 156: letters of Sor María de Ágreda to Don Francisco de Borja.

AGP Sección Administrativa, leg. 983, 12 March 1646.

AGS Estado, legs 220; 224; 227; 228; 233; 235; 244, doc. 58; 245, docs 53 and 56; 250; 247; 253; 642; 1317, fols 152 and 382; 2644; 4126. Guerra Antigua, legs 1256 and 3173. Guerra y Marina, leg. 88, fol. 359. Patronato Eclesiástico, legs 135 and 136. Registro del Sello, 9 February 1639; 16 February 1639; March 1639.

AHN Estado, leg. 2779; lib. 869, fols 118v–19r. Consejos, lib. 1290, fols 260–264; lib. 1474, no. 188; lib. 2029, fols 24r–v; leg. 51060; leg. 7133, Mesta. Consejos, Cámara de Castilla, leg. 51442, fol. 6. Consejo de Castilla, Sala de Alcaldes de Casa y Corte, fol. 33. Consejos Suprimidos, leg. 15214; leg. 15224, no. 24; legs 15220–15293. Inquisición, leg. 3205, exp. 1. *Premática en que Su Magestad da la orden que se ha de tener en la prisión y castigo de los bandoleros, y gente perdida, y que roban, y saltean en los caminos, y poblados* (AHN Consejos, leg. 51442, fol. 6).

AHNT Sección Nobleza, Osuna, caja 4256, lib. 3, doc. 13; Villalobos, Pedro de, *Discursos jurídicos políticos en razón de que a los gitanos vandoleros de estos tiempos no les vale la Iglesia para su inmunidad* (Salamanca: Diego de Cossío, 1644), caja 4248, doc. 4.

AHPM protocolo 6280, fols 412r, 413v; protocolo 9823, fols 1121v and 1124r.

BL MS Additional 24947, fols 49r, 50v, 53v–58v, 61r–63r.

BNM MS 1517, fol. 4; MS 5791, fols 263–70; MS 9577, fol. 304; MS 13163, fols 70r, 77r, 124r–v, 158r–9r. *Noticia del recibimiento i entrada de la Reyna nvestra Señora doña Maria-Ana de Avstria en la mvy noble i leal coronada villa de Madrid* (Madrid?: n. pub., 1650?; 2/61823). *Pragmática que su Magestad manda que se imprima. Sobre los Vagamundos, Ladrones, Blasphemos, Rufianes . . .* (Alcalá de Henares: En casa de Juan de Villanueva, 1566; R/14090, 26). *Pragmática que su Magestad manda se promulgue en razón de los gitanos que andan por el Reino, y otras cosas* (Madrid: Viuda de Juan González, 1633). *Cédula que SM tiene por bien, y manda, salgan del Reyno dentro de seis meses los Gitanos, que andan vagando por él* (MS 13120). Juan de Quiñones, *Discurso contra los gitanos* (Madrid: Juan González, 1631; R/31436)

Bibliography

Actas de las Cortes de Castilla, 60 vols (Madrid: Real Academia de la Historia, 1877–1974).

Ágreda, Sor María de, *Cartas de Sor María de Jesús de Ágreda y de Felipe IV*, ed. Carlos Seco Serrano, 2 vols, Biblioteca de Autores Españoles, 108–9 (Madrid: Ediciones Atlas, 1958).

Agulló y Cobo, Mercedes, 'Primera entrega documental sobre teatro en Andalucía', in *En torno al teatro del Siglo de Oro: Actas Jornadas XII–XIII* (Almería: Instituto de Estudios Almerienses, Diputación de Almería, 1996), pp. 123–6.

Aiton, Arthur, *Antonio de Mendoza: First Viceroy of New Spain* (Durham: Duke UP, 1927).

Alenda y Mira, Jenaro, *Relaciones de solemnidades y fiestas públicas de España*, 2 vols (Madrid: Sucesores de Rivadeneyra, 1903).

Allen, John J., *The Reconstruction of a Spanish Golden-Age Playhouse: El Corral del Príncipe, 1583–1744* (Gainesville: University Presses of Florida, 1983).

Alonso, Carlos, *Los apócrifos del Sacromonte (Granada): Estudio histórico* (Valladolid: Ed. Estudio Agustiniano, 1979).

Álvarez y Baena, José Antonio, *Compendio Histórico de las Grandezas de la Coronada Villa de Madrid* (Madrid: El Museo Universal, 1985).

Álvarez-Ossorio Alvariño, Antonio, 'Virtud coronada: Carlos II y la piedad de la Casa de Austria', in P. Fernández Albaladejo, J. Martínez Millán and V. Pinto Crespo (eds), *Política, religión e inquisición en la España moderna. Homenaje a Joaquín Pérez Villanueva* (Madrid: Ediciones de la Universidad Autónoma de Madrid, 1996), pp. 29–57.

Ansón Calvo, María del Carmen, 'La expulsión de los moriscos en el Campo de Cariñena', in *Destierros aragoneses. I. Judíos y Moriscos* (Zaragoza: Institución Fernando el Católico, 1988), pp. 261–72.

Aranda Doncel, J., *Los moriscos en tierras de Córdoba* (Córdoba: Publicaciones del Monte de Piedad y Caja de Ahorros de Córdoba, 1984).

Arbel, Benjamin, 'Jews in International Trade: The Emergence of the Levantines and Ponentines', in Robert Davis and Benjamin Ravid (eds), *The Jews of Early Modern Venice* (Baltimore: Johns Hopkins UP, 2001), pp. 73–96.

Astrana Marín, Luis, ed., *Vida ejemplar y heroica de Miguel de Cervantes Saavedra*, 7 vols (Madrid: Reus, 1948–58).

Aznar Cardona, Pedro, *Expulsión justificada de los moriscos españoles y suma de las excelencias cristianas de Nuestro Rey Felipe Tercero* (Huesca: Pedro Cabarte, 1612).

Bances Candamo, Francisco, *Theatro de los theatros de los passados y presentes siglos*, ed. Duncan W. Moir (London: Tamesis, 1970).

Barrios Aguilera, Manuel, *Granada morisca, la convivencia negada. Historia y textos* (Granada: Editorial Comares, 2002).

Beinart, Haim, *Los conversos ante el Tribunal de la Inquisición* (Barcelona: Riopiedras, 1983).

Benítez Sánchez-Blanco, Rafael, 'Las relaciones moriscos–cristianos viejos: entre la asimilación y el rechazo', in *Disidencias y exilios en la España moderna. Actas de la IV Reunión Científica de la Asociación Española de*

Historia Moderna, eds Antonio Mestre Sanchis and Enrique Giménez López (Alicante: CAM/Universidad de Alicante, 1997), pp. 335–46.

Benjamin, Walter, *Illuminations. Essays and Reflections*, trans. Harry Zohn, ed. Hannah Arendt (New York: Schocken Books, 1968).

Bennassar, Bartolomé, *La América española y la América portuguesa: siglos XVI–XVIII*, 3rd edn (Madrid: Akal, 1996).

Bergin, Joseph, *The Rise of Richelieu*, 2nd edn (Manchester: Manchester UP, 1997).

Bireley, Robert, *The Counter-Reformation Prince: Anti-Machiavellianism or Catholic Statecraft in Early Modern Europe* (Chapel Hill: The University of North Carolina Press, 1990).

Blanco-González, Bernardo, 'Introducción. Biografía y crítica', in *Guerra de Granada*, ed. Bernardo Blanco-González (Madrid: Castalia, 1970), pp. 7–87.

Blázquez Miguel, Juan, *Inquisición y criptojudaísmo* (Madrid: Kaydeda, 1988).

Bleda, Jaime, *Corónica de los moros de España* (Valencia: Felipe Mey, 1618 [facsimile edition with introduction by Bernard Vincent and Rafael Benítez Sánchez-Blanco: Valencia: Biblioteca Valenciana-Ajuntament de València-Universitat de València, 2001]).

Boase, Roger, 'The Morisco Expulsion and Diaspora: An Example of Racial and Religious Intolerance', in *Cultures in Contact in Medieval Spain: Historical Survey and Literary Essays for L.P. Harvey* (London: King's College London Medieval Studies, 1990), pp. 9–28.

Bocángel y Unzueta, Gabriel, *Obras completas*, ed. Trevor J. Dadson, 2 vols (Madrid: Iberoamericana and Vervuert, 2000).

Bolaños, Alvaro Félix, 'The historian and the Hesperides: Fernández de Oviedo and the limitations of imitation', *Bulletin of Hispanic Studies*, 72 (1995), 273–88.

Botero, Giovanni, *Della ragion di stato libri dieci* (Venice: I. Gioliti, 1589).

Boyarin, Jonathan, 'Space, Time, and the Politics of Memory', in *Remapping Memory: The Politics of Time Space*, ed. Jonathan Boyarin (Minneapolis: University of Minnesota Press, 1994), pp. 1–37.

Brading, D.A., *The First America. The Spanish Monarchy, Creole Patriots and the Liberal State 1492–1867* (Cambridge: CUP, 1991).

Braudel, Fernand, *The Mediterranean and the Mediterranean World in the Age of Philip II*, 2 vols (London: Harper Collins, 1972).

Brown, Jonathan and Elliott, John H., *A Palace for a King: The Buen Retiro and the Court of Philip IV*, 2nd edn (New Haven: Yale UP, 2003).

Bunes, M.A. de, *Los moriscos en el pensamiento histórico* (Madrid: Cátedra, 1983).

Burgos, Cantera, 'Fernando de Pulgar and the *conversos*', *Sefarad*, 4 (1944), 296–348.

Cabrera de Córdoba, L., *Relaciones de las cosas sucedidas en la Corte de España desde 1599 hasta 1614* (Madrid: Imprenta de J. Martín Alegría, 1857 [facsimile edition: Salamanca: Junta de Castilla y León, 1997]).

Calderón de la Barca, Pedro, *El agua mansa; Guárdate del agua mansa*, eds Ignacio Arellano and Víctor García Ruiz (Kassel: Reichenberger, 1989).

—— *El cubo de la Almudena*, in *Obras completas*, III, ed. Ángel Valbuena Prat (Madrid: Aguilar, 1952), pp. 559–85.

―― *El gran príncipe de Fez, Baltasar de Loyola*, in *Obras completas*, II, ed. Ángel Valbuena Briones (Madrid: Aguilar, 1959), pp. 1407–54.

―― *El sitio de Bredá*, in *Pedro Calderón de la Barca: Comedias*, eds D.W. Cruickshank and J.E. Varey (Farnborough/London: Gregg/Tamesis, 1973), IV, *Primera parte de comedias* (Madrid, '1640').

―― *El Tuzaní de la Alpujarra*, ed. Manuel Ruiz Lagos (Alcalá de Guadaira: Editorial Guadalmena, 1998).

―― *La segunda esposa y triunfar muriendo*, ed. Víctor García Ruiz (Kassel: Reichenberger, 1992).

Capdevila y Orozco, José, *Errantes y expulsados: normativas jurídicas contra gitanos, judíos, y moriscos* (Córdoba: Francisco Baena, 1991).

Carbajo Isla, María F., *La Población de la Villa de Madrid: desde finales del siglo XVI hasta mediados del siglo XIX* (Madrid: Siglo Veintiuno, 1987).

Caro Baroja, Julio, *Los judíos en la España moderna y contemporánea* (Madrid: Ariel, 1961).

Carrillo, Jesús, 'From Mt Ventoux to Mt Masaya: The rise and fall of subjectivity in early modern travel narrative', in Jaš Elsner and Joan-Pau Rubies (eds), *Voyages and Visions. Towards a Cultural History of Travel* (London: Reaktion, 1999), pp. 57–73.

Cascardi, Anthony J., *Ideologies of History in the Spanish Golden Age* (University Park, PA: The Pennsylvania State UP, 1997).

Case, Thomas, 'Honor, Justice, and Historical Circumstance in *Amar después de la muerte*', *Bulletin of the Comediantes*, 36 (1984), 55–69.

Ceballos, Jerónimo de, *Discurso sobre el remedio de la Monarquía Española* (Toledo: n. pub., 1620).

Censo de la Corona de Castilla, 1591, facsimile edition (Madrid: Instituto Nacional de Estadística, 1984).

Cervantes, Miguel de, *Don Quijote*, 2 vols (Madrid: Castalia, 1978).

―― *El coloquio de los perros*, in *Novelas ejemplares*, II, ed. Harry Sieber, 2 vols (Madrid: Cátedra, 1980).

―― *La gitanilla*, in *Novelas ejemplares*, I, ed. Juan Bautista Avalle-Arce, 3 vols (Madrid: Castalia, 1982).

―― *Obras Completas*, ed. Florencio Sevilla Arroyo and Antonio Rey Hazas (Centro de Estudios Cervantinos, 1993–5).

Chaves Montoya, María Teresa, 'La conquista del Viejo Mundo "América" recibe a Mariana de Austria (1649)', in Wolfram Krömer (ed.), *1492–1992: Spanien, Österreich und Iberoamerika. Akten des Siebten Spanisch-Österreichischen Symposions 16.–21. März 1992 in Innsbruck* (Innsbruck: University of Innsbruck, Institut für Sprachwissenschaft, 1993), pp. 51–65.

―― *El espectáculo teatral en la corte de Felipe IV* (Madrid: Ayuntamiento, 2004).

Cippolla, Carlo M., *Literacy and Development in the West* (Harmondsworth: Pelican, 1960).

Colás Latorre, Gregorio, 'Los moriscos aragoneses: una definición más allá de la religión y la política', *Sharq al-Andalus. Estudios Mudéjares y Moriscos*, 12 (1995), 147–61.

Corral y Rojas, Antonio de, Antonio de, *Relación del [sic] rebelión y expulsión de los Moriscos del reino de Valencia* (Valladolid: Diego Fernández de Córdoba, 1613)

Cortés, Hernán, *Cartas de relación*, ed. Angel Delgado Gómez (Madrid: Castalia, 1993).

Cotarelo y Mori, E., *Bibliografía de las controversias sobre la licitud del teatro en España* (Madrid: Tipografía de la Revista de Archivos, Bibliotecas y Museos, 1904).

Cruz, Anne J., ' "Corazón alarbe": Los moriscos, el código de honor y la crítica de la guerra en *Amar después de la muerte*', in *Actas del Congreso Internacional, IV Centenario del nacimiento de Calderón, Universidad de Navarra, septiembre, 2000*, ed. Ignacio Arellano (Kassel: Edition Reichenberger, 2002), pp. 121–32.

Cueto, Ronald, *Quimeras y sueños. Los profetas y la Monarquía Católica de Felipe IV* (Valladolid: Secretariado de Publicaciones, Universidad de Valladolid, 1994).

Dadson, T.J., 'Convivencia y cooperación entre moriscos y cristianos del Campo de Calatrava: De nuevo con Cervantes y Ricote', in *Siglos Dorados. Homenaje a Augustin Redondo*, ed. Pierre Civil, 2 vols (Madrid: Editorial Castalia, 2004), I, pp. 301–14.

—— 'Educación y movilidad social entre los moriscos del Campo de Calatrava', in *Actas del XV Congreso de la AIH, Monterrey, julio de 2004* (in press).

—— 'Literacy and Education in Early Modern Rural Spain: the Case of Villarrubia de los Ojos', in *The Iberian Book and its Readers. Essays for Ian Michael*, eds Nigel Griffin, Clive Griffin and Eric Southworth, *Bulletin of Spanish Studies*, 81 (2004), 1011–37.

—— 'Un Ricote verdadero: el licenciado Alonso Herrador de Villarrubia de los Ojos de Guadiana – morisco que vuelve', in *Memoria de la palabra. Actas del VI Congreso de la AISO, Burgos-La Rioja, 15–19 de julio 2002*, eds María Luisa Lobato and Francisco Domínguez Matito, 2 vols (Madrid: Iberoamericana-Vervuert, 2004), I, pp. 601–12.

Davila, Juan Francisco, *Relacion de los festivos aplavsos con que celebró esta Corte Catolica las alegres nueuas del feliz Desposorio del Rey nuestro Señor Don Felipe Quarto (que Dios guarde) y el cumplimiento de años de la Reyna nuestra Señora* (Madrid: Domingo García y Morras, 1649?).

Davis, Charles, 'Tacitean Elements in Diego Hurtado de Mendoza's *Guerra de Granada*', *Dispositio*, 10 (1996), 85–96.

Davis, Robert and Ravid, Benjamin (eds), *The Jews of Early Modern Venice* (Baltimore: Johns Hopkins UP, 2001).

Deleito y Piñuela, José, *El Rey se divierte* (Madrid: Alianza, 1988).

Domínguez Ortiz, Antonio, *Alteraciones Andaluzas* (Madrid: Narcea, 1973).

—— *Las Clases Privilegiadas en el Antiguo Régimen* (Madrid: Istmo, 1979).

—— 'Las rentas de los prelados de Castilla en el siglo XVII', in *Estudios de Historia económica y social de España* (Granada: Universidad de Granada, 1987), pp. 223–60.

—— *Los conversos de origen judío después de la expulsión* (Madrid: CSIC, 1955).

—— *The Golden Age of Spain: 1516–1659* (London: Weidenfeld & Nicolson, 1971).

Domínguez Ortiz, Antonio and Vincent, Bernard, *Historia de los moriscos. Vida y tragedia de una minoría* (Madrid: Alianza, 1984).

Eire, Carlos, *From Madrid to Purgatory. The Art and Craft of Dying in Sixteenth-Century Spain* (Cambridge: CUP, 1995).

Elliott, J.H., *Imperial Spain 1469–1716* (London: Edward Arnold, 1963). Spanish edition *La España imperial: 1469–1716*, trans. J. Marfany, 5th edn (Barcelona: Vicens Vives, 1986).

—— 'Self-perception and decline in early seventeenth century Spain', in *Spain and its World, 1500–1700* (New Haven: Yale UP, 1989), pp. 241–61.

—— *The Count-Duke of Olivares: The Statesman in an Age of Decline* (New Haven: Yale UP, 1986).

Elliott J.H. and de la Peña, José F. (eds), *Memoriales y Cartas del Conde-Duque de Olivares* (Madrid: Alfaguara, 1978).

Entrambasaguas, Joaquín de, *Una familia de ingenios. Los Ramírez de Prado* (Madrid: CSIC, 1943).

Ercilla, Alonso de, *La Araucana* (Salamanca: Domingo de Portonariis, 1569).

Escudero, José Antonio, *Los Secretarios de Estado y del Despacho (1472–1724)*, 4 vols (Madrid: Instituto de Estudios Administrativos, 2nd edn 1976).

Fayard, Janine, *Los miembros del Consejo de Castilla, 1621–1746*, trans. Rufina Rodríguez Sanz (Madrid: Siglo Veintiuno, 1982).

Fernández de Navarrete, Pedro, *Conservación de Monarquías y discursos políticos*, ed. Michael D. Gordon (Madrid: Instituto de Estudios Fiscales, 1982).

Feros, Antonio, 'El viejo monarca y los nuevos favoritos: los discursos sobre la privanza en el reinado de Felipe II', *Studia Histórica (Historia Moderna)*, 17 (1997), 11–36.

Fita, Fidel, 'La verdad sobre el martirio del santo niño de la guardia, o sea el proceso y quema (16 noviembre, 1491) del judío Jucé Franco en Ávila', *Boletín de la Real Academia de la Historia*, 11 (1887), 6–160.

Fonseca, Damien, *Justa expulsión de los moriscos de España, con la instrucción, apostasía y traición dellos* (Roma: Iacomo Mascardo, 1612).

Galmés de Fuentes, A., 'La conversión de los moriscos y su pretendida aculturación', in *La política y los moriscos en la época de los Austria*, dir. Rodolfo Gil Grimau (Madrid: Comunidad de Madrid, 1999), pp. 157–74.

—— *Los moriscos (Desde su misma orilla)* (Madrid: Instituto Egipcio de Estudios Islámicos en Madrid, 1993).

García-Arenal, Mercedes, 'El entorno de los plomos: historiografía y linaje', *Al-Qantara. Revista de estudios árabes*, 24:2 (2003), 295–326.

—— 'Los moriscos de la región de Cuenca según los censos establecidos por la Inquisición en 1589 y 1594', *Hispania*, 38 (1978), 151–99.

García España, E. and Molinié-Bertrand, A. (eds), *Censo de Castilla de 1591: Estudio Analítico* (Madrid: Instituto Nacional de Estadística, 1986).

García López, A., *Moriscos en tierras de Uceda y Guadalajara (1502–1610)* (Guadalajara: Diputación Provincial de Guadalajara, 1992).

García Sanz, Ángel, 'Castile 1580–1650: economic crisis and the policy of reform', in *The Castilian Crisis of the Seventeenth Century*, eds I.A.A. Thompson and B. Yun (Cambridge: CUP, 1995), pp. 13–31.

—— 'El sector agrario durante el siglo XVII: depresión y reajustes', in *Historia de España Menéndez y Pidal*, XXIII (Madrid: Espasa Calpe, 1989), pp. 161–235.

Garrido Atienza, M., *Las capitulaciones para la entrega de Granada* (Granada: Universidad de Granada, 1992), pp. 273–4.

Gerbi, Antonello, *La naturaleza de las Indias Nuevas* (Mexico: Fondo de Cultura Económica, 1978).

Gil Ayuso, Faustino (ed.), *Noticia bibliográfica de textos y disposiciones legales de Castilla impresos en los siglos XVI y XVII* (Madrid: S. Aguirre, 1935).

Gittlitz, David, *Secrecy and Deceit: The Religion of the Crypto-Jews* (Philadelphia: The Jewish Publication Society, 1996).

González Dávila, Gil, *Historia de la vida y hechos del inclito monarca, amado y santo Don Felipe Tercero*, in Pedro Salazar de Mendoza, *Monarquía de España*, III (Madrid: Ibarra, 1770–1).

—— *Teatro de las Grandezas de la Villa de Madrid* (Madrid: Publicaciones Abella, 1986 [1623]).

González Palencia, Ángel (ed.), *Archivo Histórico Español*, V (Valladolid: n. pub., 1932), *La Junta de Reformación, 1618–1625*.

González Palencia, Angel and Mele, Eugenio, *Vida y obras de Don Diego Hurtado de Mendoza*, 3 vols (Madrid: Instituto de Valencia Don Juan, 1941–3).

Goodman, David, *Spanish Naval Power, 1589–1665* (Cambridge: CUP, 1997).

Grayzel, Solomon, *The Church and the Jews in the XIIIth Century* (New York: Hermon Press, 1966).

Greer, Margaret R., 'Constituting Community: A New Historical Perspective on the *Autos* of Calderón', in *New Historicism and the Comedia: Poetics, Politics and Praxis*, ed. José A. Madrigal (Boulder, CO: Society of Spanish and Spanish-American Studies, 1997), pp. 41–67.

Guadalajara, Fray Marcos de, *Memorable expulsión y justísimo destierro de los Moriscos de España* (Pamplona: Nicolás de Assiayn, 1613).

Hamilton, Earl J., 'Las consecuencias económicas de la expulsión de los moriscos', in *Actas del I Congreso de Historia de Andalucía. Andalucía Moderna (Siglos XVI–XVII)*, II (Córdoba: Publicaciones del Monte de Piedad y Caja de Ahorros de Córdoba, 1978), pp. 69–84.

Harris, A. Katie, 'The Sacromonte and the Geography of the Sacred in Early Modern Granada', *Al-Qantara. Revista de estudios árabes*, 23:2 (2002), 517–43.

Hermengildo, Alfredo, *La 'Numancia' de Cervantes*, Biblioteca de Crítica Literaria (Madrid: Sociedad General Española de Librería, 1976).

Hobson, Anthony, *Renaissance Book Collecting: Jean Grolier and Diego Hurtado de Mendoza, Their Books and Bindings* (Cambridge: CUP, 1999).

Hurtado de Mendoza, Diego, *Guerra de Granada*, ed. Bernardo Blanco-González (Madrid: Castalia, 1970).

Ife, B.W., 'Alexander in the New World', *Renaissance and Modern Studies*, 30 (1986), 35–44.

—— 'The literary impact of the New World: Columbus to Carrizales', *Journal of the Institute of Romance Studies*, 3 (1994–95), 65–85.

Ife, B.W. and Goodwin, R.T.C., ' "Many expert narrators": History and fiction in the Spanish chronicles of the New World', in *Remapping the Rise of the European Novel* (Oxford: Voltaire Foundation), forthcoming.

Ioly Zorattini, Pier Cesare, 'Jews, Crypto-Jews and the Inquisition', in Robert Davis and Benjamin Ravid (eds), *The Jews of Early Modern Venice* (Baltimore: Johns Hopkins UP, 2001), pp. 97–116.

Janer, Florencio, *Condición social de los moriscos de España: Causas de su expulsión, y consecuencias que ésta produjo en el orden económico y político* (Madrid: Imprenta de la Real Academia de la Historia, 1857 [facsimile edition: Barcelona: Alta Fulla, 1987]).

Johnson, Carroll B., '*La Numancia* y la estructura de la ambigüedad cervantina', in *Cervantes: su obra y su mundo: Actas del I Congreso Internacional sobre Cervantes, Madrid, 1978*, ed. Manuel Criado del Val (Madrid: Edi-6, 1981), pp. 309–16.

Jowitt, Claire, ' "I am another woman": The Spanish and French Matches in Massinger's *The Renegado* (1624) and *The Unnatural Combat* (1624–5)', in Alexander Samson (ed.), *The Spanish Match: Prince Charles' Journey to Madrid, 1623* (Basingstoke: Ashgate, 2005).

Kagan, Richard L., *Students and Society in Early Modern Spain* (Baltimore: Johns Hopkins UP, 1974).

Kamen, Henry, *Spain, 1469–1714* (London: Longman, 1999).

—— *The Phoenix and the Flame. Catalonia and the Counter-Reformation* (New Haven: Yale UP, 1993).

—— *The Spanish Inquisition: A Historical Revision* (London: Phoenix, 1998).

Kendrick, T.D., *Mary of Ágreda: The Life and Legend of a Spanish Nun* (London: Routledge & Kegan Paul, 1967).

Keniston, Howard, *Francisco de los Cobos: Secretary of the Emperor Charles V* (Pittsburg: University of Pittsburg Press, 1960).

King, Willard F., 'Cervantes's *Numancia* and Imperial Spain', *Modern Language Notes*, 94: 2 (1979), 200–21.

Koningsveld, P.S. van and Wiegers, Gerard A., 'The Parchment of the "Torre Turpiana": the original document and its early interpreters', *Al-Qantara. Revista de estudios árabes*, 24: 2 (2003), 327–58.

Krantz, Albert, *Rerum Germanicarum historici clariss. Saxonia* (Frankfurt am Main: Andreas Wechel, 1580 [1520]).

La Parra-López, Santiago, 'Los moriscos y moriscas de los Borja', in *Disidencias y exilios en la España moderna: Actas de la IV Reunión Científica de la Asociación Española de Historia Moderna, Alicante, 27–30 de mayo de 1996*, ed. Antonio Mestre Sanchis (Alicante: Universidad de Alicante, 1998), pp. 435–46.

Lapeyre, H., *Geografía de la España morisca* (Valencia: Diputación Provincial, 1986).

Leblon, Bernard, *Los gitanos de España* (Barcelona: Gedisa, 2001 [1985]).

León Pinelo, Antonio de, *Anales de Madrid del año 447 al de 1658*, ed. Pedro Fernández Martín (Madrid: Instituto de Estudios Madrileños, 1971).

Lewis-Smith, Paul, 'Cervantes's *Numancia* as Tragedy and Tragicomedy', *Bulletin of Hispanic Studies*, 64 (1986), 15–26.

Lewy, Guenter, *Constitutionalism and Statecraft during the Golden Age of Spain:*

A Study of the Political Philosophy of Juan de Mariana, S.J. (Geneva: Droz, 1960).

Lynch, John, *The Hispanic World in Crisis and Change, 1598–1700* (Oxford: Blackwell, 1992).

Mackay, Ruth, *The Limits of Royal Authority: Resistance and Obedience in Seventeenth-Century Castile* (Cambridge: CUP, 1999).

McKendrick, Melveena, *Theatre in Spain 1490–1700* (Cambridge: CUP, 1989).

Maiso González, Jesús, 'La cuestión morisca en Bulbuente, 1576–1700', in *Estudios del Departamento de Historia Moderna. Facultad de Filosofía y Letras, Zaragoza* (Zaragoza: Universidad, 1976), pp. 247–77.

Malcolm, Alistair, 'Don Luis de Haro and the Political Elite of the Spanish Monarchy in the Mid-Seventeenth Century' (unpublished doctoral thesis, University of Oxford, 1999).

—— 'La práctica informal del poder. La política de la Corte y el acceso a la familia real durante la segunda mitad del reinado de Felipe IV', *Reales Sitios*, 38 (2001), 38–48.

—— 'Spanish Queens and Aristocratic Women at the Court of Madrid, 1598–1665', in Christine Meek and Catherine Lawless (eds), *Public Life, Private Life: Women in Medieval and Early Modern Europe* (Dublin: Four Courts, 2005), pp. 160–80.

Manrique, Ángel, *Socorro del clero al estado* (Salamanca, 1624; repr. Madrid: n. pub., 1814).

Marañón, Gregorio, *El conde-duque de Olivares. La pasión de mandar*, 26th edn (Madrid: Espasa Calpe, 1998).

—— *Expulsión y diáspora de los moriscos españoles* (Madrid: Taurus, 2004).

Maravall, José Antonio, *Teoría del estado en España en el Siglo XVII* (Madrid: Centro de Estudios Constitucionales, 1997).

Marmol Carvajal, Luis del, *Historia del rebelión y castigo de los moriscos del reino de Granada*, ed. Angel Galán (Málaga: Editorial Arguval, 1991).

Márquez Villanueva, Francisco, *El problema morisco (desde otras laderas)* (Madrid: Ediciones Libertarias, 1991).

Martínez Gil, Fernando, *Muerte y Sociedad en la España de los Austrias* (Madrid: Siglo Veintiuno, 1993).

Martz, Linda, 'Pure Blood Statutes in Sixteenth Century Toledo: Implementation as Opposed to Adoption', *Sefarad*, 54 (1994), 83–106.

Mendo, Andrés, *Principe perfecto y ministros aiustados documentos politicos y morales en emblemas*, 3rd edn (Lyon: Horacio Boissat and George Remeus, 1662).

Meneses García, E. (ed.), *Correspondencia del Conde de Tendilla, 1508–1513*, 2 vols (Madrid: Real Academia de la Historia, 1973–4).

Metford, J.C.J., 'The Enemies of the Theatre in the Golden Age', *Bulletin of Hispanic Studies*, 28 (1951), 76–92.

Molinié-Bertrand, A., 'Le Clergé dans le Royaume de Castille à la fin du XVIe siècle', *Revue d'histoire économique et sociale*, 51 (1978), 5–53.

Moncada, Sancho de, *Restauración política de España*, ed. Jean Vilar Berrogain (Madrid: Instituto de Estudios Fiscales, 1974 [1619]).

Morales, Ambrosio de, *La Coronica General de España que continuaua prosiguiendo adelante de los cinco libros que el Maestro Florián de Ocampo* . . . (Alcalá: Juan Iñiguez de Lequerica, 1574).

Nader, Helen, *The Mendoza Family in the Spanish Renaissance, 1350–1550* (New Brunswick: Rutgers UP, 1979).

Nalle, Sara T., *God in La Mancha. Religious Reform and the People of Cuenca, 1500–1650* (Baltimore: Johns Hopkins UP, 1992).

—— 'Literacy and Culture in Early Modern Castile', *Past and Present*, 125 (1989), 65–96.

Netanyahu, Benzion, *The Origins of the Inquisition in 15th Century Spain* (New York: Random House, 1995).

Novísima recopilación de las leyes de España, 4 vols (Paris: Mégico, 1831).

O'Connor, Thomas Austin, *Love in the 'Corral': Conjugal Spirituality and Anti-Theatrical Polemic in Early Modern Spain* (New York: Peter Lang, 2000).

Oehrlein, Josef, 'El actor en el Siglo de Oro: imagen de la profesión y reputación social', in *Actor y técnica de representación del teatro clásico español*, ed. José María Borque (London: Tamesis, 1989), pp. 17–33.

Okely, Judith, *The Traveller-Gypsies* (Cambridge: CUP, 1983).

Otero Torres, Dámaris, 'Amor y silencio: Ecos del discurso minoritario en *Amar después de la muerte*', in El escritor y la escena VII: Estudios sobre teatro español y novohispano de los Siglos de Oro. El espectador y el crítico: problemas de recepción, ed. Ysla Campbell (Ciudad Juárez: Universidad Autonóma de Ciudad Juárez, 2000), pp. 195–203.

Oviedo y Valdés, Gonzalo Fernández de, *Historia general y natural de las Indias, islas y tierra firme del mar Océano*, ed. José Amador de los Ríos, Biblioteca de Autores Españoles, 118–22 (Madrid, 1959 [1851–5]). Part I (books 1–19; 362,610 words) can be consulted at http://ems.kcl.ac.uk/content/etext/ e026.html.

Pagden, Anthony, *European Encounters with the New World* (New Haven: Yale UP, 1993).

—— *The Fall of Natural Man. The American Indian and the Origins of Comparative Ethnology* (Cambridge: CUP, 1982).

—— *Lords of All the World. Ideologies of Empire in Spain, Britain and France c.1500–c.1800* (New Haven: Yale UP, 1995).

Parker, Alexander A., *The Mind and Art of Calderón: Essays on the Comedia* (Cambridge: CUP, 1988).

Pellicer, José de, *Avisos históricos* (Madrid: Taurus, 1965).

Pérez de Guzmán, Torcuato, *Los gitanos herreros de Sevilla* (Sevilla: Ayuntamiento, 1982).

Pérez de Hita, Ginés, *Segunda parte de las guerras civiles de Granada*, ed. Joaquín Gil Sanjuan (Granada: Editorial Universidad de Granada, 1998).

Pérez Villanueva, Joaquín (ed.), *Felipe IV y Luisa Manrique de Lara, Condesa de Paredes de Nava. Un epistolario inédito* (Salamanca: Ediciones de la Caja de Ahorros y Monte de Piedad de Salamanca, 1986).

Plutarch, *Plutarch's Lives*, ed. G.P. Gould, trans. Bernadotte Perrin, The Loeb Classical Library, 11 vols (London: Heinemann, 1982), IX, 'Demetrius and Antony; Pyrrhus and Caius Marius'.

Pulgar, Hernando del, *Crónica de los Reyes Católicos*, ed. Juan de la Mata Carriazo (Madrid: Espasa Calpe, 1943).

Pullen, Brian, *The Jews of Europe and the Inquisition of Venice, 1550–1670* (Oxford: Basil Blackwell, 1983).

Puyol Buil, Carlos, *Inquisición y política en el reinado de Felipe IV. Los procesos de Jerónimo de Villanueva y las monjas de San Plácido, 1628–1660* (Madrid: CSIC, 1993).

Pym, Richard J., 'Negotiated Voices: the *Vida* of Santa Teresa de Jesús', *Bulletin of Hispanic Studies*, 77 (2000), 225–38.

—— 'The Pariah Within: Early Modern Spain's Gypsies', *Journal of Romance Studies*, 4:2 (2004), 21–35.

Rawlings, Helen, *Church, Religion and Society in Early Modern Spain* (Basingstoke: Palgrave, 2002).

Regalado, Antonio, *Calderón: Los orígenes de la modernidad en la España del Siglo de Oro*, 2 vols (Barcelona: Destino, 1995).

Rojas, Agustín de, *El viaje entretenido*, Libro 2 (Madrid: Águila, 1945).

Romanos, Melchora, 'Ficción y realidad histórica en *El Tuzaní de la Alpujarra* o *Amar después de la muerte* de Pedro Calderón de la Barca', in *Calderón: Protagonista eminente del Barroco europeo*, eds Kurt Reichenberger and Theo Reichenberger (Kassel: Edición Reichenberger, 2000), pp. 355–72.

Roth, Cecil, *A History of the Marranos* (Philadelphia: Jewish Publication Society, 1932).

Ruiz Martín, Felipe, 'Demografía Eclesiástica', in *Diccionario de Historia Eclesiástica de España*, ed. Q. Aldea, T. Marín and J. Vives, 4 vols (Madrid: CSIC, 1972–5), II, pp. 682–733.

—— 'La población española al comienzo de los tiempos modernos', *Cuadernos de Historia*, 1 (1967), 189–202.

Rupp, Stephen, *Allegories of Kingship: Calderón and the Anti-Machiavellian Tradition* (University Park, PA: Pennsylvania State UP, 1996).

Saavedra Fajardo, Diego de, *Empresas políticas*, 2nd edn [Milan, 1643], ed. Sagrario López (Madrid: Cátedra, 1999).

Salas, Alberto M., *Tres cronistas de Indias* (México: Fondo de Cultura Económica, 1986).

Salazar de Mendoza, Pedro de, *Memorial de el hecho de los gitanos* (Toledo? n. pub., 1618?).

—— *Monarquía de España*, III (Madrid: Ibarra, 1770–1).

Sánchez Ortega, María Helena, *La Inquisición y los gitanos* (Madrid: Taurus, 1988).

—— *Los gitanos españoles: el período borbónico* (Barcelona: Castellote, 1977).

San Román, Teresa de, *La diferencia inquietante: Viejas y nuevas estrategias culturales de los gitanos* (Madrid: Siglo Veintiuno, 1997).

Santa María, Fray Juan de, *República y policía christiana para reyes y príncipes y para los que en el govierno tienen sus vezes*, 3rd edn (Barcelona: Geronymo Margarit, 1617).

Sharpe, Kevin, *The Personal Rule of Charles I* (New Haven: Yale UP, 1992).

Shergold, N.D., *A History of the Spanish Stage from Medieval Times to the End of the Seventeenth Century* (Oxford: Clarendon Press, 1967).

Shergold, N.D. and Varey, J.E., 'Datos históricos sobre los primeros teatros de

Madrid: prohibiciones de autos y comedias y sus consecuencias (1644–1651)', *Bulletin Hispanique*, 72 (1960), 286–325.

—— *Fuentes para la historia del teatro en España, I: Representaciones palaciegas: 1603–1699* (London: Tamesis, 1982).

—— *Fuentes para la historia del teatro en España, II: Genealogía, origen y noticias de los comediantes de España* (London: Tamesis, 1985).

Sieber, Diane M., 'El monstruo en su laberinto: cristianos en las Alpujarras de *Amar después de la muerte*', in *Actas del XIII Congreso de la Asociación Internacional de Hispanistas*, 4 vols (Madrid: Castalia, 2000), I, pp. 740–6.

Simerka, Barbara, *Discourses of Empire: Counter-Epic Literature in Early Modern Spain* (University Park, PA: Pennsylvania State UP, 2003).

Spivakovsky, Erika, 'A Jewess of Venice', *The Chicago Jewish Forum*, 19 (1960–1), 129–37.

—— *Son of the Alhambra: Don Diego Hurtado de Mendoza, 1504–1575* (Austin: University of Texas Press, 1970).

Stradling, R.A., *Philip IV and the Government of Spain, 1621–1665* (Cambridge: CUP, 1988).

Tapia, Serafín de, *La comunidad morisca de Ávila* (Salamanca: Ediciones Universidad de Salamanca, 1991).

—— 'Los moriscos de Castilla la Vieja, ¿una identidad en proceso de disolución?', *Sharq al-Andalus. Estudios Mudéjares y Moriscos*, 12 (1995), 179–95.

Thompson, I.A.A., 'Castile', in *Absolutism in Seventeenth-Century Europe*, ed. John Miller (London: Macmillan, 1990), pp. 69–98.

Tomás y Valiente, Francisco, *Los validos en la monarquía española del siglo XVII*, 2nd edn (Madrid: Siglo Veintiuno, 1990).

Tyler, Richard W. and Elizondo, Sergio D., *The Characters, Plots, and Settings of Calderón's Comedias* (Lincoln, NB: Society of Spanish and Spanish-American Studies, 1981).

Ugarte de Hermosa y Salcedo, Francisco, *Origen de los dos goviernos divino i humano i forma de su exercicio en lo tenporal* (Madrid: G. Morras, 1655).

Varey, J.E. and Davis, Charles, *Fuentes para la historia del teatro en España XX: Los corrales y los hospitales de Madrid: 1574–1615* (Madrid: Támesis, 1997).

—— *Fuentes para la historia del teatro en España XXI: Los corrales de comedias y los hospitales de Madrid: 1615–1849* (Madrid: Támesis, 1997).

Varey, J.E. and Salazar, A.M., 'Calderón and the Royal Entry of 1649', *Hispanic Review*, 34 (January 1966), 1–26.

Varey, J.E. and Shergold, N.D. 'Datos históricos sobre los primeros teatros de Madrid: prohibiciones de autos y comedias y sus consecuencias (1644–1651)', *Bulletin Hispanique*, 72 (1960), 286–325.

Vazquez, Alberto and Selden Rose, R. (eds), *Algunas Cartas de Don Diego Hurtado de Mendoza escritas 1538–1552* (New Haven: Yale UP, 1935).

Vega Carpio, Lope de, *El asalto de Mastrique*, in *Obras de Lope de Vega*, 27, *Crónicas y leyendas dramáticas de España*, ed. Marcelino Menéndez Pelayo, Biblioteca de autores españoles, 225 (Madrid: Atlas, 1969), pp. 1–59.

—— *El nuevo mundo descubierto por Cristóbal Colón*, ed. Robert M. Shannon (New York: Peter Lang, 2001).

Veliz, Zahira, 'Signs of Identity in *Lady with a Fan* by Diego Velázquez: Costume and Likeness Reconsidered', *Art Bulletin*, 86 (March 2004), 75–95.

Vicens Vives, J., 'The Decline of Spain in the Seventeenth Century', in *The Economic Decline of Empires*, ed. C.M. Cipolla (London: Methuen, 1970), pp. 121–67.

Vilar, Jean, *Literatura y Economía. La figura satírica del arbitrista en el Siglo de Oro* (Madrid: Revista de Occidente, 1973), pp. 59–102.

Villalón, Cristobal de, *Viaje de Turquía*, ed. Fernando García Salinero (Madrid: Cátedra, 1986).

Vincent, Bernard, 'L'Albaicín de Grenade au XVIe siècle (1527–1587)', *Mélanges de la Casa de Velázquez*, 7 (1971), 187–222.

—— 'Amor y matrimonio entre los moriscos', in *Minorías y marginados en la España del siglo XVI* (Granada: Diputación Provincial, 1987), pp. 47–71.

Vitse, Marc, *Elements pour une théorie du théâtre espagnol du XVIIe siècle* (Toulouse: Université de Toulouse-Le Mirail, 1988).

Whicker, Jules, ' "La caballería bajo fuego": La representación de la virtud militar española en *El asalto de Mastrique* de Lope y *El sitio de Bredá* de Calderón', in *Calderón 2000: Homenaje a Kurt Reichenberger en su 80 cumpleaños. Actas del Congreso Internacional IV centenario del nacimiento de Calderón. Universidad de Navarra, septiembre 2000* (Kassel: Reichenberger, 2002), pp. 411–23.

Wilson, E.M., 'Nuevos documentos sobre las controversias teatrales: 1650–1681', in Jaime Sánchez Romeralo and Norbert Poulussen (eds), *Actas del Segundo Congreso Internacional de Hispanistas celebrado en Nijmegen del 20 al 25 de agosto de 1965* (Nijmegen: Instituto Español de la Universidad de Nimega, 1967), pp. 155–70.

Wilson, E.M. and Moir, D.M., *Historia de la literatura española. Siglo de oro: teatro, 1492–1700*, trans. Carlos Pujol (Barcelona: Ariel, 1985).

Wilson, Margaret, ' "Si África llora, España no ríe": A Study of Calderón's *Amar después de la muerte* in Relation to its Source', *Bulletin of Hispanic Studies*, 61 (1984), 419–25.

Wiseman, T.P., 'The publication of *De Bello Gallico*', in *Julius Caesar as Artful Reporter: The war commentaries as political instruments*, eds Kathryn Welch and Anton Powell (London: Duckworth, 1998), pp. 1–9.

Zabaleta, Juan de, *El día de fiesta por la tarde*, ed. Cristóbal Cuevas García (Madrid: Clásicos Castalia, 1983).

Zizek, Slavoj, *The Sublime Object of Ideology* (London: Verso, 1989).

INDEX

Absolutism in Spain, x, 41, 93, 95
Ágreda, Sor María de, 96, 99, 109n. 43;
  correspondence with Philip IV of
  Spain, 97, 98, 100, 105, 106n. 37,
  110–11, 111n. 47, 112
Aitona, Marquis of, Francisco de
  Moncada, 96
Alba, Duke of, Fernando Álvarez de
  Toledo, 132, 133, 135
Alcázar palace, Madrid, 106, 109, 110
Alonso de Granada y Venegas (Ben Omar),
  60
Alpujarras, Second Rebellion of the, 13,
  54, 62, 114, 117, 118, 126, 132
Amezqueta, Pedro de, 51, 53, 96n. 13
Arauco (Mapuche) Indians, 135, 137, 141
arbitristas, 25, 26, 29, 32, 33, 36, 40, 46;
  Ceballos, Jerónimo de, 27, 33, 39;
  Fernández de Navarrete, Pedro, 27, 33;
  Manrique, Ángel, 27, 31; Moncada,
  Sancho de, 26, 31, 33, 44; Salazar de
  Mendoza, Pedro, 31n. 12, 44
Arce y Reinoso, Diego de (appointment as
  Inquisitor General), 96
Austria, Don Juan de (1545–78), 79, 113,
  118, 121, 122, 123, 126–7, 129, 130,
  132, 133
authority: cultural authority, classical and
  biblical sources of, ix, 145, 148, 154–5,
  155, 156, 157; authority gendered as
  male, 82, 83 (inversion of); royal/
  imperial authority, 10, 24, 41, 93–4,
  149
Ayuntamiento of Madrid (re-opening of the
  theatres), 107

Baltasar Carlos, Prince (1629–46), 106
Boccaccio, Giovanni, *Decameron*, 63
Bocángel, Gabriel, *El nuevo Olimpo*, 106,
  107; *La piedra cándida*, 106n. 38
Buen Retiro palace, Madrid, 99

Caesar, Julius, 146

Calderón, Inés de, 'La Calderona', 79
Calderón de la Barca, Pedro, Plays:
  Andrómeda y Perseo, 81; *El alcalde de
  Zalamea* (*El garrote más bien dado*),
  54n. 45, 87; *El cubo de la Almudena*,
  128; *El gran príncipe de Fez, don
  Baltasar de Loyola*, 129; *El sitio de
  Bredá*, 132, 133, 137n. 11, 142n.14; *El
  Tuzaní de la Alpujarra* (*Amar después
  de la muerte*), 113–30; *Guárdate del
  agua mansa*, 109–10; *La fiera, el rayo
  y la piedra*, 111n. 48; *La niña de
  Gómez Arias*, 115n. 6; *La segunda
  esposa y triunfar muriendo*, 94
Calderón, Rodrigo, 3
Calvinism, 58
Carranza, Bartolomé, 63
Castro, Guillén de, *La fuerza de la
  costumbre*, 83
Catalonia, revolt in 1640, 95; numbers of
  clergy, 29
Catholic Church, 55, 135
Catholic Monarchs, 2n. 3, 42, 48, 114
Ceballos, Jerónimo de, 27, 33, 39
Cervantes Saavedra, Miguel de, 25, 75n. 7;
  Works: *Coloquio de los perros*, 16, 19;
  Don Quijote, 13, 14, 23n. 51, 59; *La
  gitanilla*, 50n. 32; *El cerco de
  Numancia*, 131–44; *Los baños de
  Argel*, 59
Charles I of England (1600–49), 58
Charles I of Spain (1519–56); Charles V,
  Holy Roman Emperor (1519–58), 42,
  121, 124
Charles II of Spain (1665–1700), 49n. 27,
  52, 56
Charles III of Spain (1759–88), 49n. 28, 56
Chumacero, Juan, President of the Council
  of Castile, 99–104 *passim*, 107, 108,
  111
Church (Spanish Catholic), 26–40; and the
  Council of Trent, 26, 28, 58, 61, 65;
  and the *moriscos*, 19, 24; opposition to